Directory of Companies

Offering

DIVIDEND REINVESTMENT

PLANS

22nd Edition

Sumie Kinoshita
Editor

Evergreen Enterprises LLC
P O Box 763
Laurel, Maryland 20725-0763

Cover Design by

Jeff Calvert
KC Graphics
Laurel, Maryland

Dedicated to:

Jean Tigner, Evergreen partner and accountant; David Knetsch and Lorinda Stracke, printing advisers; to all Investor Relations officials of DRP issuers; Paul Ort Sr and Postal Service and United Parcel customer reps, who all helped get the directories out; and DRP investors, who made suggestions for improvements and their support for the directory. And to Nuchine Nobari, a fellow directory publisher, for her advice and sympathy. Also to Kumi, Keiko and Emi Kinoshita, my sister-in-law and nieces, and Tony Walz, my nephew-in law, for helping me with trade shows and stuffing envelopes.

And especially to all the production and press people, bulk mail handlers, messengers, drivers, and delivery persons , who make everything happen.

Additional copies of this Directory may be ordered from

EVERGREEN ENTERPRISES LLC
P O Box 763 - Dept 22CVR
Laurel, MD 20725-0763
(301) 549-3939

Directory of Companies Offering

DIVIDEND REINVESTMENT PLANS

TABLE OF CONTENTS

ISBN 0-933183-31-3

1st Edition published February 1982
2nd Edition published April 1984
3rd Edition published February 1986
4th Edition published February 1987
5th Edition published February 1988
6th Edition published February 1989
7th Edition published February 1990
8th Edition published February 1991
9th Edition published March 1992
10th Edition published March 1993
11th Edition published March 1994
12th Edition published March 1995
12th Edition, 2nd Printing published October 1995
13th Edition published March 1996
14th Edition published March 1997
15th Edition published March 1998
16th Edition published April 1999
17th Edition published April 2000
18th Edition published April 2001
19th Edition published March 2002
20th Edition published May 2003
21st Edition published May 2004
22nd Edition published May 2005

DIVIDEND REINVESTMENT PLANS

From the Editor

This will be Evergreen's final edition of the Directory and, as I retire from the working world, it gives me an opportunity to look back over the past 24 years to consider the dividend reinvestment plan (DRP) concept.

Much has changed in the stock market and in the mechanics of trading stocks. In 1981, when I was faced with making decisions on buying stocks, I searched for a list of companies that offered DRPs. Unfortunately, the library didn't have such a list. So, I put one together for myself.

I had learned about DRPs when AT&T began their plan in the early '70s. When AT&T discontinued their employee stock purchase plan, they offered a DRP to all shareholders.

In 1982 when the first edition of the *Directory of Companies Offering Dividend Reinvestment Plans* was published (if the production of that early edition can be described as publishing), DRPs were very primitive.

Optional cash payments were invested quarterly along with dividends. The upper limits of optional cash payments were $20,000; most of the plans did not impose any buy costs; and many more plans offered discounts.

Now the plans have upper limits of $120,000 to $250,000 a year; very few companies absorb all the costs of purchasing; and only a limited number of plans offer discounts.

On the other hand, there are many more features and conveniences: partial reinvestment so that we might spend some of the dividends, electronic deposit of dividends into our bank accounts, automatic withdrawal of funds from our bank accounts to buy more stock, and purchase and sale of shares without going through a broker.

These developments display a widening of opportunities for all investors. My original desire in putting together the DRP list was to help lower middle-class workers like me. I still feel that by investing a small portion of our salaries over the course of 25 to 40 years, we should be able to retire comfortably.

Dividend reinvestment plans are not an exciting way to invest, but it does impose discipline in our execution of financial plans. I hope I have contributed to helping others find a way to execute their plan. I have heard from quite a number of readers who have expressed their thanks for my effort and I greatly appreciate that.

Even Playing Field

However, all our efforts will be negated if the playing field is not even. Attorney General Eliot Spitzer of New York pointed out that 100 years ago Theodore Roosevelt railed against "the failure of ethics in the business leadership and perverse effect on our economy of the cartels that he was pursuing."

I hope you will read the remarks of Eliot Spitzer printed in Appendix B. (*Business Ethics, Regulation and The "Ownership Society."*)

As I mentioned last year, my confidence in the U S stock market was shaken because of the many cases of deceit and fraud evidenced in small part by the convictions of CEOs of WorldCom and Adelphia and officers at Enron. Also as evidenced by the apparent malfeasance of officials such as former U S Securities and Exchange (SEC) Commissioner Harvey Pitt and former New York Stock Exchange Chairman Richard Grasso.

I am heartened by recent events. Attorney General Spitzer, SEC Chairmen Arthur Levitt and William H Donaldson and Senator Paul Sarbanes (D-MD) have come to the defense of the American investing public in the manner of the muckrakers of the 1890's and President Teddy Roosevelt. And I thank them and their staffs for their work on my behalf. *(See full text of Public Law 107-204 (the Sarbanes-Oxley Act of 2002) at www.gpo.gov and also Appendix B of the 20th edition of the* Directory of Companies Offering Dividend Reinvestment Plans *for excerpts from PL 107-204.)*

The 1930s saw ground breaking legislation passed to protect U S investors, such as the Securities Act of 1933, Securities Exchange Act of 1934, Public Utility Holding Company Act of 1935, Trust Indenture Act of 1939, Investment Company Act of 1940, and Investment Advisers Act of 1940. These laws were not comprehensive enough to deal with new dodges in the 1990s.

The business community has expressed dismay over the cost of compliance with the new regulations. Eliot Spitzer maintains that "self-regulation failed utterly." My contention has always been that laws and regulations are passed primarily because of previous wrongdoing, not because law makers take it into their heads to make life difficult for others.

Researching Stocks

I began publication of this directory to assist small investors participate in the stock market through DRPs. I have advised readers that because a company offers a plan does not necessarily indicate its suitability as an investment for a conservative, small investor. I have long cautioned DRP investors to investigate the companies before investing their money. I now add that after buying a stock, investors *must* continue research and oversight of management and performance of the stock in the market.

With the advent of the internet, much more information is available to the individual investor. However, again I caution investors to look into who is giving the advice and what their interest is in the securities they are evaluating. Remember that "free" usually has an underlying cost.

We rearranged some of the entries in the directory and added another feature. The new feature listing is the transfer and/or gifting of shares to another person or account. Another feature, dividend deposit has been repositioned. Consequently a line "div deposit/gifting" has been added. The dividend deposit feature is very convenient and was easily incorporated in dividend reinvestment when computers made partial reinvestment possible.

Good luck in your investing future! I hope to find a new organization to take over the directory and hope you will support their effort, if I do.

Sumie Kinoshita

Laurel, Maryland
May 2005

DIVIDEND REINVESTMENT PLANS

Dividend reinvestment plans (DRP) are plans in which dividends, rather than being paid to stockholders by check, are invested in stock. In most cases, a plan participant may also purchase additional shares with optional cash payments. The reinvested dividends usually are not issued as stock certificates, but are held in "book entry" form—computer recordkeeping accounts. However, in most cases, upon request the shareholder will receive certificates.

Statements of plan holdings are sent quarterly to participants after dividends are reinvested. Investors are advised to keep the year-end statement until the shares are sold for income tax purposes. [If the plan administrator does not provide a cumulative statement of all transactions during the year, you will have to keep each statement you receive.] The statements assist the shareholder to establish the cost basis of the shares that will determine the capital gains (or loss) when the shares are sold.

Price of Shares

Shares are purchased by the plan's agent in quantity and may be stock purchased from the company of original issue or treasury shares; or they may be purchased on the open market *(see Source of Shares)*. When purchased from the company, a price is established based on the selling price on the market, either on a particular date, such as the dividend payment date, or an average of five days prior to a specific date, or some other formula.

Some companies offer the shareholder a **discount** off the market price, usually 3 to 5 percent. In some cases the discount applies only to reinvested dividends; in a limited number of cases, the discount applies to both dividends and cash payments. In other cases the discount is given only on original issue or treasury shares, not on shares purchased on the market. *(For list of plans offering discounts, see Appendix A.)*

Costs to Investors

A number of companies pick up the costs of administration so that all dividends and cash payments are used for purchasing additional shares of stock. Some plans assess the plan participant an administrative service charge (e.g., 5 percent up to $2 or $3 an investment) and/or a pro rata share of the brokerage fees (usually 10¢ or 12¢ a share).

In some cases, the service charge is a flat fee, e.g., $1.00 or $2.50 or $5.00, for each reinvested dividend payment or cash payment. In these cases, small accounts are charged a proportionately high fee, especially if the dividend paid is low.

A recent development has been the drop in fees for EFT (electronic funds transfer) for cash payments. So, a cash payment made by check can cost $5, whereas a one-time EFT payment will be $3.50, while an automatic monthly EFT payment will be $2.

With the drop in fees charged by discount and online brokers, the investor is advised to compare costs of plan transactions with those discount resources. Many brokers are also offering reinvestment of dividends in brokerage accounts, some at no cost. However, brokerage accounts will, of course, impose a regular commission on additional cash purchases.

Termination Fees Many plans assess a fee (from $5 to $15) when the stockholder terminates the DRP account or requests certificates. The administrator will send a certificate for full shares and sell the remaining fractional shares. Some plans will sell all shares and pass on the cash proceeds from the sale, less transfer taxes, brokerage and termination fees, if applicable.

A growing number of plans allow for **partial sales** of plan shares. Thus, the plan participant may request the plan administrator to sell a certain number of shares without terminating the plan. In all cases, the shareholder will be assessed pro-rata brokerage fees and transfer taxes. In some cases, an additional service charge may be assessed for this service.

Requirements for Eligibility
A number of plans require that the shares be held in the name of the individual investor (shareholder of record), rather than held by nominees or brokers in "street name" accounts. Those plans that do allow for nominee or broker account participation caution that there may be an additional charge made by these holders of shares that would reduce the cost savings of participating in DRPs. A few plans require a certain number of shares be owned (e.g. one, 25 or 50) in order to participate in the DRP. Generally, there are no restrictions on the residency of the shareholder. However, in some instances, the DRP restricts participation to certain countries, e.g., U S residents only, or Canadian residents only for some Canadian plans.

The laws of the investor's resident country may restrict participation.

Direct Initial Purchase
Although most plans require that initial purchase of stock be made on the market through a broker, a number of companies feature initial purchase of stock from the company. That is, investors do not have to purchase the first shares from a broker, but may buy them from the company itself or through the administrator of the plan. Online services are also available for purchase of initial shares. *(See Appendix A for a list of direct initial purchase (DIP) plans and the ADR (American Depositary Receipts) section for non-U S and non-Canadian plans.)*

Share Certificates
Accounts are maintained by the administrator or its agent in the individual shareholder's name. When the shareholder desires certificates, the plan administrator will issue them for whole shares. *(See Costs to Investors.)*

Because the reinvested shares are held in a computerized account, fractional shares may be assigned to each shareholder. Fractional shares are usually computed from three to five decimal points.

In addition, quite a number of companies offer a custodial service for shareholders where the stock certificates held by the owner may be sent to the plan administrator. The certificate shares are combined with the plan shares, reducing administrative costs for the company and providing a safekeeping service for the shareholder.

Combining certificate shares with your plan shares could present problems if the shareholder sells only a portion of the plan shares. The IRS assumes that the first shares purchased are the first shares sold, unless the investor specifically requests specific shares be sold.

Tax Considerations
Detailed record keeping and advanced planning is necessary before selling DRP shares to minimize payment of disadvantageous short-term capital gain taxes. *(See the most recent IRS publications, Pub 550–Investment Income and Expenses and Pub 17--Your Federal Income Tax for Individuals, regarding cost basis and holding period.)*

DIVIDEND REINVESTMENT PLANS

Recent tax law changes have greatly reduced (until 2008) the tax rate (5% or 15%) for dividends and capital gains. *(See Appendix B,* Directory of Companies Offering DRPS, *21st ed, for PL108-27, Title III, for text of the 2003 tax reduction law.)*

Cash Purchases of Additional Stock

Most plans allow optional cash payments for the purchase of additional shares. The cash payment limits generally range from as little as $10 a month to as much as $250,000 a year. Cash payments are voluntary and do not have to be made on a regular basis or in any specified amount within the payment limits. Thus, the investor can time payments, to a certain degree, to fluctuations in market price, or whenever s/he has any spare cash available.

Dates when the cash purchases are invested vary with each plan; some plans invest on a monthly basis, others on a quarterly basis; a few invest on a weekly or daily basis. Most plans will invest cash payments on dates other than the dividend payment dates. However, many plans, although they have provisions for monthly or bi-quarterly investments, will only invest cash payments when enough funds have been accumulated to purchase 100-share lots.

Thus, investors should determine from the plan prospectus or brochure the exact terms and dates and time their cash purchases. Interest is not paid on cash sent to the administrator.

A growing number of plans provide for transfer from bank accounts of cash (EFT - electronic funds transfer) to purchase additional shares. Many plans provide for automatic monthly or quarterly transfers, a few allow for single transactions.

Types of Plans

Plans generally fall into four categories: full dividend reinvestment, partial dividend reinvestment, cash purchase only, and a combination. Some plans require that all dividends be reinvested; some specify percentages of dividends be reinvested; while others specify the number of shares that will participate in the plan (**partial reinvestment**).

In most cases, dividends paid on plan shares (those shares that are held by the administrator) must be reinvested. Some plans require that cash payments may be made only if the shareholder participates in the dividend reinvestment plan.

Others allow the shareholder to receive all dividend payments and participate only in the cash option feature of the plan. For those shareholders receiving cash dividends (either all or partial), companies are providing a direct deposit of dividends to their bank accounts.

A few plans provide for using their DRP as an Individual Retirement Arrangement (IRA) plan. *(See Appendix A.)*

Source of Shares

Dividend reinvestment plans get the shares for their participants in several ways. The plan administrator buys shares from the company or on the open market.

Shares purchased from the company may be either original issue or treasury shares. Original issue shares are authorized, but unissued shares that have been registered with the Securities and Exchange Commission (SEC). Treasury shares are previously issued shares that the company has repurchased and holds in its treasury. Proceeds from shares purchased with original issue or treasury shares are used by the company for general corporate purposes.

Market shares are purchased on a stock exchange, over the counter, or through negotiated sales from an independent owner. The company does not receive any proceeds from market purchase plans.

Canadian Plans

Certain restrictions are imposed on Canadian companies with regard to U S investors so that careful investigation prior to purchase of Canadian stocks by U S residents is advised. Canadian companies must file with the U S Securities and Exchange Commission in order for their U S shareholders to participate in their DRPs. However, U S shareholders may participate in Canadian stock dividend plans, even though the plan is not registered with the U S SEC. [Please note that Canadian companies that do not trade on U S exchanges may have symbol designations similar to U S-listed companies.]

Other Non-U S Plans

Many non-U S companies offer American depositary receipts (ADRs) that are traded on U S exchanges. They are also known as ADSs (American depositary shares). ADRs offer Americans a simpler way of investing in foreign stocks rather than trying to execute trades on an overseas market. ADRs are not actual stocks, but represent the foreign shares that are held in trust by a financial institution. Although ADRs make ownership of foreign securities much simpler, the responsibility of keeping track of the underlying stock and its financial market still rests with the investor. In addition, taxes may be levied on dividends. *(See ADR section, beginning on page 9.)*

How the Information Was Gathered

Many readers have asked how we obtained the listings of companies for this directory. Beginning in 1984, we contacted all investor relations departments and many bank administrators and requested copies of DRP prospectuses and brochures. We extracted our information from these company publications.

We send annual questionnaires to all companies listed in the Directory to update the information. In some instances, the company does not wish to be involved in the details of the DRP and the bank administrator handles all correspondence and queries from the shareholder and general public. In general, we rely on direct contact by mail and phone with the company or administrator for our information.

KEY TO DIRECTORY LISTINGS

Beginning on page 23 is a list of U S and Canadian companies that offer dividend reinvestment plans (DRP). Addresses and telephone numbers are provided so that requests for current information regarding the plans may be made.

Although a company has a DRP, investment may not be suitable if the company has a poor dividend or financial history. Additionally, fees may be imposed that would make smaller accounts absorb a proportionally greater amount of fees per share. The requirement for listing in this directory is that the security be publicly traded on a major stock exchange or through the national market system of NASDAQ (National Association of Securities Dealers Automated Quotations).

DIVIDEND REINVESTMENT PLANS

Key to Stock Exchanges
A letter appears after company name and indicates the primary **exchange** on which the stock is listed.

(A)–American Stock Exchange
(N)–New York Stock Exchange
(NDQ)–National Market

System-NASDAQ
(O)–Over the Counter Market
(T)–Toronto Stock Exchange

[In 1999 the Canadian financial community restructured their markets. Equity trading was concentrated on the Toronto Exchange.]

The trading **symbol** for the company appears after the exchange listing.

Dividends
The dollar amount of dividends paid per year is given, e.g., (div/yr: $0.46).

In some cases, companies have suspended dividends. We continue coverage if we have previously listed the company and the plan accepts new participants. Usually these plans provide for cash purchases without reinvestment of dividends. In most cases, these companies intend to reinstate dividends when financial circumstances warrant.

Other companies that have never paid dividends and have no plans to do so are listed because they have DIP (direct initial purchase) and cash purchase features.

S&P Ranking System
The rankings for common stocks were obtained from *Standard & Poor's Net Advantage*, April 2005. The ranking scores are based on past earnings and dividends which are adjusted by various factors, such as growth, stability, size and cyclicality. The ranking scores represent:

A +	Highest	B +	Average	C	Lowest
A	High	B	Below Average	D	Reorganizing
A –	Above Average	B –	Lower		

Companies with no ranking indicates that S&P does not rank the company or the ranking was unavailable. The ranking system for equities is different from the debt rating system for bonds. (For more information on the S&P ranking system see S&P's Net Advantage, *Stock Guide* or *CreditWeek*. See also, *S&P Outlook*, March 19, 2003, *A + Stocks Pass Test of Time*.)

Since S&P is constantly re-evaluating their rankings, the scores presented are just an indication of the company's position at a certain period of time.

Plan Features
Type of industry—A short description of the major line of business is provided for each company.

Country—Country of parent is indicated if not a U S company. Some U S companies are legally registered in an offshore tax haven and those countries are indicated.

Addresses and telephone numbers—Addresses and phone numbers are those given by companies for investor queries. Abbreviations after phone numbers indicate the department that handles the DRP (e.g., CpSecy, InvRe, or Treas - see glossary).

Generally, to get information on dividend reinvestment plans, ask (or click) for the Investor Relations or Shareholder Relations Department. A second phone number is given for fax queries to company investor relations departments. A third telephone number is given, usually for the administrator (admr) of the plan. Some companies have all queries handled by their plan administrator, in those cases, the address of the administrator is listed. If an investor relations department accepts electronic mail, we have listed the e-mail address. Internet addresses are also provided.

Costs—Generally fees are charged for (1) administrative services and (2) pro-rata brokerage commissions. Plans in which the company picks up the service charges and brokerage fees are designated "no cost." Otherwise, the two-part cost structure is indicated. No designation means both charges are imposed. There are usually fees charged when selling shares or terminating the plan and the investor should read the prospectus or brochure before purchasing the stock.   [margin note ✹ means "no cost"]

Discount—Discounts off market price are indicated (1) for reinvested dividends only [e.g., 5% disc-div] or (2) for both dividends and cash payments [e.g., 3% disc-div/cash or 5%-div/3%-cash].   [margin note: %]

Cash limits—Most plans impose minimum and maximum limits on cash purchases, as well as a time limit. For example, $10-5,000/qtr would indicate a minimum payment of $10 and a maximum of $5,000 total per quarter. EFT (electronic funds transfer) indicates that payments may be made from investor's bank account electronically.

Investment period for cash purchases—Cash purchase payments usually are made on a monthly or quarterly basis. In most cases, the payments are made at the same time dividends are reinvested. In addition, some plans purchase shares on a bi-quarterly basis: the dividend payment date and the 45th day thereafter, or on common and preferred dividend dates. In other plans, monthly purchases are made if the plan administrator has received enough cash from participants to purchase 100-share lots. The purchase period per year is indicated in parentheses ( ) after the cash limit amounts. Quarterly investments are indicated by (4), monthly by (12), etc.

DIP-Direct initial purchase—The minimum amount to begin participation in the DRP is listed for those plans that allow direct purchase without going through a broker.   [margin note: ★]

Partial/Cash-only option— "Partial DR option" or "part. DR" indicates that the plan allows participants to reinvest only a portion of dividends while receiving dividend payments directly on the remaining portion. "Cash only option" indicates that plan allows participants to send in cash payments to the plan while still receiving their dividends in cash. Generally dividends on shares in the plan must be reinvested.

Safekeeping—Owner-held share safekeeping service. The plan will accept certificates held by the shareholder into the plans. Dollar amount is the fee charged for the service.

Partial sales—"Part. sale" or "p. sale" indicate the plan administrator will sell plan shares for the participant without terminating the plan. Usually a pro-rata brokerage fee, transfer taxes and a service charge will be deducted. A check for the proceeds will then be sent to the plan participant.

Div deposit—Dividends can be deposited directly to investor's bank account.

Gifting/transfer— Shares may be transferred to another person or account.

Eligibility—"Record" or "rec" indicates that the plan specifically limits the plan to individual shareholders; beneficial owners whose shares are held in "street name" brokerage accounts are not eligible. Most plans are for common

6

stockholders; those plans that are open to preferred and bond holders are indicated. In the case of plans that accept preferred dividends and bond interest, they are usually reinvested in common shares. If the preferred dividend is reinvested in preferred shares and common into common, that is indicated.

Residency—Most plans are open to all shareholders. Residency restrictions imposed by a company are indicated. Although most companies allow non-US residents to participate, participation is determined by the laws of the investor's resident country.

Notes—Special provisions or limitations are indicated.

Glossary of Abbreviations

admr - administrator, also referred to as transfer agent.

ADR or ADS - American Depositary Receipt or Share, represents the foreign stock held by a U S fiduciary (bank or trustee). ADRs trade on U S stock markets like common stocks.

American Association of Individual Investors, 625 N Michigan Ave, Chicago, IL 60611, 312-280-0170, www.aaii.com

American Society of Corporate Secretaries Inc, 521 Fifth Ave, New York, NY 10175, 212-681-2015, www.ascs.org

ann - annual

AsstSecy - Assistant Corporate Secretary

bd - bonds

B/O - beneficial owner, a shareholder who deposits shares with a broker or trustee, also known as "street name" accounts. The broker or nominee keeps all shares for clients in a commingled account.

book entry - ownership of shares are recorded on company books (computer logs) without issuing paper certificates.

bkg - brokerage

cash - optional cash purchases

CDN - Canada

C$ - Canadian dollar

cg - capital gains

Chp 11- Chapter 11 bankruptcy declared–company intends to reorganize and continue operations. Chp 7 bankruptcy indicates the company intends to cease operations.

co # - company telephone number

c/o - care of

comm - common stock

Contr - controller

CpSecy - Corporate Secretary's Office

CpTrust - Corporate Trust Dept

deb or deben - debenture

DIP - direct initial purchase of shares from the company or transfer agent, without first going to a broker.

disc - discount

div - dividend

div deposit - dividends are electronically deposited to investor's bank account

DR - dividend reinvestment

DRP - dividend reinvestment plan

EFT - electronic funds transfer. Cash payments may be made by transferring funds from the investor's bank account or dividends may be deposited directly to a bank account. Funds may be transferred automatically on a monthly or quarterly basis, in other instances, a single transfer may be arranged.

GC - General Counsel, a corporate officer responsible for legal matters

Gift/transfer of shares - Shares from a DRP may be transferred to another account or into certificates in another name. Some plans will send a gift certificate as a means of notification to the recipient.

GPO - Government Printing Office, 732 North Capitol St, N E, Washington, D C 20401, 202-512-1800, 866-512-1800, www.gpo.gov.

gp - group

int - interest on bonds or debentures

InvRe - Investor Relations Dept

issuer - the term used by the financial community for "company". An entity that "issues" stocks.

mgt - management

mo - month

NAIC - National Assn of Investors Corp, P O Box 220, Royal Oak, MI 48068, 248-583-6242, www.better-investing.org

NASD - National Association of Securities Dealers, Broker Check Dept, 9509 Key West Ave, Rockville, MD 20850, 301-590-6500, www.nasd.com

NASDAQ - National Association of Securities Dealers Automated Quotations of NASD

NDQ - National Market System of NASDAQ

no cost-orig iss - no service or brokerage fees when shares are purchased from company using original issue shares

no residency restrictions - foreign residents eligible for plan, subject to their own country's laws

original issue - authorized, but unissued shares, that have been registered with the Securities and Exchange Commission

part. sale or p. sale - admr will sell a portion of plan shares, deduct costs of sale and send check to plan participant.

plc - public limited company (United Kingdom)

pref - preferred or preference stock

pymt - payment

qt or qtr - quarter, dividend payment quarter

REIT - real estate investment trust

s-a - semi-annual

SEC - Securities & Exchange Commission, Market Regulation Division, 450 5th St, NW, Washington, DC 20549, 202-942-8088, www.sec.gov

sfkg - safekeeping (owner-held shares accepted into plan)

sh or shs - share or shares

ShRel or ShSvc - Shareholder Relations Dept or Shareholder Services Dept

Ste - suite

svc - service

StkTr - Stock Transfer Dept

TransAg - Transfer Agent. The entity (usually a bank) that handles stock ownership recordkeeping, dividend payments, etc.

Treas - Treasurer's Office

yr - year

American Depositary Receipts (ADRs)

American Depositary Receipts (ADR) represent non-US/non-Canadian registered shares that are held in trust by a financial institution. ADRs are also known as American Depositary Shares (ADS). New York registry shares are similar to ADRs, except the owners' names are registered on the books of the parent company. ADRs, on the other hand, are held in "street name".

Although ADRs make ownership of foreign securities much simpler than holding the actual shares, the responsibility of keeping track of the underlying stock and its financial market still rests with the investor.

Following is a list of ADRs that have DRP and DIP features. These ADRs are Level II and Level III shares, which requires the issuers to register with the U S Securities and Exchange Commission and follow all reporting requirements. (For more information on types of ADRs, see websites of Bank of New York and J P Morgan Chase Bank, see Transfer Agents, p 22.)

Plan details and telephone numbers are listed on page 22. Most plans are sponsored by banks, who are the American transfer agent for the issues. In those cases where the parent company has registered the U S division with the Securities and Exchange Commission or the U S office of the company maintains an investor relations or shareholder relations department, we list the plan in the main body of the directory with U S address and phone numbers and the features of the plan. Canadian companies do not go through the ADR process, since U S residents may purchase Canadian stocks on US or Canadian exchanges.

ABN AMRO Holdings NV (N-ABN) (div/yr: $0.92) banks/banking-NETHERLANDS
c/o JP Morgan Chase Bank   800-428-4237 admr

AEGON NV (N-AEG) (div/yr: $0.45) insurance-life/health, investment products-NETHERLANDS
See main entry for details of plan.   410-576-4577 InvRe

AFP Provida SA (N-PVD) (div/yr: $ 1.22) fin svcs-pension investments-CHILE
c/o Bank of New York   800-345-1612 admr

AMVESCAP plc (N-AVZ) (div/yr: $0.28) fin svcs-investment mgmt svcs-UK
c/o Bank of New York   800-345-1612 US IR

APT Satellite Co Ltd (N-ATS) (div/yr: $0.00) telecomm-satellite svcs-HONG KONG
c/o Bank of New York   800-345-1612 admr

ARM Holdings plc (NDQ-ARMHY) (div/yr: $0.03) tech-design microprocessors-UK
c/o Bank of New York   800-345-1612 admr

ASML Holding NV (NDQ-ASML) (div/yr: $0.00) mfg-lithographic systems-SWEDEN
c/o JP Morgan Chase Bank   800-428-4237 admr

AXA (N-AXA) (div/yr: $0.67) insurance/fin svcs-FRANCE
c/o EquiServe   800-437-8736 admr

Acambis plc (NDQ-ACAM) (div/yr: $0.00) biotechnology-UK
c/o Bank of New York   800-345-1612 admr

Adecco SA (N-ADO) (div/yr: $0.18) svcs-staffing-SWITZERLAND
c/o JP Morgan Chase Bank   800-428-4237 admr

Advantest Corp (N-ATE) (div/yr: $ 0.12) mfg-electronics-JAPAN
c/o JP Morgan Chase   800-428-4237 admr

Ahold (Royal Dutch) Ltd NV (N-AHO) (div/yr: $0.00) retail-global supermarket chains-NETHER
c/o Bank of New York   800-345-1612 US IR

Akzo Nobel (NDQ-AKZOY) (div/yr: $ 1.54) mfg-chemicals/petrochemicals -NETHERLANDS
c/o Citibank N A   877-248-4237 admr

Alcatel SA (N-ALA) (div/yr: $0.00) [S&P ranking: B] telecommunications-FRANCE
c/o Bank of New York   800-345-1612 admr

‹ **Allianz AG** (N-AZ) (div/yr: $0.18) fin svcs-insurance/banking/asset mgmt-GERMANY
c/o JP Morgan Chase Bank   800-428-4237 admr

Allied Domecq plc (N-AED) (div/yr: $ 1.22) food/bev-supermarkets/hotels/restaurants-UK
c/o JP Morgan ADR Group   800-428-4237 admr

Allied Irish Banks plc (N-AIB) (div/yr: $ 1.51) banking-IRELAND
c/o Bank of New York   800-345-1612 US IR

Altana AG (N-AAA) (div/yr: $0.86) drug/pharmaceuticals-GERMANY
c/o Bank of New York   800-345-1612 admr

Alto Palermo SA (NDQ-APSA) (div/yr: $0.24) real estate-property mgmt-ARGENTINA
c/o Bank of New York   800-345-1612 admr

Aluminum Corp of China Ltd (N-ACH) (div/yr: $ 2.13) mfg-aluminum products-CHINA
c/o Bank of New York   800-345-1612 admr

Amcor Ltd (NDQ-AMCR) (div/yr: $0.88) mfg-paper/packaging-AUSTRALIA
c/o JP Morgan Chase Bank   800-428-4237 admr

America Movil SA de CV (N-AMX) (div/yr: $0.24) telecommunications-MEXICO
c/o JP Morgan ADR Group   800-428-4237 admr

Andina SA (Embotelladora) (N-AKO) (div/yr: $0.49) food/bev-beverage prod/distr-Coca-Cola-CHILE
c/o Bank of New York   800-345-1612 admr

AngloGold Ashanti Ltd (N-AU) (div/yr: $0.56) metals/mining-gold-SO AFRICA
c/o Bank of New York   800-345-1612 admr

Ansell Ltd (NDQ-ANSL) (div/yr: $0.42) mfg-rubber/plastics-AUSTRALIA
c/o JP Morgan Chase Bank   800-428-4237 admr

Aracruz Celulose SA (N-ARA) (div/yr: $0.97) mfg-eucalpytus kraft pulp/paper-BRAZIL
c/o JP Morgan Chase Bank   800-428-4237 admr

Arcadis NV (NDQ-ARCAF) (div/yr: $0.44) retail-merchandising-NETHERLANDS
c/o Bank of New York   800-345-1612 US adm

Asia Satellite Telecommunications Holdings (N-SAT) (div/yr: $0.45) telecomm-satellite transpon-
der capacity-HONG KONG
c/o Bank of New York   800-345-1612 admr

AstraZeneca plc (N-AZN) (div/yr: $0.94) drugs/pharmaceuticals-UK
c/o JP Morgan Chase Bank   800-428-4237 US IR

Atlas Pacific Ltd (NDQ-APCFY) (div/yr: $0.00) metal/mining-gold mines/pearl farming-AUSTRALIA
c/o Bank of New York   800-345-1612 US IR

BE Semiconductor Industries NV (NDQ-BESI) (div/yr: $0.00) mfg-semiconductor packaging-
NETHERLANDS
c/o Bank of New York   800-345-1612 admr

BG Group plc (N-BRG) (div/yr: $ 0.35) energy-oil/gas-UK
c/o JP Morgan Chase   800-428-4237 admr

BHP Billiton Ltd (N-BHP) (div/yr: $ 0.46) metals/mining-AUSTRALIA
c/o JP Morgan Chase   800-428-4237 admr

BHP Billiton Ltd (N-BBL) (div/yr: $ 0.46) metals/mining-AUSTRALIA
c/o JP Morgan Chase   800-428-4237 admr

BOC Group plc (The) (N-BOX) (div/yr: $ 1.54) misc-diversified indus-chemical/drugs/food-UK
c/o JP Morgan Chase Bank   800-428-4237 admr

BP plc (N-BP) (div/yr: $ 1.77) energy-petroleum-UK
See main entry for details of plan.   877-272-2723 admr

BT Group plc (N-BT) (div/yr: $ 1.66) telecommunications-UK
c/o JP Morgan Chase Bank   800-428-4237 US IR

Banco Bilbao Viz Argentaria SA (N-BBV) (div/yr: $0.47) banks/banking-SPAIN
c/o Bank of New York   800-345-1612 admr

Banco Bilbao Viz Chile (N-BB) (div/yr: $0.53) banking-CHILE
c/o Bank of New York   800-345-1612 admr

Banco de Chile (N-BCH) (div/yr: $ 2.38) banks/banking-CHILE
c/o JP Morgan Chase   800-428-4237 admr

Banco Frances SA (BBVA) (N-BFR) (div/yr: $0.45) banks/banking-ARGENTINA
c/o Bank of New York   800-345-1612 admr

Banco Itau Holding Financeira SA (N-ITU) (div/yr: $ 1.43) banks/banking-BRAZIL
c/o Bank of New York   800-345-1612 admr

Banco Santander Central Hispano SA (N-STD) (div/yr: $0.43) banking-SPAIN
See main entry for details of plan.   800-428-4237 admr

Banco Santander Chile (N-SAN) (div/yr: $ 1.46) banks/banking-BRAZIL
c/o Bank of New York   800-345-1612 admr

Bank of Ireland (Governor & Co) (N-IRE) (div/yr: $ 2.19) banks/banking-IRELAND
c/o Bank of New York   800-345-1612 admr

Barclays plc (N-BCS) (div/yr: $ 1.80) banks/banking-UK
c/o Bank of New York   800-345-1612 admr

Bayer AG (N-BAY) (div/yr: $0.56) mfg-chemicals-GERMANY
c/o Bank of New York   800-345-1612 admr

Bennetton Group SpA (N-BNG) (div/yr: $0.64) mfg-textiles, apparel-ITALY
c/o JP Morgan Chase Bank   800-428-4237 admr

Blue Square-Israel Ltd (N-BSI) (div/yr: $0.53) retail-supermarkets/dept stores-ISRAEL
c/o Bank of New York   800-345-1612 admr

Braskem SA (N-BAK) (div/yr: $0.84) mfg-petrochemicals-BRAZIL
c/o Bank of New York   800-345-1612 admr

British Airways plc (N-BAB) (div/yr: $0.00) transportation-airlines-UK
c/o JP Morgan Chase Bank   800-428-4237 US IR

British Sky Broadcasting Group plc (N-BSY) (div/yr: $0.55) entertainment - broadcasting-UK
c/o Bank of New York   800-345-1612 admr

Buenaventura SA (Comp de Minas) (N-BVN) (div/yr: $0.33) metals/mining-gold& silver-PERU
c/o Bank of New York   800-345-1612 admr

Buhrmann NV (N-BUH) (div/yr: $0.00) retail-office supplies-NETHERLANDS
c/o Bank of New York   800-345-1612 admr

Bunzl plc (N-BNL) (div/yr: $ 1.28) mfg-paper/plastic products-UK
c/o Bank of New York   800-345-1612 admr

Business Objects SA (NDQ-BOBJ) (div/yr: $0.00) svcs-develop decision-making software-FRANCE
c/o Bank of New York   800-345-1612 admr

CNOOC Ltd (N-CEO) (div/yr: $ 2.05) energy-oil/gas-HONG KONG
c/o JP Morgan Chase   800-428-4237 admr

Cable & Wireless plc (N-CWP) (div/yr: $ 0.24) telecommunications-UK
c/oCitibank   800-808-8010 admr

Cadbury Schweppes plc (N-CSG) (div/yr: $ 0.93) food/beverage-candy, soft drinks, food products-UK
c/o JP Morgan Chase Bank   800-428-4237 admr

Canon Inc (N-CAJ) (div/yr: $ 0.47) mfg-office/optical equipment-JAPAN
c/o JP Morgan Chase Bank   800-428-4237 admr

Carnival plc (N-CUK) (div/yr: $0.80) publishing/entertainment-UK
c/o JP Morgan Chase Bank   800-428-4237 admr

Cervecerias Unidas SA (CIA) (N-CU) (div/yr: $ 0.77) food/bev-beverages-CHILE
c/o JP Morgan Chase   800-428-4237 admr

Cemex (N-CX) (div/yr: $ 1.02) mfg-cement-MEXICO
c/o Citibank NA   800-808-8010 admr

Chicago Bridge & Iron Co NV (N-CBI) (div/yr: $0.09) svcs-engineering/construction-NETHER
c/o Bank of New York   800-345-1612 US IR

China Airlines Co Ltd (N-ZNH) (div/yr: $0.83) trans-regional scheduled airline-CHINA
c/o Bank of New York   800-345-1612 admr

China Eastern Airlines Corp (N-CEA) (div/yr: $0.00) trans-scheduled airlines-CHINA
c/o Bank of New York   800-345-1612 admr

China Mobile (Hong Kong) Ltd (N-CHL) (div/yr: $0.26) telecomm-cellular telephone svc-HONG
KONG
c/o Bank of New York   800-345-1612 admr

China Unicom Ltd (N-CHU) (div/yr: $0.12) telecom-wireless svc-HONG KONG
c/o Bank of New York   800-345-1612 admr

Chunghwa Telecom Co Ltd (N-CHT) (div/yr: $ 1.33) telecomm-land line/wireless svc-TAIWAN
c/o Bank of New York   800-345-1612 admr

Coca Cola Hellenic Bottling Co SA (N-CCH) (div/yr: $0.24) food-beverage -GREECE
c/o Bank of New York   800-345-1612 admr

Coca-Cola FEMSA SA de CV (N-KOF) (div/yr: $0.30) food-prod/markets/distr soft drinks-MEXICO
c/o Bank of New York   800-345-1612 US IR

Colt Telecom Group plc (NDQ-COLT) (div/yr: $0.00) telecomm-high bandwidth data/internet/voice
svc-UK
c/o Bank of New York   800-345-1612 admr

Controladora Comercial Mexicana SA (N-MCM) (div/yr: $0.22) retail-MEXICO
c/o Bank of New York   800-345-1612 admr

Converium Holding AG (N-CHR) (div/yr: $0.36) insurance-SWITZERLAND
c/o Bank of New York   800-345-1612 admr

DIVIDEND REINVESTMENT PLANS ADRs

Credit Suisse Group (N-CSR) (div/yr: $ 1.67) banks/banking - SWITZERLAND
c/o Mellon Investor Svcs 866-249-2593 admr

Cresud SA (NDQ-CRESY) (div/yr: $0.07) food-production-ARGENTINA
c/o Bank of New York 800-345-1612 admr

Cristalerias de Chile SA (N-CGW) (div/yr: $0.50) mfg-glass containers-CHILE
c/o Bank of New York 800-345-1612 admr

DRDGold Ltd (NDQ-DROOY) (div/yr: $0.00) metals/mining-gold-S AFRICA
c/o Bank of New York 800-345-1612 admr

DaimlerChrysler AG (N-DCX) (div/yr: $ 1.93) mfg-automobiles-GERMANY
c/o Bank of New York 800-345-1612 admr

Danone Groupe (N-DA) (div/yr: $ 0.35) food/beverage-packaged foods-FRANCE
c/o Citibank N A 800-808-8010 admr

Dassault Systemes SA (NDQ-DASTY) (div/yr: $0.31) svcs-CAD/CAM software dev-FRANCE
c/o JP Morgan Chase Bank 800-428-4237 admr

Delhaize (Etablissements) SA (N-DEG) (div/yr: $ 1.12) food-supermarkets-Food Lion-BELGIUM
See main entry for details of plan. 800-345-1612 admr

Desarrolladora Homex SA de CV (N-HXM) (div/yr: $ 0.00) real estate-MEXICO
c/o JP Morgan Chase 800-428-4237 admr

Deutsche Telekom AG (N-DT) (div/yr: $0.64) telecommunications-GERMANY
c/o Citibank 800-808-8010 admr

Diageo plc (N-DEO) (div/yr: $ 2.10) food/bev-Burger King/Guiness/Pillsbury-UK
c/o Bank of New York 800-345-1612 admr

Dialog Semiconductor plc (NDQ-DLGS) (div/yr: $0.00) mfg-circuit solutions to wireless indus-GERMANY
c/o Bank of New York 800-345-1612 admr

Distribucion & Servicio (D&S) SA (N-DYS) (div/yr: $ 0.30) retail services-CHILE
c/o JP Morgan Chase 800-428-4237 admr

Dr Reddy's Laboratories Ltd (N-RDY) (div/yr: $ 0.11) drugs/pharmaceuticals-INDIA
c/o JP Morgan Chase 800-428-4237 admr

Ducati Motor Holding SpA (N-DMH) (div/yr: $0.00) mfg-motorcyles-ITALY
c/o Bank of New York 800-345-1612 admr

ENI SpA (N-E) (div/yr: $ 4.30) energy-oil & gas exploration/dev/distr-ITALY
c/o JP Morgan Chase Bank 800-428-4237 admr

E.ON AG (N-EON) (div/yr: $ 1.01) energy-special chem/telecom/real estate-GERMANY
c/o JP Morgan Chase Bank 800-428-4237 admr

Eidos plc (NDQ-EIDSY) (div/yr: $0.00) tech-dev interactive software products-UK
c/o Bank of New York 800-345-1612 admr

Elan Corp plc (N-ELN) (div/yr: $0.00) health-drug delivery technology-IRELAND
c/o Bank of New York 800-345-1612 US IR

Electrolux AB (NDQ-ELUXY) (div/yr: $ 1.65) consumer prod-appliances-SWEDEN
c/o JP Morgan Chase Bank 800-428-4237 admr

Embraer-Empresa Brasileira de Aeronautica SA (N-ERJ) (div/yr: $ 1) mfg-jet/turboprop aircraft-BRAZIL
c/o JP Morgan Chase Bank 800-428-4237 admr

Embratel Participacoes (N-EMT) (div/yr: $0.00) telecomm-telecommunications svcs-BRAZIL
c/o Bank of New York   800-345-1612 admr

Empresas ICA Sociedad Controladora SA de CV (N-ICA) (div/yr: $0.00) svcs-const-MEXICO
c/o Bank of New York   800-345-1612 US IR

Enodis plc (N-ENO) (div/yr: $0.00) mfg-food service equipment-UK
c/o Bank of New York   800-345-1612 admr

Epcos AG (N-EPC) (div/yr: $0.00) mfg-electronic components-GERMANY
c/o JP Morgan Chase Bank   800-428-4237 admr

Equant NV (N-ENT) (div/yr: $0.00) tech-data network svcs-NETHERLANDS
c/o JP Morgan Chase Bank   800-428-4237 admr

Ericsson (Telefonaktiebolaget L M) (NDQ-ERICY) (div/yr: $0.00) telecommunications - SWEDEN
c/o Citibank N A   877-248-4237 admr

Espirito Santo Financial Group SA (N-ESF) (div/yr: $0.10) fin svcs-financial services in Portugal-
LUXEMBOURG
c/o Bank of New York   800-345-1612 admr

Fiat SpA (N-FIA) (div/yr: $0.00) mfg-automobiles, farm equip-ITALY
c/o JP Morgan Chase Bank   800-428-4237 admr

Flamel Technologies SA (NDQ-FLML) (div/yr: $0.00) drugs/pharmaceuticals-FRANCE
c/o Bank of New York   800-345-1612 admr

Fomento Economico Mexicano SA (N-FMX) (div/yr: $0.60) food/bev-Coca Cola bottler -MEXICO
c/o Bank of New York   800-345-1612 admr

France Telecom (N-FTE) (div/yr: $0.29) telecommunications-FRANCE
c/o Bank of New York   800-345-1612 admr

Freeserve plc (NDQ-FREE) (div/yr: $0.00) tech-Internet access svc-UK
c/o Bank of New York   800-345-1612 admr

Fresenius Medical Care AG (N-FMS) (div/yr: $0.38) drug/pharmaceuticals-GERMANY
c/o JP Morgan Chase Bank   800-428-4237 admr

Gallaher Group plc (N-GLH) (div/yr: $ 2.39) cons prod-tobacco products-UK
c/o Bank of New York   800-345-1612 admr

GlaxoSmithKline plc (N-GSK) (div/yr: $ 1.83) drug/pharmaceuticals-UK
c/o Bank of New York   800-345-1612 admr

Gol Linhas Aereas Inteligentes SA (N-GOL) (div/yr: $0.25) enter-travel & leisure services-BRAZIL
c/o Bank of New York   800-345-1612 admr

Grupo Aeroportuario del Sureste SA de CV (N-ASR) (div/yr: $0.49) svcs-operates airport in Can-
cun-MEXICO
c/o Bank of New York   800-345-1612 admr

Grupo Casa Saba SA de CV (N-SAB) (div/yr: $0.00) distr-pharmaceuticals/cosmetics-MEXICO
c/o Bank of New York   800-345-1612 admr

Grupo Elektra SA de CV (N-EKT) (div/yr: $0.40) retail-electronics/appliances-MEXICO
c/o Bank of New York   800-345-1612 admr

Grupo Iusacell (N-CEL) (div/yr: $0.00) telecommunications-cellular-MEXICO
c/o Bank of New York   800-345-1612 admr

Guangshen Railway Co Ltd (N-GSH) (div/yr: $0.60) trans-railroads-CHINA
c/o JP Morgan Chase Bank   800-428-4237 admr

HEAD NV (N-HED) (div/yr: $0.00) consumer prod-sporting goods -NETHERLANDS
c/o Bank of New York   800-345-1612 admr

HSBC Holdings plc (N-HBC) (div/yr: $ 3.35) banking/asset mgmt-UK
c/o Bank of New York   800-345-1612 admr

Hanson plc (N-HAN) (div/yr: $ 1.70) mfg-bldg materials-UK,
See main entry for details of plan.   877-248-4237 admr

Harmony Gold Mining Co Ltd (N-HMY) (div/yr: $0.11) metals/mining-gold-S AFRICA
c/o Bank of New York   800-345-1612 admr

Havas (NDQ-HAVS) (div/yr: $0.07) misc-advertising-FRANCE
c/o JP Morgan Chase Bank   800-428-4237 admr

Hellenic Telecommunications (N-OTE) (div/yr: $0.21) telecomm-telecommunications svcs-GREECE
c/o Bank of New York   800-345-1612 admr

Honda Motor Co Ltd (N-HMC) (div/yr: $ 0.38) mfg-automobiles-JAPAN
c/o JP Morgan Chase Bank   800-428-4237 admr

Huaneng Power International Inc (N-HNP) (div/yr: $ 1.64) energy-power plant operator-CHINA
c/o Bank of New York   800-345-1612 admr

ICICI Bank Ltd (N-IBN) (div/yr: $0.33) banks/banking-INDIA
c/o Deutsche Bank Trust Co   800-749-1873 admr

ILOG SA (NDQ-ILOG) (div/yr: $0.00) svcs-computer software/hardware-FRANCE
c/o J P Morgan Chase   800-428-4237 admr

ING Groep NV (N-ING) (div/yr: $0.99) insurance/investment svcs-NETHERLANDS
c/o JP Morgan Chase Bank   800-428-4237 admr

IRSA Inversiones y Representaciones SA (N-IRS) (div/yr: $0.00) real estate invest-ARGENTINA
c/o Bank of New York   800-345-1612 admr

Imperial Chemical Industries plc (N-ICI) (div/yr: $0.54) [S&P ranking: B-] mfg-chemicals-UK
See main entry for details of plan.   800-749-1687 admr

Imperial Tobacco Group Ltd (N-ITY) (div/yr: $ 1.88) consumer prod-cigarettes/tobacco products-UK
c/o Citibank N A   800-808-8010 admr

InfoVista SA (NDQ-IVTA) (div/yr: $0.00) svcs-software-FRANCE
c/o Bank of New York   800-345-1612 admr

Infosys Technologies LTD (NDQ-INFY) (div/yr: $0.72) software svcs exporter-INDIA
c/o Deutsche Bank Trust Co   800-301-3517 admr

Insignia Solutions (NDQ-INSG) (div/yr: $0.00) svcs-software for mobile phones-UK
c/o Bank of New York   800-345-1612 admr

International Power (N-IPR) (div/yr: $0.00) energy-builds & operates elec power plants-UK
c/o Bank of New York   800-345-1612 admr

Iona Technologies plc (NDQ-IONA) (div/yr: $0.00) software svcs-IRELAND
c/o Deutsche Bank Trust Co   800-749-1873 admr

Jilin Chemical Industrial Co Ltd (N-JCC) (div/yr: $0.00) mfg-chemical products-CHINA
c/o Bank of New York   800-345-1612 admr

Kookmin Bank (N-KB) (div/yr: $0.45) banks/banking-KOREA
c/o Bank of New York   800-345-1612 admr

Koor Industries Ltd (N-KOR) (div/yr: $0.00) diversified-telecomm/elec/chem/food-ISRAEL
c/o Bank of New York   800-345-1612 admr

Korea Electric Power Corp (N-KEP) (div/yr: $0.41) utility-electric-KOREA
c/o Bank of New York   800-345-1612 admr

Kubota (N-KUB) (div/yr: $ 0.38) mfg-machinery-JAPAN
c/o JP Morgan Chase Bank   800-428-4237 admr

Kyocera Corp (N-KYO) (div/yr: $0.71) mfg-ceramic products/office eq-JAPAN
c/o Citibank N A   877-248-4237 admr

Lafarge (N-LR) (div/yr: $ 1.46) mfg-construction/building materials-FRANCE
c/o JP Morgan Chase Bank   800-428-4237 admr

Lan Chile SA (N-LFL) (div/yr: $0.83) trans-passenger/cargo airlines-CHILE
c/o Bank of New York   800-345-1612 admr

Lihir Gold Ltd (NDQ-LIHRY) (div/yr: $0.00) metals/mining-gold mining-AUSTRALIA
c/o Bank of New York   800-345-1612 admr

Lloyds TSB Group plc (N-LYG) (div/yr: $ 2.46) banks/banking-UK
c/o Bank of New York   800-345-1612 admr

Logitech International (NDQ-LOGI) (div/yr: $0.00) mfg-computer peripherals-SWITZERLAND
c/o Bank of New York   800-345-1612 admr

Luxottica Group SpA (N-LUX) (div/yr: $0.25) consumer prod-design/mfg-eyeglass frames-ITALY
c/o Bank of New York   800-345-1612 admr

Macronix International Co Ltd (NDQ-MXICY) (div/yr: $0.00) mfg-integrated circuits-TAIWAN
c/o Bank of New York   800-345-1612 admr

Magyar Tavkozlesi Vallalat Rt (MATAV) (N-MTA) (div/yr: $ 1.43) telecommunications-HUNGARY
c/o JP Morgan Chase Bank   800-428-4237 admr

Makita Corp (NDQ-MKTAY) (div/yr: $0.19) mfg-electrical equip-JAPAN
c/o Bank of New York   800-345-1612 admr

Masisa SA (N-MYS) (div/yr: $ 1.44) mfg-particle board-CHILE
c/o Bank of New York   800-345-1612 admr

Matav-Cable Systems Media Ltd (NDQ-MATV) (div/yr: $0.00) telecomm-cable TV-ISRAEL
c/o Bank of New York   800-345-1612 admr

Matsushita Electric Industrial Co Ltd (N-MC) (div/yr: $0.14) consumer prod-electronics-JAPAN
c/o JP Morgan Chase Bank   800-428-4237 admr

MetroGas SA (N-MGS) (div/yr: $0.00) utility-gas-ARGENTINA
c/o Bank of New York   800-345-1612 admr

Metso Corp (N-MX) (div/yr: $0.45) mfg-pulp machinery-FINLAND
c/o Bank of New York   800-345-1612 admr

Mitsubishi Tokyo Financial Group (N-MTF) (div/yr: $0.06) banks/banking-JAPAN
c/o Bank of New York   800-345-1612 admr

NEC Corp (NDQ-NIPNY) (div/yr: $0.06) mfg-office equipment-JAPAN
c/o Bank of New York   800-345-1612 admr

Nacional Telefonos de Venezuela CA (N-VNT) (div/yr: $ 2.09) telecomm-fixed line communications -VENEZUELA
c/o Bank of New York   888-269-2377 admr

Naspers Ltd (NDQ-NPSN) (div/yr: $0.58) publishing/enter-books/pay TV/internet-S AFRICA
c/o Bank of New York   800-345-1612 admr

National Australia Bank Ltd (N-NAB) (div/yr: $ 6.11) banks/banking-AUSTRALIA
c/o Bank of New York   800-345-1612 admr

Natuzzi SpA (N-NTZ) (div/yr: $0.17) consumer prod-household produ/furniture-ITALY
c/o Bank of New York   800-345-1612 admr

NetEase.com Inc (NDQ-NTES) (div/yr: $0.00) telecomm-interactive/wireless svc-CHINA
c/o Bank of New York   800-345-1612 admr

News Corp (The) (N-NWS) (div/yr: $0.06) publishing-newspapers/TV broadcasting-UK
c/o Citibank N A   877-248-4237 admr

Nice Systems Ltd (NDQ-NICE) (div/yr: $0.00) misc-technology-ISRAEL
c/o Bank of New York   800-345-1612 admr

Nippon Telephone & Telegraph Corp (N-NTT) (div/yr: $0.27) telecomm-wireless-JAPAN
c/o Bank of New York   800-345-1612 admr

Nissin Co Ltd (N-NIS) (div/yr: $0.21) fin svc-diversified financial svcs-JAPAN
c/o Bank of New York   800-345-1612 admr

Nokia Corp (N-NOK) (div/yr: $0.36) telecomm-cellular eq mfg/svcs-FINLAND
c/o Citibank Shareholder Services   877-CITI-ADR admr

Nomura Holdings Inc (N-NMR) (div/yr: $0.17) fin svcs-securities brokerage-JAPAN
c/o Bank of New York   800-345-1612 admr

Norsk Hydro AS (N-NHY) (div/yr: $ 1.39) energy-oil/gas, fertilizers, metals-NORWAY
c/o JP Morgan Chase Bank   800-428-4237 admr

Novartis AG (N-NVS) (div/yr: $0.75) drugs/pharmaceuticals-SWITZERLAND
c/o JP Morgan Chase Bank   800-428-4237 InvRe

Novo Nordisk of North America Inc (N-NVO) (div/yr: $0.62) drug/pharm-mfg insulin & indus enzymes-DENMARK
c/o JP Morgan Chase Bank   212-867-0123 US #

Novogen Ltd (NDQ-NVGN) (div/yr: $0.00) drug/pharm-phenolic technology products -AUSTRALIA
c/o Bank of New York   800-345-1612 admr

Oce NV (NDQ-OCENY) (div/yr: $0.64) mfg-office equipment-NETHERLANDS
c/o JP Morgan Chase Bank   800-428-4237 admr

Open-Joint/Vimpel Communications (N-VIP) (div/yr: $0.00) telecommunications-RUSSIA
c/o Bank of New York   800-345-1612 admr

POSCO (N-PKX) (div/yr: $ 1.61) mfg-steel-KOREA
c/o Bank of New York   800-345-1612 admr

PT Indosat Tbk (N-IIT) (div/yr: $0.67) telecomm-wired svcs-INDONESIA
c/o Bank of New York   800-345-1612 admr

Partner Communications Co Ltd (NDQ-PTNR) (div/yr: $0.00) telecommunications-ISRAEL
c/o JP Morgan Chase Bank   800-428-4237 admr

Pearson plc (N-PSO) (div/yr: $0.48) publishing-books/newspaper-Financial Times -UK
c/o Bank of New York   800-345-1612 admr

Perdigao SA (N-PDA) (div/yr: $ 1.24) food/bev-poultry/pork producer -BRAZIL
c/o Bank of New York   800-345-1612 admr

PetroChina Co Ltd (N-PTR) (div/yr: $ 3.18) energy-oil/gas explo/prod/refining-CHINA
c/o Bank of New York   800-345-1612 admr

Philips Electronics NV (Koninklijke) (N-PHG) (div/yr: $ 0.51) mfg-electronics-NETHERLANDS
c/o Citibank N A   800-808-8010 admr

Pioneer Corp (N-PIO) (div/yr: $0.23) cons prod-mfg hi-fi equip-JAPAN
c/o Citibank N A   877-248-4237 admr

Portugal Telecom (N-PT) (div/yr: $0.40) telecommunications-svcs-PORTUGAL
c/o Bank of New York   800-345-1612 admr

Prudential plc (N-PUK) (div/yr: $0.89) insurance-UK
c/o JP Morgan Chase Bank   800-428-4237 admr

Publicis Groupe SA (N-PUB) (div/yr: $0.27) misc-advertising-FRANCE
c/o Bank of New York   800-345-1612 admr

Quilmes Industrial SA (N-LQU) (div/yr: $0.00) food/bev-beer-LUXEMBOURG
c/o Bank of New York   800-345-1612 admr

Quinenco SA (N-LQ) (div/yr: $0.00) misc-diversified-fin svcs, food, telecomm-CHILE
c/o Bank of New York   800-345-1612 admr

Randgold Resources Ltd (N-GOLD) (div/yr: $0.00) metals/mining-gold mining-CHANNEL ISLANDS
c/o Bank of New York   800-345-1612 admr

Rank Group (The) plc (NDQ-RANKY) (div/yr: $0.55) rec/enter-film/TV prod/movie theaters/resorts-UK
c/o JP Morgan Chase Bank   800-428-4237 admr

Reed Elsevier plc (N-ENL) (div/yr: $0.65) publishing/information svcs-UK
c/o Bank of New York   800-345-1612 admr

Repsol YPF SA (N-REP) (div/yr: $0.49) energy-integrated oil distr-SPAIN
c/o Bank of New York   800-345-1612 admr

Reuters Group plc (NDQ-RTRSY) (div/yr: $ 1.10) publishing-wire svc/market & trading info-UK
c/o JP Morgan Chase Bank   800-428-4237 admr

Rhodia SA (N-RHA) (div/yr: $ 0.52) mfg-specialty chemicals-FRANCE
c/o Citibank NA   800-808-8010 admr

Rinker Group Ltd (N-RIN) (div/yr: $0.00) construction/building materials-AUSTRALIA
c/o JP Morgan Chase Bank   800-428-4237 admr

Rio Tinto plc (N-RTP) (div/yr: $ 3.08) metals/mining/energy-AUSTRALIA
c/o Bank of New York   800-345-1612 admr

Royal Dutch Petroleum Co (N-RD) (div/yr: $ 3.44) [S&P ranking: B +] energy-petroleum-
NETHERLANDS
c/o JP Morgan Chase Bank   800-428-4237 admr

Ryanair Holdings (NDQ-RYAAY) (div/yr: $0.00) trans-airline-ISRAEL
c/o Bank of New York   800-345-1612 admr

SCOR (N-SCO) (div/yr: $0.00) insurance-FRANCE
c/o Bank of New York   800-345-1612 admr

SGL Carbon AG (N-SGG) (div/yr: $ 0.00) mgf-chemicals-GERMANY
c/o JP Morgan Chase Bank   800-428-4237 admr

STMicroelectronics NV (N-STM) (div/yr: $0.09) mfg-semiconductors-NETHERLANDS
c/o Bank of New York   800-345-1612 admr

Sadia SA (N-SDA) (div/yr: $ 2.11) food/bev-poultry/pork/grains/pasta producer-BRAZIL
-/o Bank of New York   800-345-1612 admr

San Paolo IMI SA (Istituo Bancario) (N-IMI) (div/yr: $0.88) banks/banking-ITALY
c/o JP Morgan Chase Bank   800-428-4237 admr

Sanofi-Aventis SA (N-SNY) (div/yr: $0.71) drugs/pharmaceutical-FRANCE
c/o Bank of New York   800-345-1612 admr

Sappi Ltd (N-SPP) (div/yr: $0.30) mfg-paper/paper products-So AFRICA
c/o Bank of New York   800-345-1612 admr

Sasol Ltd (N-SSL) (div/yr: $0.72) energy-synfuels, coal & chemicals-S AFRICA
c/o Bank of New York   800-345-1612 admr

Schering AG (N-SHR) (div/yr: $ 1.01) drugs/pharmaceuticals-GERMANY
c/o JP Morgan Chase Bank   800-428-4237 admr

Scottish Power plc (N-SPI) (div/yr: $ 1.42) utility-electric-UK
c/o JP Morgan Chase Bank   800-428-4237 admr

Senetek plc (OTC-SNTKY) (div/yr: $0.00) drugs/pharmaceuticals-biotech development-UK
c/o Bank of New York   800-345-1612 admr

Serono SA (N-SRA) (div/yr: $0.16) dru/phar-dev genetic therapeutic prods-SWITZERLAND
c/o Bank of New York   800-345-1612 admr

Shire Pharmaceuticals Group plc (NDQ-SHPGY) (div/yr: $0.71) drug/pharmaceuticals-UK
c/o JP Morgan Chase Bank   800-428-4237 admr

Siemens AG (N-SI) (div/yr: $ 1.28) svcs/mgf-electrical engineering & electronics -GERMANY
c/o JP Morgan Chase Bank   800-428-4237 admr

Signet Group plc (N-SIG) (div/yr: $0.55) retail-jewelry-UK
c/o Bank of New York   800-345-1612 admr

Sinopec Shanghai Petrochemical (N-SHI) (div/yr: $0.97) energy-petroleum producer-CHINA
c/o Bank of New York   800-345-1612 admr

Skillsoft plc (NDQ-SKIL) (div/yr: $0.00) svcs-elearning software-IRELAND
See main entry for details of plan.   800-345-1612 admr

Smith & Nephew plc (N-SNN) (div/yr: $0.47) healthcar products-UK
c/o Bank of New York   800-345-1612 admr

Sociedad Quimica y Minera (N-SQM) (div/yr: $ 1.19) mfg-nitrates-CHILE
c/o Bank of New York   800-345-1612 admr

Sodexho Alliance SA (N-SDX) (div/yr: $0.91) food/agribusiness/tobacco FRANCE
c/o Bank of New York   800-345-1612 admr

Sony Corp (N-SNE) (div/yr: $0.23) consumer prod-mfg TV, radio, video monitors-JAPAN
c/o JP Morgan Chase Bank   800-428-4237 admr

Spirent plc (N-SPM) (div/yr: $0.00) network software- UK
c/o Bank of New York   800-345-1612 admr

Statoil ASA (N-STO) (div/yr: $0.39) energy-oil & gas exporation/production -NORWAY
c/o Bank of New York   800-345-1612 admr

TDK (N-TDK) (div/yr: $ 0.57) mfg-electronic storage media-JAPAN
c/o Citibank NA   800-808-8010 admr

THOMSON SA (N-TMS) (div/yr: $0.24) consumer prod-electronics-FRANCE
c/o JP Morgan Chase Bank   800-428-4237 admr

TIM Participacoes SA (N-TSU) (div/yr: $ 0.84) telecommunications-BRAZIL
c/o JP Morgan Chase Bank   800-428-4237 admr

Technip SA (N-TKP) (div/yr: $ 2.07) energy-oil/gas industry svcs-FRANCE
c/o JP Morgan Chase Bank   800-428-4237 admr

TOTAL SA (N-TOT) (div/yr: $ 3) energy-oil & gas exp/dev/prod-FRANCE
c/o Bank of New York   800-345-1612 admr

TV Azteca SA (N-TZA) (div/yr: $ 1) rec/ent-television-MEXICO
c/o Bank of New York   800-345-1612 admr

Tatneft (AO) (N-TNT) (div/yr: $0.00) energy-oil & gas div/prod-RUSSIA
c/o Bank of New York   800-345-1612 admr

Tele Centro Oeste Celular Part (N-TRO) (div/yr: $0.53) telecomm-cellular svcs-BRAZIL
c/o Bank of New York   800-345-1612 admr

Tele Leste Celular Part (N-TBE) (div/yr: $0.00) telecomm-cellular svcs-BRAZIL
c/o Bank of New York   800-345-1612 admr

Tele Norte Celular Part (N-TCN) (div/yr: $0.35) telecomm-cellular svcs-BRAZIL
c/o Bank of New York   800-345-1612 admr

Tele Norte Leste Part (N-TNE) (div/yr: $ 1.04) telecomm-telecommunications svcs-BRAZIL
c/o Bank of New York   800-345-1612 admr

Telecom Argentina STET-France Telecom SA (N-TEO) (div/yr: $0.00) telecom-svcs-ARGENTINA
c/o JP Morgan Chase Bank   800-428-4237 admr

Telecom Italia SpA (N-TI) (div/yr: $ 1.43) telecommunications-ITALY
c/o JP Morgan Chase Bank   800-428-4237 admr

Telefonos de Mexico SA de CV (N-TMX) (div/yr: $ 1.25) telecommunications-MEXICO
c/o JP Morgan Chase Bank   800-428-4237 admr

Telekom Austria (N-TKA) (div/yr: $0.23) telecomm-landline/mobile svcs -AUSTRIA
c/o Bank of New York   800-345-1612 admr

Telekomunikasi Indonesia PT (N-TLK) (div/yr: $0.00) telecomm-satellite svcs-INDONESIA
c/o Bank of New York   800-345-1612 admr

Telemig Celular Part SA (N-TMB) (div/yr: $0.91) telecomm-cellular svcs-BRAZIL
c/o Bank of New York   800-345-1612 admr

Telesp Celular Part SA (N-TCP) (div/yr: $0.00) telecomm-cellular svcs-BRAZIL
c/o Bank of New York   800-345-1612 admr

Telkom SA Ltd (N-TKG) (div/yr: $0.72) telecomm-fixed line systems-S AFRICA
c/o Bank of New York   800-345-1612 admr

Telstra Corp Ltd (N-TLS) (div/yr: $0.76) telecomm-telecomm svcs-AUSTRALIA
c/o Bank of New York   800-345-1612 admr

Tenaris SA (N-TS) (div/yr: $ 1.69) energy-oil/gas related svcs-LUXEMBOURG
c/o JP Morgan Chase Bank   800-428-4237 admr

Teva Pharmaceuticals Industries Ltd (NDQ-TEVA) (div/yr: $0.19) drugs/pharm/vet prod-ISRAEL
c/o Bank of New York   800-345-1612 admr

Tompkins plc (N-TKS) (div/yr: $0.95) misc-ind & consumer prod/mgmt svcs -UK
c/o Bank of New York   800-345-1612 admr

Toyota Motor Corp (N-TM) (div/yr: $0.96) mfg-autos/pre-fab housing -JAPAN
c/o Bank of New York   800-345-1612 admr

Transportadora de Gas del Sur SA (N-TGS) (div/yr: $0.00) energy-natural gas trans-ARGENTINA
c/o Bank of New York   800-345-1612 admr

Tricom SA (OTC-TRICY) (div/yr: $0.00) telecomm-telecomm svcs-DOMINICAN REP
c/o Bank of New York   800-345-1612 admr

Ultrapar Participacoes (N-UGP) (div/yr: $0.71) energy-dist/liq petroleum gas/chem/petrochem-BRAZIL
c/o Bank of New York   800-345-1612 admr

Unilever NV (N-UN) (div/yr: $ 1.81) [S&P ranking: B +] misc-diversified international concern-NETHERLANDS
c/o JP Morgan Chase Bank   800-428-4237 admr

Unilever plc (N-UL) (div/yr: $ 1.42) misc-diversified int'l concern-UK
c/o JP Morgan Chase Bank   800-428-4237 admr

Vale do Rio Doce Comp (N-RIO) (div/yr: $0.58) metals/mining-BRAZIL
c/o JP Morgan Chase Bank   800-428-4237 admr

Van der Moolen Holding NV (N-VDM) (div/yr: $0.21) fin svcs-securities brokerage-NETHERLANDS
c/o Bank of New York   800-345-1612 admr

Veolia Environnement (N-VE) (div/yr: $0.62) svcs-water/waste mgt/energy-FRANCE
c/o Bank of New York   800-345-1612 admr

Vina Concha y Toro SA (N-VCO) (div/yr: $0.68) food/bev-wine producer/exporter-CHILE
c/o Bank of New York   800-345-1612 admr

Vivendi Universal (N-V) (div/yr: $0.00) entertainment-FRANCE
c/o Bank of New York   800-345-1612 admr

Vodafone Group plc (N-VOD) (div/yr: $0.56) telecomm-mobile phone svc-UK
c/o Bank of New York   800-345-1612 admr

Volvo AB (NDQ-VOLVY) (div/yr: $ 1.50) mfg-trucks, buses*/jet & ind engines-SWEDEN
See main entry for details of plan.   212-418-7432 InvRe

Votorantim Celulose e Papel SA (N-VCP) (div/yr: $0.59) mft-forest products/paper-BRAZIL
c/o Bank of New York   800-345-1612 admr

WMC Resources Ltd (N-WMC) (div/yr: $ 1.12) mining/energy-AUSTRALIA
c/o Bank of New York   800-345-1612 admr

Waterford Wedgwood plc (NDQ-WATFZ) (div/yr: $0.12) consumer prod-glass/ceramics-IRELAND
c/o Bank of New York   800-345-1612 admr

Wavecom SA (NDQ-WVCM) (div/yr: $0.00) svc-wireless voice/data applications-FRANCE
c/o Bank of New York   800-345-1612 admr

Westpac Banking Corp (N-WBK) (div/yr: $ 3.17) banks/banking-AUSTRALIA
c/o JP Morgan Chase Bank   800-428-4237 admr

Wipro Ltd (N-WIT) (div/yr: $ 0.33) svcs-software-INDIA
c/o JP Morgan Chase Bank   800-428-4237 admr

Wolseley plc (N-WOS) (div/yr: $0.94) distr-plumbing/central heat equip-UK
c/o Bank of New York   800-345-1612 admr

Xenova Group plc (NDQ-XNVA) (div/yr: $0.00) drugs/pharmaceuticals-UK
c/o Bank of New York   800-345-1612 admr

YPF Sociedad Anomina (N-YPF) (div/yr: $ 4.29) energy-oil/natural exp/dev/prod-ARGENTINA
c/o Bank of New York   800-345-1612 admr

Yanzhou Coal Mining Co Ltd (N-YZC) (div/yr: $0.69) metals/mining-coal mining-CHINA
c/o Bank of New York   800-345-1612 admr

ADR Transfer Agents

A number of large banks handle the transfer agency functions of record keeping and processing ADRs and New York registry shares. In many cases U S investors may purchase the initial ADRs directly from the bank. Because the bank serves as the transfer agent, shareholders deal directly with the entity performing administrative functions. The following are descriptions of the four plans, which are sponsored and administered by the banks, not the company. In addition, ADRs and New York shares are traded on U S exchanges, they may be purchased through a broker. (*See Costs to Investors, Introduction.*)

Bank of New York
Global BuyDIRECT
PO Box 11258 Church St Sta
New York, NY 10286-1258
 800-345-1612
 610-382-7836
e-mail: shareowner-svcs@bankofny.com
www.adrbny.com
NOTE: *$5 + 10¢/sh cash pymts

Buy fees: 5% to $5 + 10¢/sh - div
$50-100,000/yr EFT*(52)
DIP: $200 + $10 + 10¢/sh
part. DR/cash-only
sfkg-$10/p. sale-$10 + 10¢/sh
ADR
gifting $5

Citibank N A
150 Royal St
Canton, MA 02021
 877-248-4237 admr
 212-657-5107 fax #
 212-657-1698 admr
 www.citibank.com/adr
NOTE: *$5 + 10¢/sh cash purch, EFT from a U S bank/ Citibank plans vary with each company, inquire for current individual plan

Buy fees: 10¢/sh-div*
$50-100,000/yr EFT*(52)
DIP: $250 + $5 + bkg fee
partial DR option
sfkg-free/p. sale-$10 + 12¢/sh
New York shs/U S res only

Deutsche Bank Trust Co Americas
DB-Direct
P O Box 338
South Hackensack, NJ 07606-1938
800-301-3517
www.melloninvestor.com
www.adr.db.com
NOTE: *cash pymt fees: 6 ¢/sh + $2 auto mo EFT/$3 single EFT/$5 check

Buy fees: 5% to $5 + 6¢/sh(no cost for <100shs)-div*
$50-250,000/yr EFT*
DIP: $250 + $15 + 6¢/sh
part. DR/cash-only
sfkgfree/p. sale-$15 + 12¢/sh
ADR
gifting free

J P Morgan Chase Bank
Global Invest Direct
P O Box 43013
Providence, RI 02940-3013
 800-428-4237
 800-749-1687 DIP
www.adr.com/shareholder
NOTE: *cash pymt-$5+12¢/sh/ daily sales, sales by telephone or internet

Buy fees: 5% to $2.50-div*
$50-100,000/yr EFT (52)
DIP: $250 + $18
part. DR/cash-only
sfkg-free/p. sale-$5 + 12¢/sh
ADR

A

AAR Corp (N-AIR) (div/yr: $0.00) mfg-aviation industry
1100 N Wood Dale Rd
Wood Dale, IL 60191
 800-446-2617 admr
 630-227-2059 fax #
 630-227-2040 CorpSecy
 www.aarcorp.com
Buy fees: no cost-div*
$50-250,000/yr EFT(12)
part. DR/cash-only
sfkg-free/p. sale-$15 + 12¢/sh
rec common
✂
NOTE: *cash pymt fee ($5 by check $2/EFT) + 3¢/sh/co does not pay div

ADC Telecommunications Inc (NDQ-ADCT) (div/yr: $0.00) [S&P ranking: B] mfg-telecommunications equipt
P O Box 1101
Minneapolis, MN 55440
 800-929-6782 admr
 952-917-0892 fax #
 952-938-8080 InvRe
 e-mail: investor@adc.com
 www.adc.com/
Buy fees: 5¢/sh
$50-250,000/yr EFT(52)
DIP: $500 + $10 ($50/mo)
sfkg-free/p. sale-$10 + 15¢/sh
rec common
gifting $10
★
NOTE: telephone transactions

AEGON NV (N-AEG) (div/yr: $ 0.53) insurance-life/health, investment products-NETHER
1111 N Charles St
Baltimore, MD 21201
 800-808-8010 admr
 410-347-8685 fax #
 410-576-4577 InvRe
 e-mail: mpappas@aegonusa.com
 www.aegon.com
Buy fees: 10¢/sh-div*
$50-100,000/yr EFT*(52)
DIP: $250 + $15 + 10¢/sh
part. DR/cash-only
sfkg-free/p. sale-$10 + 12¢/sh
NY registry shares/US res only
★
NOTE: *$5 + 10¢/sh for cash pymts

AFLAC Inc (N-AFL) (div/yr: $ 0.44) [S&P ranking: A] insurance
1932 Wynnton Rd
Columbus, GA 31999-0001
 800-235-2667 ShSvc
 706-596-3488 fax #
 706-596-3264 InvRe
 e-mail: jdiblasi@aflac.com
 www.aflac.com
Buy fees: no cost
$50-250,000/yr EFT(52)
DIP: $1,000
part. DR/cash-only
sfkg-free/p. sale-bkg fee
rec common/no residency restrict.
div deposit/gifting free
✂
★

AGL Resources Inc (N-ATG) (div/yr: $ 1.24) [S&P ranking: A-] utility-gas
P O Box 4569   Loc 1080
Atlanta, GA 30302-4569
 877-ATG-NYSE DRP
 404-584-3419 fax #
 800-866-1543 admr
 www.aglresources.com
Buy fees: no cost
25-5,000/mo EFT(24)
DIP: $250
part. DR/cash-only
sfkg-free/p. sale-avail
rec common
div deposit/gifting free
✂
★

AK Steel Holding Corp (N-AKS) (div/yr: $0.00) [S&P ranking: C] mfg-steel (carbon flat-rolled)
703 Curtis St
Middletown, OH 45043-0001
 513-425-5792 Treas
 513-425-5958 fax #
 800-837-2755 admr
 e-mail: greg.kuzma@aksteel.com
 www.aksteel.com
Buy fees: no cost
$25-4,000/mo(12)
sfkg-avail
common
✂

ALLTEL Corp (N-AT) (div/yr: $ 1.52) [S&P ranking: B +] telecommunications
✂ 50 Executive Parkway   Buy fees: no cost
Hudson, OH 44236 $50-25,000/qtr EFT(12)
330-963-1469 ShrSv   sfkg-free
888-243-5445 admr   rec common
e-mail: shareholder.services@alltel.com
www.alltel.com

AMB Property Corp (N-AMB) (div/yr: $ 1.76)   REIT-industrial properties
✂ Pier 1, Bay 1   Buy fees: no cost
San Francisco, CA 94111 $500-5,000/mo
★ 800-331-9474 amdr   DIP: $500
415-477-2065 fax #   p. sale-$15
415-394-9000 InvRe   div deposit
e-mail: ir@amb.com
www.amb.com

AMCOL International (N-ACO) (div/yr: $ 0.36) [S&P ranking: B +] metals/mining-bentonite/trans/specialty chemicals
1500 W Shur Dr, Ste 500   Buy fees: no svc chg
Arlington Heights, IL 60004-7803 $25-2,000/mo EFT(12)
800-937-5449 admr   partial DR option
847-394-7890 fax #   sfkg-free/p. sale-avail
847-394-8730 ShrSv   rec common
e-mail: invest@amcol.com   div deposit
www.amcol.com

AMCORE Financial Inc (NDQ-AMFI) (div/yr: $ 0.68) [S&P ranking: A-] banking/mortgage banking/fin svcs
P O Box 1537/501 7th St   Buy fees: no cost
✂ Rockford, IL 61110-0037 $10-7,500/qtr EFT(12)
815-968-2241 co #   partial DR option
815-961-7728 fax #   sfkg-free/p. sale-avail
800-468-9716 admr   rec common 1 sh min
www.AMCORE.com   div deposit

AMETEK Inc (N-AME) (div/yr: $ 0.24) [S&P ranking: A-] mfg-precision instruments
P O Box 1764   Buy fees: 2%to$2.50 + 10¢/sh
Paoli, PA 19301 $25-10,000/day(250)
610-647-2121 co #   DIP: $250+ $2.50 + 10¢/sh
610-296-8485 fax #   sfkg-$7.50/p. sale-$15 + 10¢/sh
★ 877-854-0864 admr   common
e-mail: investor.info@ametek.com div deposit
www.ametek.com

AMLI Residential Properties Trust (N-AML) (div/yr: $ 1.92) [S&P ranking: B +] REIT-multifamily residential units
✂ 125 S Wacker Dr Ste 3100   Buy fees: no cost
Chicago, IL 60606 $50-25,000/qtr(4)
312-443-1477 InvRe   sfkg-free/p. sale-avail
312-443-0909 fax #   rec common
800-730-6001 admr
e-mail: invest@amli.usa.com
www.amli.com

AT&T Corp (N-T) (div/yr: $ 0.95) [S&P ranking: B] telecommunications
c/o EquiServe Trust Co NA   Buy fees: no bkg fee*
P O Box 43007 $100-250,000/yr(52)
Providence, RI 02940-3007   partial DR option
 800-348-8288 admr   sfkg-free/p. sale-$20 + 7¢/sh
 908-221-2528 fax #   rec comm 1 sh min**
 908-221-2000 InvRe   div deposit/gifting avail
 e-mail: attir@att.com
 www.att.com/ir
NOTE: *svc chg: div-10% to $1 & cash-$5/purchase/**pref div & deb/bonds/note int purchases common/may sell or transfer shs on internet/certificate no longer issued

AVX Corp (N-AVX) (div/yr: $ 0.15) [S&P ranking: B-] mfg-electronic components
P O Box 867   Buy fees: no cost
Myrtle Beach, SC 29577-0867 $20-2,000/mo(12)
 800-937-5449 admr   partial DR option
 843-444-0424 fax #   sfkg-avail
 843-448-9411 InvRe   rec common
 e-mail: finance@avxcorp.com
 www.avxcorp.com

Abbott Laboratories (N-ABT) (div/yr: $ 1.10) [S&P ranking: A] health care products
c/o EquiServe   Buy fees: no cost
P O Box 1681 $10-20,000/yr(8)
Boston, MA 02105-1681   cash-only option
 847-937-6100 ShSvc   sfkg-free/p. sale-avail
 888-332-2268 admr   rec common/no residency restrict.
 www.abbott.com

Acadia Realty Trust (N-AKR) (div/yr: $ 0.69) [S&P ranking: B] REIT-shopping centers
1311 Mamaroneck Ave Ste 260   Buy fees: 2% to $2.50 + *
White Plains, NY 10605 $25-10,000/day EFT(240)
 914-288-8100 InvRe   DIP: $250 + $2.50 +10¢/sh
 888-200-3164 admr   part. DR/cash-only
 ww.acadiarealty.com   sfkg-$7.50/p. sale-$15 + 10¢/sh
                                             div deposit/gifting free
NOTE: * 10¢/sh-div/$2.50 + 10¢/sh-cash purch

Acuity Brands Inc (N-AYI) (div/yr: $ 0.60) mfg-lighting fixtures, specialty products
1170 Peachtree St NE Ste 2400   Buy fees: no cost
Atlanta, GA 30309-3002 $25-100,000/yr EFT(52)
 800-432-0140 admr   DIP: $500 + $15
 404-853-1457 AsstSecy   partial DR option
 e-mail: shareholderservices@acuitybrands.co   sfkg-free/p. sale-$10 + 10¢/sh
 www.acuitybrands.com   common
                                             div deposit/gifting free

Advanta Corp (NDQ-ADVNB) (div/yr: $ 0.30) fin svcs-financial products/credit card proc-
essing
PO Box 844 - 300 Welsh Rd   Buy fees: no cost
Springhouse, PA 19477   0-5% disc-div/cash*
 800-851-9673 admr $50-3,000/mo**(12)
 215-659-9479 fax #   DIP: $1,500
 215-444-5335 InvRe   part. DR/cash-only
 www.advanta.com   sfkg-free***/p. sale-avail
                                             comm Cl A#* & B-25 sh
NOTE: *call 800/299-3150 for disc amt/**approval for greater amt/***safekeeping only for Cl
B shares/ # reinvests in Cl B

Aetna Inc (N-AET) (div/yr: $ 0.02) fin svcs/health insurance
151 Farmington Ave
Hartford, CT 06156-3215
   800-446-2617 admr
   860-293-1361 fax #
★ 860-273-3945 ShrRe
   www.aetna.com

Buy fees: div 5%to$3 + 3¢/sh
$50-250,000/yr*EFT(52)
DIP: $500 + $10 + 10¢/sh**
sfkg-free/p. sale-$15 + 10¢/sh
common

NOTE: *$5 + 10¢/sh cash pymts/$1 EFT fee + 10¢/sh/**or $50 by EFT for 10 consecutive pymts/free trans of shs

Agere Systems Inc (N-AGR/A) (div/yr: $0.00) mfg-chipsets for hard drives/mobile phones/telecom
1110 American Parkway NE
Allentown, PA 18109
   866-243-7347 admr
   610-712-6011 co #
   www.agere.com

p. sale-$7.50 + 10¢/sh
common Class A & B

NOTE: book entry registration for shares, may sell through transfer agent/no div paid by company

Air Products & Chemicals Inc (N-APD) (div/yr: $ 1.28) [S&P ranking: B +] mfg-industrial gases/chemicals
   7201 Hamilton Blvd
★ Allentown, PA 18195-1501
   877-322-4941 admr
   610-481-5765 fax #
   610-481-8657 CorpSecy
   e-mail: info@apci.com
   www.airproducts.com

Buy fees: 2% to $2.50* + 10¢/sh
$100-200,000/yr(52)
DIP: $500 + $2.50 + 10¢/sh
part. DR/cash-only
sfkg-$7.50/p. sale-$15 + 10¢/sh
rec common/no residency restrict.
div deposit/gifting avail

Alaska Communications Systems Group Inc (NDQ-ALSK) (div/yr: $ 0.18) telecomm-local, long distance, wireless,internet
   600 Telephone Ave
★ Anchorage, AK 99503
   800-870-2426 admr
   800-234-9383 CpCom
   e-mail: investors@acsalaska.com
   www.acsalaska.com

Buy fees: 6¢/sh
$25-20,000/mo EFT
DIP: $500 + 6¢/sh
part. DR/cash-only
p. sale-$15 + 12¢/sh
common/no residency restrict.

Albany International Corp (N-AIN) (div/yr: $ 0.32) [S&P ranking: B] mfg-paper-making fabric
✂ c/o Computershare Investor Services
   P O Box A3309
   Chicago, IL 60690
   312-360-5395 ShSvc
   518-447-6343 fax #
   518-445-2284 ShSvc
   e-mail: investor_relations@albint.com
   www.albint.com

Buy fees: no cost
$10-5,000/month(12)
part. DR/cash-only
sfkg-free/p. sale-avail
rec common Cl A

NOTE: board will consider div pymts on qtrly basis

Albemarle Corp (N-ALB) (div/yr: $ 0.60) [S&P ranking: B +] mfg-specialty chemicals
✂ 330 S 4th St
   Richmond, VA 23229
   800-622-6757 admr
   804-788-6000 InvRe
   www.albemarle.com

Buy fees: no cost
$25-1,000/month(12)
cash-only option
sfkg-free
common

Albertson's Inc (N-ABS) (div/yr: $ 0.76) [S&P ranking: A-] food-supermarkets/drug stores
PO Box 20 $25-10,000/day(4)
Boise, ID 83726-0020   DIP: $250
888-788-5081 admr   part. DR/cash-only
208-395-6672 fax #   sfkg-$7.50
208-395-6208 co #   common
www.albertsons.com

★

Alcan Inc (N-AL) (div/yr: $ 0.60) [S&P ranking: B-] metals/mining-CDN
P O Box 6090   Buy fees: no cost
Montreal, Que H3C 3A7, Canada   US$100-15,000/qtr or (12)
514-848-8000 ShSvc   C$100-25,000/qtr
514-848-1465 fax #   part. DR/cash-only
800-387-0825 admr   common/no residency restrict.
e-mail: investor.relations@alcan.com   div deposit in Canada only
www.alcan.com

✂

Alcoa Inc (N-AA) (div/yr: $ 0.60) [S&P ranking: B +] metals/mining
201 Isabella St   Buy fees: no cost
Pittsburgh, PA 15212-5858 $25-5,000/mo EFT(12)
412-553-4545 co #   part. DR/cash-only
412-553-4498 fax #   rec comm/pref-1 sh
800-317-4545 admr
e-mail: investor.relations@alcoa.com
www.alcoa.com

✂

Alexander & Baldwin Inc (NDQ-ALEX) (div/yr: $ 0.90) [S&P ranking: B +] trans-shipping/real estate/agribusiness
PO Box 3440   Buy fees: no cost
Honolulu, HI 96801   no cash plan
808-525-8450 CorpSecy   sfkg-free/p. sale-$10
808-525-6678 fax #   rec common 25 sh min
800-356-2017 admr
e-mail: invrel@abinc.com
www.alexanderbaldwin.com

✂

Alfa Corp (NDQ-ALFA) (div/yr: $ 0.34) [S&P ranking: A] insurance
P O Box 11000   Buy fees: no cost
Montgomery, AL 36191-0001 $25-5,000/qtr(4)
877-611-7981 admr   part. DR/cash-only
334-394-3087 fax #   p. sale-avail
334-613-4500 ShrSv   rec common
e-mail: srutledge@alfains.com
www.alfains.com

✂

Aliant Inc (CDN) (T-AIT.C) (div/yr: $ 1.12) telecommunications-CDN
P O Box 820   Buy fees: no cost
Charlottetown, PEI C1A, 7M1Canada   to C$10,000/qtr(4)
877-248-3113 admr   rec common/US res not elig
902-429-8755 fax #
902-486-2363 InvRe
e-mail: investor.relations@aliant.ca
www.aliant.ca   NOTE: div in Canadian dollars

✂

Allegheny Energy Inc (N-AYE) (div/yr: $0.00) [S&P ranking: C] utility-elec
10435 Downsville Pke   Buy fees: 3% to $3.00*
Hagerstown, MD 21740-1766 $50-10,000/qtr(4)
301-665-2704 CorpSecy   part. DR/cash-only
301-665-2739 fax #   sfkg-free/p. sale-$15 + bkg
800-526-0801 admr   rec common/no residency restrict.
e-mail: investorinfo@alleghenypower.com
www.alleghenyenergy.com
NOTE: *$3.00 fee for cash purchases/$5-20 for duplicate statements

Allegheny Technologies Inc (N-ATI) (div/yr: $ 0.24) [S&P ranking: B-] mfg-specialty metals
6 PPG Place Ste 1000   Buy fees: no cost-div
Pittsburgh, PA 15222-5479 $100-10,000/mo*EFT(52)
✂ 412-394-2800 ShSvc   DIP: $1,000 + $5 + 12¢/sh
412-394-2805 fax #   partial DR option
★ 800-406-4850 admr   sfkg-free/p. sale-$15 + 12¢/sh
www.alleghenytechnologies.com   rec common-30 sh min

Allergan Inc (N-AGN) (div/yr: $ 0.40) [S&P ranking: B] mfg-pharmaceutical prods for vi-
sion/skin/neurologic conditions
P O Box 19534   Buy fees: no cost
✂ Irvine, CA 92623-9534 $10-50,000/yr(12)
781-575-2000 admr   part. DR/cash-only
714-246-4774 fax #   sfkg-free/p. sale-avail
714-246-4500 CorpSecy   common
e-mail: corpinfo@allergan.com
www.allergan.com

Allete Inc (N-ALE) (div/yr: $ 1.20) [S&P ranking: A-] utility-electric/real estate
✂ 30 W Superior St   Buy fees: no cost
Duluth, MN 55802-2093 $10-100,000/yr EFT(12)
★ 800-535-3056 ShrSv   DIP: $250
218-720-2502 fax #   part. DR/cash-only
218-723-3974 ShrSv   sfkg-free/p. sale-avail*
e-mail: shareholder@allete.com   common/U S residents only
www.allete.com   gifting avail
NOTE: *sale of up to 200 shs/year

Alliant Energy Inc (N-LNT) (div/yr: $ 1.05) [S&P ranking: B] utility-elec holding co
PO Box 2568   Buy fees: 50¢/per qtr-div
Madison, WI 53701-2568 $25-360,000/yr EFT(24)
800-356-5343 ShSvc   DIP: $250 or $25/mo EFT
★ 608-458-3321 fax #   part. DR/cash-only
608-458-3407 CorpSecy   sfkg-free/p. sale-$15 + 7.5¢/sh
e-mail: joniaeschbach@alliantenergy.com   rec common/no residency restrict.
www.alliantenergy.com/   div deposit/gifting free

Allstate Corp (The) (N-ALL) (div/yr: $ 1.28) [S&P ranking: B +] insurance-property-casualty
3075 Sanders Rd Dept G2H   Buy fees: 5% to $3 + 3¢/sh*
Northbrook, IL 60062-7127 $100-150,000/yr EFT(52)
★ 800-355-5191 admr   DIP: $500* + $10 + 3¢/sh
847-402-9116 fax #   part. DR/cash-only
847-402-2607 ShrSv   sfkg-free/p. sale-$15 + 12¢/sh
www.allstate.com   rec comm
                                          div deposit/gifting avail
NOTE: *for div, $5 + 3¢/sh by check, free EFT/**$50/mo min EFT

Altria Group Inc (N-MO) (div/yr: $ 2.92) [S&P ranking: A +] consumer prod-tobacco/Philip
Morris, foods/Kraft
120 Park Ave   Buy fees: 5% to $3 + 3¢/sh*
★ New York, NY 10017-5592 $10-60,000/yr EFT(104)
800-442-0077 admr   DIP: $500 + $5 + 3¢/sh
917-663-5794 fax #   part. DR/cash-only
917-663-4000 AsstSecy   sfkg-avail/p. sale-$15 + 12¢/sh
www.altria.com   rec common/no residency restrict.
                                          div deposit/gifting avail
NOTE: *plus enrollment fee $10 (cash purch fee: $5/check, $2.50/EFT + 3¢/sh)

AmSouth Bancorp (N-ASO) (div/yr: $ 1) [S&P ranking: A-] banking
P O Box 11426   Buy fees: no cost
Birmingham, AL 35202 $10-5,000/qtr EFT*(4)   ✂
  800-284-4100 5359   part. DR/cash-only
  205-326-4072 fax #   sfkg-free/p. sale-avail
  205-560-3478 CpTrs   rec common
  www.amsouth.com
NOTE: *EFT of dividends to an AmSouth bank acct

Amegy Bank of Texas (NDQ-ABNK) (div/yr: $0.00) banks/banking
P O Box 27459   Buy fees: no cost
Houston, TX 77027-7459 $50-10,000/mo EFT   ✂
  877-484-5037 admr   DIP: $250
  713-232-1115 InvRe   part. DR/cash-only   ★
  www.swbanktx.com   p. sale-$15 + 12¢/sh
                                       no residency restrict.

AmerUs Group Inc (N-AMH) (div/yr: $ 0.40) [S&P ranking: B] insurance-individual life & annuity products
699 Walnut St Dept H-75   Buy fees: 5%to$2.50 + 12¢/sh
Des Moines, IA 50306-1555 $50-15,000/mo EFT*(12)
  800-304-9709 admr   DIP: $1,000 + $10 + 12¢/sh   ★
  515-362-3648 fax #   cash-only option
  515-362-3693 InvRe   sfkg-free/p. sale-$15 + 12¢/sh
  www.amerus.com   rec comm-50 shs min/no residency restrict.
                                       div deposit/gifting free

NOTE: *cash pymt fees: 12¢/sh + $3 EFT/$5 check

Amerada Hess Corp (N-AHC) (div/yr: $ 1.20) [S&P ranking: B] energy-petroleum
c/o Bank of New York   Buy fees: no cost   ✂
P O Box 11258 Church St Sta $50-5,000/qtr(12)
New York, NY 10286   partial DR option
  212-997-8500 CorpSecy   p. sale-avail
  212-536-8291 fax #   rec common
  800-432-0140 admr
  e-mail: investorrelations@hess.com
  www.hess.com

Ameren Corp (N-AEE) (div/yr: $ 2.54) [S&P ranking: A-] utility-electric
P O Box 66887   Buy fees: 4¢/sh-market shs
St Louis, MO 63166-6887 $25-120,000/yr EFT(24)   ★
  800-255-2237 InvSv   DIP: $250 + 4¢/sh**
  314-554-2888 fax #   part. DR/cash-only
  314-554-3502 InvSv   sfkg-free/p. sale-4¢/sh
  e-mail: invest@ameren.com   rec comm/pref*/no residency restrict.
  www.ameren.com   div deposit
NOTE: *pref of Union Electric and Central Illinois Pub Svc/**must be of legal age to enroll in plan

AmeriServe Financial Inc (PA) (OTC-ASRV) (div/yr: $0.00) [S&P ranking: C] banks/banking
216 Franklin St, PO Box 430   Buy fees: no cost   ✂
Johnstown, PA 15907-0430 $10-2,000/mo
  800-317-4445 admr   sfkg-avail/p. sale-$10
  814-255-9700 CorpSecy   rec common
  www.ameriservfinancial.com   div deposit
NOTE: co does not pay div

AmeriVest Properties Inc (A-AMV) (div/yr: $ 0.13) REIT-office buildings
1780 S Bellaire St, Ste 100
Denver, CO 80222
800-884-4225 admr
303-296-7353 fax #
303-297-1800 InvRe
e-mail: ir@amvproperties.com
www.amvproperties.com

Buy fees: no cost-orig iss
3% disc-div
no cash plan
partial DR option
sfkg-free/p. sale-avail
record common

American Electric Power Inc (N-AEP) (div/yr: $ 1.40) [S&P ranking: B] utility-electric
1 Riverside Plaza/PO Box 16631
Columbus, OH 43216-6631
800-955-4740 admr
614-716-3288 fax #
614-716-2840 InvRe
e-mail: corpcomm@aep.com
www.aep.com

Buy fees: no cost
$25-150,000/yr EFT(52)
DIP: $250 or $25/mo + $10
part. DR/cash-only
sfkg-free*/p. sale-$5 + 12¢/sh
rec common
gifting free

NOTE: *cert insurance provided/IRA/internet access to acct

American Express Co (N-AXP) (div/yr: $ 0.48) [S&P ranking: A-] fin svcs/travel
200 Vesey St
New York, NY 10285-4814
800-463-5911 admr
212-619-9230 fax #
212-640-5101 ShSvc
www.americanexpress.com

Buy fees: div 75c + 6¢/sh *
$50-10,000/mo EFT + (12)
DIP: $1,000 + $6 + 6¢/sh
sfkg-free/p. sale-$10 + 12¢/sh
rec comm-min 10 shs
div deposit

NOTE: *cash $5 + 6¢/sh/ + EFT fee $3 + 6¢/sh

American Greetings Corp (N-AM) (div/yr: $ 0.32) [S&P ranking: B-] consumer prod-cards/gift-wrap
10500 American Rd
Cleveland, OH 44144-2398
216-252-7300 InvRe
216-252-6777 fax #
800-622-6757 admr
e-mail: information@americangreetings.com
www.americangreetings.com

Buy fees: no cost
$100-10,000/qtr(4)
sfkg-avail/p. sale-avail
rec comm 10 sh min/no residency restrict.

American Power Conversion Corp (NDQ-APCC) (div/yr: $ 0.40) [S&P ranking: B +] mfg-power availability solutions
132 Fairgrounds Rd
West Kingston, RI 02892
800-733-5001 admr
800-788-2208 InvRe
e-mail: investorrelations@apcc.com
www.apc.com

Buy fees: no cost-div*
$50/mo min&max*EFT(12)
sfkg-free/p. sale-$15
rec common
div deposit/gifting avail

NOTE: *cash purch fees: auto EFT-$2.50, check-$5

American States Water Co (N-AWR) (div/yr: $ 0.90) [S&P ranking: B +] utility-water
630 E Foothill Blvd
San Dimas, CA 91773-9016
877-463-6297 admr
909-394-0711 fax #
909-394-3600 co #
e-mail: investorinfo@aswater.com
www.aswater.com

Buy fees: no cost
$100-20,000/yr EFT(52)
DIP: $500
sfkg-avail/p. sale-avail
rec common/no residency restrict.
div deposit

DIVIDEND REINVESTMENT PLANS

DIVIDEND REINVESTMENT PLANS A

American Tower Corp (N-AMT) (div/yr: $0.00) svcs-leases antenna space to wireless/radio/TV

116 Huntington Ave	Buy fees: no cost
Boston, MA 02116	**
800-524-4458 admr	$500-10,000/mo(24)
617-375-7500 InvRe	DIP: $1,000 + $10
e-mail: ir@amertower.com	part. DR/cash-only
www.americantower.com	sfkg-avail/p. sale-$15 + 12¢/sh
	comm Cl A
	gifting avail

✂

★

NOTE: **0-5% discount on approved amts >$10,000/co does not pay div

Anadarko Petroleum Corp (N-APC) (div/yr: $ 0.72) energy-natural gas/oil production

1201 Lake Robbins Dr	Buy fees: no cost
The Woodlands, TX 77380-1000	5% disc*-div
888-470-5786 admr	$50-10,000/mo EFT(52)
832-636-8232 fax #	DIP: $1,000
832-636-1000 CorpSecy	part. DR/cash-only
www.anadarko.com	sfkg-free/p. sale-$15 + 15¢/sh
	comm-25 shs min
	div deposit

✂

%

★

NOTE: *0-3% disc on cash purchases over $10,000 may be available; for threshold prices info call 212-273-8200

Angelica Corp (N-AGL) (div/yr: $ 0.44) [S&P ranking: B-] svcs/sales-hospital laundry svc & retail uniforms

424 S Woods Mill Rd	Buy fees: no cost
Chesterfield, MO 63017-3406	$10-3,000/qtr(4)
314-854-3800 ShrSv	sfkg-free
314-854-3949 fax #	rec common
800-884-4225 admr	
www.angelica.com	

✂

Anheuser-Busch Cos (N-BUD) (div/yr: $ 0.98) [S&P ranking: A+] beverages/brewing

One Busch Place	Buy fees: no cost
St Louis, MO 63118-1852	$25-5,000/mo EFT(12)
888-213-0964 admr	sfkg-free/p. sale-5 cents/sh
314-577-3251 fax #	rec common/no residency restrict.
314-577-2663 InvRe	div deposit
www.anheuser-busch.com	

✂

Aon Corp (N-AOC) (div/yr: $ 0.60) [S&P ranking: B+] insurance-insurance broker

c/o EquiServe Trust Co	Buy fees: no cost
P O Box 2598 # 4675	$25-1,000/month(12)
Jersey City, NJ 07303-2598	partial DR option
800-446-2617 admr	p. sale-$10 + bkg
312-381-3793 fax #	common
312-381-1000 ShrSv	div deposit
www.aon.com	

✂

Apache Corp (N-APA) (div/yr: $ 0.32) [S&P ranking: B+] energy-petroleum/gas indus

2000 Post Oak Blvd, #100	Buy fees: no cost
Houston, TX 77056-4400	$50-25,000/qtr(12)
713-296-6504 CorpSecy	part. DR/cash-only
713-296-6805 fax #	sfkg-avail/p. sale-$10 + 10¢/sh
800-468-9716 admr	rec common/no residency restrict.
www.apachecorp.com	

✂

31

Applera Corp-Biosystems Group (N-ABI) (div/yr: $ 0.17) [S&P ranking: B] misc-biotechnology
R&D/software
c/o EquiServe Trust Co   Buy fees: no cost
✂ P O Box 43010   no cash plan
Providence, RI 02940-3010   partial DR option
 800-345-5224 admr   sfkg-free/p. sale-avail
 650-554-2920 fax #   common
 650-554-2479 InvRe
 e-mail: greublm@appliedbiosystems.com
 www.applera.com

Applied Industrial Technologies Inc (N-AIT) (div/yr: $ 0.48) [S&P ranking: B +] distr-bearings
& power transmission components
✂ P O Box 6925   Buy fees: no cost
Cleveland, OH 44115 $10-1,000/mo(12)
 800-988-5891 admr   sfkg-free/p. sale-$5
 216-426-4845 fax #   rec common
 216-426-4212 co #
 www.appliedindustrial.com

✂ **Aqua America Inc** (N-WTR) (div/yr: $ 0.52) [S&P ranking: A-] utility-water
762 W Lancaster Ave   Buy fees: no cost
% Bryn Mawr, PA 19010   5% disc-div
 800-205-8314 admr $50-250,000/yr EFT(154)
★ 610-645-1061 fax #   DIP: $500
 610-645-1196 ShrRe   partial DR option
 e-mail: info@aquaamerica.com   sfkg-free/p. sale-$15 + 12¢/sh
 www.aquaamerica.com   rec comm-min 5 shs*
                                          div deposit
NOTE: *max 100,000 shs/IRA-no ann fee (min $50 for shareholder/$500 for non-share-
holder) call 800/472-7428

Arbitron Inc (N-ARB) (div/yr: $ 0.10) svcs-market research to radio/TV/advertising cos
142 W 57th St   Buy fees: cash pymt*
New York, NY 10019 $100-120,000/yr
 800-524-4458 admr   DIP: $500 ($200 for*
★ 212-887-1390 fax #   sfkg-free/p. sale-$10 + 10¢/sh
 212-887-1300 InvRe
 e-mail: ir@arbitron.com
 www.arbitron.com
NOTE: *$2.50 + 10¢/sh/**shareholders) + $7.50/co does not pay div

Arch Chemicals Inc (N-ARJ) (div/yr: $ 0.80) mfg-specialty chemicals
P O Box 5204   Buy fees: div-5% to $3 + 10¢/sh-div*
Norwalk, CT 06856-5204 $50-250,000/yr*EFT(52)
 866-857-2223 admr   DIP: $500 + $10 + 10c\sh
★ 203-229-2613 fax #   part. DR/cash-only
 203-229-2804 InvRe   sfkg-free/p. sale-$15 + 10¢/sh
 www.archchemicals.com   rec common
                                          div deposit/gifting free
NOTE: *cash pymts: 10¢/sh + $2 EFT/$5 check

✂ **Archer Daniels Midland** (N-ADM) (div/yr: $ 0.34) [S&P ranking: B +] food processing & distri-
bution
P O Box 1470   Buy fees: no cost-div*
Decatur, IL 62525 $10-60,000/yr(12)
 888-470-5512 admr   part. DR/cash-only
 217-424-7224 fax #   sfkg-avail/p. sale-$15 + 12¢/sh
 217-424-4647 InvRe   rec common/no residency restrict.
 e-mail: info@admworld.com
 www.ADMworld.com
NOTE: *cash pymt fees: 6¢/sh + $2 EFT/$5 check

Archstone-Smith Trust (N-ASN) (div/yr: $ 1.73) REIT-apartments
9200 E Panorama Cir Ste 400 . . . . Buy fees: no cost-div*
Englewood, CO 80112 . . . . 0-5% disc-div/cash**
800-982-9293 admr . . . . $200-5,000/mo EFT(12)
720-873-6489 fax # . . . . DIP: $200 + 6¢/sh
303-708-5959 InvRe . . . . part. DR/cash-only
www.archstonesmith.com . . . . sfkg-avail/p. sale-$15 + 12¢/sh
comm-legal age/no residency restrict.
div deposit
NOTE: *cash pymt fee: 6¢/sh/**discount only on orig issue shs

Arrow Financial Corp (NDQ-AROW) (div/yr: $ 0.92) [S&P ranking: A-] banking
250 Glen St . . . . Buy fees: no cost
Glens Falls, NY 12801 . . . . $100-10,000/qtr(12)
518-793-4121 CpTrs . . . . DIP: $300
518-745-1976 fax # . . . . cash-only option
800-937-5449 admr . . . . p. sale-avail
www.arrowfinancial.com . . . . rec common/no residency restrict.

Artesian Resources Corp (NDQ-ARTNA) (div/yr: $ 0.87) [S&P ranking: B +] utility-water
664 Churchmans Rd . . . . Buy fees: no cost
Newark, DE 19702 . . . . $100-10,000/qtr(12)
800-368-5948 admr . . . . partial DR option
302-453-6943 InvRe . . . . comm Cl A non-voting
www.artesianwater.com

ArvinMeritor Inc (N-ARM) (div/yr: $ 0.40) mfg-auto parts
2135 W Maple Rd . . . . Buy fees: no cost
Troy, MI 48084 . . . . $50-100,000/yr EFT(12)
248-435-1000 Treas . . . . DIP: $500 + $10
248-435-1393 fax # . . . . part. DR/cash-only
800-483-2277 admr . . . . sfkg-free/p. sale-$15 + 12¢/sh
e-mail: investor.relations@arvinmeritor.com . . . rec common
www.arvinmeritor.com/investor . . . . gifting free
NOTE: TDD: 201-222-4955

Ashland Inc (N-ASH) (div/yr: $ 1.10) [S&P ranking: B] mfg-chem/energy & road construction
P O Box 391/Investor Relations . . . . Buy fees: no cost
Covington, KY 41012 . . . . $25-5,000/mo(52)
800-622-6757 admr . . . . DIP: $500
859-815-5788 fax # . . . . part. DR/cash-only
859-815-4454 ShSvc . . . . sfkg-free/p. sale-$10 + bkg
e-mail: investor_relations@ashland.com . . . . . . rec common
www.ashland.com

Associated Banc-Corp (NDQ-ASBC) (div/yr: $ 1) [S&P ranking: A] banking
1200 Hansen Rd . . . . $50-50,000/yr EFT(4)
Green Bay, WI 54304 . . . . part. DR/cash-only
800-622-6757 admr . . . . sfkg-free/p. sale-avail
920-491-7010 fax # . . . . rec common
920-491-7000 InvRe . . . . div deposit
www.associatedbank.com

Associated Estates Realty Corp (N-AEC) (div/yr: $ 0.68) REIT-residential properties
5025 Swetland Court . . . . Buy fees: no cost
Richmond Heights, OH 44143-1467 . . . . $100-5,000/mo EFT(12)
800-622-6757 x8572 . . . . DIP: $100 + $50
216-797-8801 fax # . . . . part. DR/cash-only
216-797-8798 InvRe . . . . p. sale-avail
e-mail: ir@aecrealty.com . . . . common
www.aecrealty.com . . . . gifting avail

Astoria Financial Corp (N-AF) (div/yr: $ 0.80) [S&P ranking: A-] S&L/savings bank
1 Astoria Federal Plaza $50-5,000/qtr(4)
Lake Success, NY 11042-1085   p. sale-$15 + fees
  800-851-9677 admr   common
  516-327-3000 co #
  e-mail: ir@astoriafederal.com
  www.astoriafederal.com

Atmos Energy Corp (N-ATO) (div/yr: $ 1.24) [S&P ranking: B +] utility-natural gas
✂ P O Box 650205   Buy fees: no cost
  Dallas, TX 75265-0205 $25-100,000/yr EFT(52)
★   800-543-3038 admr   DIP: $1,250
  972-855-3040 fax #   part. DR/cash-only
  972-855-3729 ShrRe   sfkg-free/p. sale-$15 + 5¢/sh
  e-mail: investorrelations@atmosenergy.com rec comm-min 50 shs
  www.atmosenergy.com   div deposit/gifting free*
  NOTE: *minimum transfer of 50 shs to another person/acct

Auburn National Bancorp Inc (NDQ-AUBN) (div/yr: $ 0.48) banks/banking
P O Box 3110   Buy fees: bkg fee
Auburn, AL 36831-3110 $100-5,000/qtr EFT*(4)
  800-368-5943 admr   sfkg-avail
  334-887-4690 fax #   rec comm
  334-887-4675 InvRe   div deposit
  e-mail: investorrelations@auburnbank.com
  www.auburnbank.com
  NOTE: *only bank customers may participate in cash purchase feature

Avery Dennison Corp (N-AVY) (div/yr: $ 1.52) [S&P ranking: A] mfg-office supplies/labels
✂ 150 N Orange Grove Blvd   Buy fees: no cost-div
  Pasadena, CA 91103-7090 $100-150,000/yr*(12)
★   800-649-2291 admr   DIP: $500 + $10 + 3¢/sh or $50/mo EFT
  626-304-2251 fax #   partial DR option
  626-304-2032 InvRe   sfkg-free/p. sale-$15 + 12¢/sh
  e-mail: investorcom@averydennison.com   rec common
  www.averydennison.com   div deposit/gifting free

Aviall Inc (N-AVL) (div/yr: $0.00) [S&P ranking: B-] mfg-aviation parts and aftermarket svcs
✂ P O Box 619048   Buy fees: no cost
  Dallas, TX 75261-9048 $25-15,000/qtr
  800-730-4001 admr   sfkg-avail/p. sale-5% to $10
  972-586-1702 fax #   rec comm-10shs min/no residency restrict.
  972-586-1703 InvRe
  e-mail: investorrelations@aviall.com
  www.aviall.com

Avista Corp (N-AVA) (div/yr: $ 0.54) utility-electric/gas
P O Box 3647   Buy fees: no cost-orig iss
✂ Spokane, WA 99220-3647   to $100,000/yr(12)
  800-642-7365 admr   sfkg-free/p. sale-avail
  509-495-8725 fax #   common/no residency restrict.
  509-495-2930 InvRe
  www.avistacorp.com

Avon Products Inc (N-AVP) (div/yr: $ 0.66) [S&P ranking: A] consumer prod-cosmetics
1345 Ave of the Americas   Buy fees: no cost
✂ New York, NY 10105-0196 $10-5,000/month(12)
  800-519-3111 admr   sfkg-free
  212-282-6035 fax #   rec common
  212-282-5320
  e-mail: individualinvestor@avon.com
  www.avon.com

B

BB&T Corp (N-BBT) (div/yr: $ 1.40) [S&P ranking: A-] banking
P O Box 1290
Winston-Salem, NC 27102-1290
252-246-4606 admr
336-733-3132 fax #
800-682-6902 33477
e-mail: ShareholderServices@bbandt.com
www.bbandt.com
NOTE: *EFT of cash pymts monthly

Buy fees: no cost
$25-10,000/mo EFT(52)
part. DR/cash-only
sfkg-free/p. sale-avail
rec common
gifting avail

BCE Inc (N-BCE) (div/yr: $ 1.32) [S&P ranking: B] telecomm-CDN
1000 de La Gauchetiere St #3700
Montreal, QUE H3B 4Y7, Canada
800-339-6353 admr
514-786-3970 fax #
514-786-3885 InvRe
e-mail: lyne.roy@bell.ca
www.bce.ca
NOTE: *Bell Canada/BCE bond interest & pref div subj to separate C$20,000 limit, purchases comm

Buy fees: no cost
up to US$20,000/yr*(12)
p. sale-avail
comm/pref/bonds*/no residency restrict.

BNP Residential Properties Inc (A-BNP) (div/yr: $ 1) [S&P ranking: B-] REIT
301 S College St Ste 3850
Charlotte, NC 28202-6024
800-829-8432 adnr
704-944-2039 fax #
704-944-0100 co #
e-mail: investor.relations@bnproperties.com
www.bnp-residential.com

Buy fees: no cost
$25-25,000/qtr(4)
part. DR/cash-only
sfkg-free/p. sale-avail
rec common

BP plc (N-BP) (div/yr: $ 1.77) energy-petroleum-UK
4101 Winfield Rd - 3W
Warrenville, IL 60555
877-638-5672 admr
630-821-3456 fax #
800-638-5672 ShSvc
e-mail: shareholderus@bp.com
www.bp.com/investors/alive
NOTE: online transactions at www.adr.com/access

Buy fees: no cost
US$50-250,000/yr EFT(104)
DIP: US$250
part. DR/cash-only
sfkg-free/p. sale-$15 + 12¢/sh
ADR-3 shs min/US & Can res
div deposit/gifting free

Baker Hughes Inc (N-BHI) (div/yr: $ 0.46) [S&P ranking: B] mfg-drilling equip
P O Box 4740
Houston, TX 77210-4740
713-439-8668 InvRe
713-439-8699 fax #
800-526-0801 admr
www.bakerhughes.com

Buy fees: no cost
$10-1,000/qtr(12)
cash-only option
sfkg-free/p. sale-avail
rec common

Baldor Electric Co (N-BEZ) (div/yr: $ 0.60) [S&P ranking: A] mfg-industrial electric motors
P O Box 2400
Fort Smith, AR 72902
800-509-5586 admr
479-649-6280 fax #
479-646-4711 Legal
www.baldor.com

Buy fees: no cost
$50-10,000/mo(12)
DIP: $50
part. DR/cash-only
sfkg-free
rec common
div deposit

Baldwin Technology Co Inc (A-BLD) (div/yr: $0.00) [S&P ranking: C] mfg-printing equipment
12 Commerce Dr   Buy fees: no cost
Shelton, CT 06484   no cash plan
✂ 203-402-1004 InvRe   sfkg-free
203-402-5500 fax #   rec common A&B*
800-368-5948 admr
e-mail: hposter@baldwintech.com
www.baldwintech.com
NOTE: *Cl B purchases comm A/div omitted since 3/92

Ball Corp (N-BLL) (div/yr: $ 0.40) [S&P ranking: B +] mfg-containers/aerospace system/divers prods
P O Box 5000   Buy fees: no cost
✂ Broomfield, CO 80038-5000   5% disc-div
800-446-2617 admr $25-2,000/mo(12)
% 303-460-2127 fax #   cash-only option
303-460-2126 CorpSecy   p. sale-avail
www.ball.com   rec common/no residency restrict.

BancTrust Financial Group Inc (NDQ-BTFG) (div/yr: $ 0.52) [S&P ranking: B +] banks/banking
100 St Joseph St   Buy fees: no cost-orig iss
✂ Mobile, AL 36652 $100-2,000/qtr(4)
800-368-5948 admr   partial DR option
251-431-7800 InvRe   sfkg-$5/p. sale-$15 + bkg
www.bantrustfinancialgroupinc.com

BancorpSouth Inc (N-BXS) (div/yr: $ 0.76) [S&P ranking: A-] banking
PO Box 789   Buy fees: no cost
✂ Tupelo, MS 38802-0789 $25-5,000/qtr EFT(4)
800-568-3476 admr   p. sale-avail
662-680-2006 fax #   common
662-680-2084 CorpSecy   div deposit
www.bancorpsouth.com

✂ **Bandag Inc** (N-BDG) (div/yr: $ 1.32) [S&P ranking: B] mfg-pre-cured tread rubber
2905 N Hwy 61   Buy fees: no cost
Muscatine, IA 52761-5886 $50-10,000/qtr*(12)
800-445-7524 admr   part. DR/cash-only
563-262-4461 fax #   sfkg-free
563-262-1461 ShrSv   rec common & Cl A/no residency restrict.
e-mail: jhenderson@bandag.com
www.bandag.com
NOTE: *per class of stock/each class reinvests in same class

✂ **Bank Mutual Corp (WI)** (NDQ-BKMU) (div/yr: $ 0.24) banks/banking
4949 W Brown Deer Rd   Buy fees: no cost
Brown Deer, WI 53223 $100-2,500/mo(12)
800-368-5948 admr   partial DR option
414-354-1500 InvRe   sfkg-avail/p. sale-$10
www.bankmutualcorp.com   comm-50 shs min

Bank of America Corp (N-BAC) (div/yr: $ 1.80) [S&P ranking: A-] banking
100 N Tryon St   Buy fees: no cost
✂ Charlotte, NC 28255-0001 $50-120,000/yr EFT(52)
800-642-9855 admr   DIP: $990 + $10
★ 704-386-0420 fax #   part. DR/cash-only
800-521-3984 CorpSecy   sfkg-free/p. sale-$15 + 8¢/sh
www.bankofamerica.com   common
                                        gifting free

Bank of Granite Corp (NDQ-GRAN) (div/yr: $ 0.52) [S&P ranking: B +] banking
P O Box 128
Granite Falls, NC 28630-0128
800-368-5948 admr
828-496-2116 fax #
828-496-2022 InvRe
www.bankofgranite.com
NOTE: *qtrly EFT of cash pymts
$100-2,000/qtr EFT*(4)
rec comm 100 sh min

Bank of Hawaii Corp (N-BOH) (div/yr: $ 1.32) [S&P ranking: B +] banking
P O Box 2900 Dept 232
Honolulu, HI 96846-0001
800-509-5586 admr
808-537-8131 fax #
808-537-8878
www.boh.com
Buy fees: no cost
$25-5,000/qtr EFT(12)
part. DR/cash-only
sfkg-free/p. sale-avail
common/no residency restrict.
div deposit

Bank of Montreal (N-BMO) (div/yr: $ 1.84) [S&P ranking: A +] banking-CDN
100 King St West, 21st Flr
Toronto, ONT M5X 1A1, Canada
416-867-6785 admr
416-867-6793 fax #
416-867-6786 CorpSecy
e-mail: corp.secretary@bmo.com
www.bmo.com
Buy fees: no cost
US/C$40,000/yr(12)
p. sale-avail
comm/pref Cl A & B
div deposit to Cdn bank

Bank of New York Co Inc (N-BK) (div/yr: $ 0.80) [S&P ranking: A-] banking
48 Wall St
New York, NY 10286-0001
800-432-0140 ShRel
212-495-1727 CorpSecy
e-mail: shareowner-svcs@bankofny.com
www.bankofny.com
Buy fees: no cost
$50-150,000/yr EFT(52)
DIP: $1,000 + $7.50
cash-only option
sfkg-free/p. sale-$10 + 5¢/sh
rec comm/bond
gifting avail

Bank of Nova Scotia (N-BNS) (div/yr: $ 1.28) [S&P ranking: A] banking-CDN
40 King St W, 10th Fl Scotia Pz
Toronto, ONT M5H 1H1, Canada
800-564-6253 admr
416-866-4048 fax #
416-866-4790 co #
e-mail: investorrelations@scotiabank.com
www.scotiabank.com
NOTE: *US residents eligible for stock dividend option only
Buy fees: no cost
C$100/mo-20,000/yr(12)
comm/pref/deb/no residency restrict.

Banner Corp (NDQ-BANR) (div/yr: $ 0.64) [S&P ranking: B +] banks/banking
10 S First Ave
Walla Walla, WA 99362
303-262-0600 admr
509-526-8891 fax #
509-526-8894 vp
www.bannerbank.com
NOTE: $25 certificate issuance fee
Buy fees: no cost
$50-1,500/month(12)
part. DR/cash-only
sfkg-avail/p. sale-$15
rec comm-min 100 shs
div deposit

Banta Corp (N-BN) (div/yr: $ 0.68) [S&P ranking: B] svcs-printing
PO Box 8003
Menasha, WI 54952-8003
800-278-4353 admr
920-751-7792 fax #
920-751-7777 co #
www.banta.com
Buy fees: no cost
$25-7,500/qtr EFT(12)
part. DR/cash-only
sfkg-free
rec common

Bard (C R) Inc (N-BCR) (div/yr: $ 0.48) [S&P ranking: B +] health care products
730 Central Ave
Murray Hill, NJ 07974-1139
✂ 800-828-1639 admr
908-277-8078 fax #
★ 908-277-8000 co #
www.crbard.com

Buy fees: no cost-div
$25-no max* EFT(52)
DIP: $250 + $15 + bkg fee
part. DR/cash-only
sfkg-free/p. sale-$15 + 12¢/sh
rec common
div deposit/gifting free

NOTE: *cash pymt fees: $1 EFT fee + $15 + 3¢/sh

Barnes Group Inc (N-B) (div/yr: $ 0.80) [S&P ranking: B] mfg/distr-mach
✂ P O Box 489
Bristol, CT 06011-0489
860-583-7070 Legal
860-589-3507 fax #
800-288-9541 admr
www.barnesgroupinc.com

Buy fees: no cost
$10-10,000/qtr(4)
p. sale-avail
common

Bausch & Lomb Inc (N-BOL) (div/yr: $ 0.52) [S&P ranking: B] cons products-health care prod
✂ c/o Mellon Bank NA
P O Box 3339
South Hackensack, NJ 07606
888-581-9377 admr
585-338-8551 fax #
585-338-5802 InvRe
e-mail: dritz@bausch.com
www.bausch.com

Buy fees: no cost
$25mo-60,000/yr(12)
cash-only option
sfkg-free
rec common
div deposit

Baxter International Inc (N-BAX) (div/yr: $ 0.58) [S&P ranking: B +] health care prod/svc
c/o EquiServe Trust Co NA
✂ P O Box 2598 # 4675
Jersey City, NJ 07303-2598
781-575-2723 admr
847-948-3948 fax #
847-948-2000 StkSv
www.baxter.com

Buy fees: no cost
$25-25,000/yr EFT(12)
part. DR/cash-only
sfkg-free
rec common
div deposit

Beckman Coulter Inc (N-BEC) (div/yr: $ 0.56) [S&P ranking: B +] mfg-laboratory instruments
✂ P O Box 3100
Fullerton, CA 92834-3100
714-773-7620 InvRe
714-773-8613 fax #
201-324-1644 admr
www.beckmancoulter.com

Buy fees: no cost
$10-60,000/yr(12)
part. DR/cash-only
sfkg-free
common

Becton, Dickinson & Co (N-BDX) (div/yr: $ 0.72) [S&P ranking: A] health care products
c/o EquiServe Trust Co NA
✂ P O Box 2598 # 4675
Jersey City, NJ 07303-2598
★ 800-446-2617 admr
201-847-7178 InvRe
www.bd.com

Buy fees: no cost-div; 3¢/sh on cash
$50-1million/yr(52)
DIP: $250 + bkg fee
partial DR option
sfkg-free/p. sale-$15 + 15¢/sh
common/no residency restrict.
div deposit/gifting free

Bedford Property Investors Inc (N-BED) (div/yr: $ 2.04) REIT
✂ 270 Lafayette Cir
Lafayette, CA 94549
% 800-948-5872 admr
925-283-5697 fax #
★ 925-283-8910 co #
www.bedfordproperty.com

Buy fees: no cost
0-3% disc-cash*
$100-5,000/month(12)
DIP: $1,000
part. DR/cash-only
p. sale-$15 + 12¢/sh

NOTE: *monthly amts over $5,000 must obtain (800/756-8200) a waiver and may receive a 0-3% discount

BellSouth Corp (N-BLS) (div/yr: $ 1.08) [S&P ranking: A-] telecommunications

1155 Peachtree St N E #14B06
Atlanta, GA 30309-3610
  888-266-6778 admr
  404-249-2060 fax #
  404-249-5977 co #
  www.bellsouth.com/investor

Buy fees: no cost
$50-100,000/yr EFT(52)
DIP: $490 + $10
part. DR/cash-only
sfkg-free/p. sale-$10 + 8¢/sh
rec common 5 sh min
div deposit/gifting free

NOTE: account transactions by phone/internet

Bemis Co (N-BMS) (div/yr: $ 0.72) [S&P ranking: A] mfg-flexible packaging & pressure sensitive mats

222 59th St Ste 2300
Minneapolis, MN 55402-4099
  800-468-9716 admr
  612-376-3180 fax #
  612-376-3000 InvRe
  www.bemis.com

Buy fees: no cost
$25-2,000/qtr EFT(12)
cash-only option
sfkg-free/p. sale-avail

Best Buy Co Inc (N-BBY) (div/yr: $ 0.44) [S&P ranking: B +] retail-computer/applicance chain stores

7601 Penn Ave S
Richfield, MN 55423
  877-498-8861 admr
  612-291-6111 InvRe
  e-mail: moneytalk@bestbuy.com
  www.bestbuy.com

Buy fees: 5%to$3 + 3¢/sh-div*
$50-250,000/yr(104)
DIP: $500 + 13 + 3¢/sh**
part. DR/cash-only
sfkg-avail/p. sale-$15 + 12¢/sh
common-1 sh min
gifting avail

NOTE: *cash pymt fees: 3¢/sh + $5 ck/$2.50 EFT/**or $50 + $2.50 + 3¢/sh for 10 mo

Black & Decker Corp (N-BDK) (div/yr: $ 1.12) [S&P ranking: B +] consumer prod-power tools/appliances

701 E Joppa Rd
Towson, MD 21286
  800-432-0140 admr
  410-716-2933 fax #
  410-716-2890 CorpSecy
  e-mail: lucy.bosley@bdk.com
  www.bdk.com

Buy fees: no cost
$25-100,000/y ($10,000/mo limit)*EFT(52)
part. DR/cash-only
sfkg-free
rec common

Black Hills Corp (N-BKH) (div/yr: $ 1.28) [S&P ranking: B +] utility-electric

P O Box 1400
Rapid City, SD 57709-1400
  605-721-1700 InvRe
  605-721-2597 fax #
  800-468-9716 admr
  e-mail: rrbasham@bh-corp.com
  www.blackhillscorp.com

Buy fees: no cost-ori orig iss shs*
$200-50,000/qtr(12)
cash-only option
sfkg-free
rec common
div deposit

NOTE: */bkg fee on market shares

Blair Corp (A-BL) (div/yr: $ 0.60) [S&P ranking: B-] retail-mail order-apparel

220 Hickory St
Warren, PA 16366-0001
  800-622-6757 admr
  814-723-3600 co #
  ww.blair.com

Buy fees: no cost
$25-5,000/month(52)
DIP: $100 + $100 fee
part. DR/cash-only
sfkg-avail/p. sale-$10 + fees
common

Block (H & R) Inc (N-HRB) (div/yr: $ 0.88) [S&P ranking: A-] fin svcs-tax preparation svcs
4400 Main St
Kansas City, MO 64111-1812
816-701-4443 ShSvc
816-753-8538 fax #
888-213-0968 admr
e-mail: investorrelations@hrblock.com
www.hrblock.com

Buy fees: no svc chg
$25-2,000/month(12)
p. sale-avail
common

Blyth Inc (N-BTH) (div/yr: $ 0.42) [S&P ranking: B +] consumer prod-home decor items-candles, gifts
One E Weaver St
Greenwich, CT 06831-5118
★ 800-446-2617 admr
203-552-6660 InvRe
www.blyth.com

Buy fees: no cost-div-orig iss*
$50-125,000/yr*EFT(52)
DIP: $240 + $10 + 10¢/sh*
part. DR/cash-only
sfkg-free/p. sale-$15 + 12¢/sh
common/residents of AZ,FL**
gifting free

NOTE: *cash pymt fees:10¢/sh + $2 EFT, $5 check (no bkg fee for orig iss purchases)
/**MD, ND & RI residents not eligible

Bob Evans Farms Inc (NDQ-BOBE) (div/yr: $ 0.48) [S&P ranking: A-] food-restaurants
3776 S High St
★ Columbus, OH 43207-0863
614-492-4952 StkRe
614-497-4459 fax #
614-492-4920 InvRe
www.bobevans.com

Buy fees: no svc chg
$50-20,000/mo EFT*(20)
DIP: $100
part. DR/cash-only
sfkg-free/p. sale-10¢/sh
rec common*/no residency restrict.
div deposit/gifting free

NOTE: *$25 EFT min amt

Boeing Co (N-BA) (div/yr: $ 1) [S&P ranking: B +] mfg-airplanes
100 N Riverside m/c 5003-5016
Chicago, IL 60606-1596
312-544-2835 InvRe
888-777-0923 admr
www.boeing.com

Buy fees: $1 + bkg fee
$50-100,000/yr EFT(52)
part. DR/cash-only
sfkg-free/p. sale-$10 + bkg
rec comm-50 sh min
div deposit/gifting avail

Borders Group Inc (N-BGP) (div/yr: $ 0.36) [S&P ranking: B] retail-book store chain
100 Phoenix Dr
Ann Arbor, MI 48104
★ 800-446-2617 admr
734-477-4538 fax #
734-477-1794 InvRe
www.bordersgroupinc.com

Buy fees: 5%to$3 + 3¢/sh-div
$50-250,000/yr EFT(104)
DIP: $500 + $13 + 3¢/sh
part. DR/cash-only
sfkg-avail/p. sale-$15 + 12¢/sh
rec common/no residency restrict.

NOTE: *cash pymt fees: 3¢/sh + $2.50 auto EFT; $5 single EFT/check

Borg-Warner Inc (N-BWA) (div/yr: $ 0.56) [S&P ranking: B +] mfg-auto powertrain parts
200 S Michigan Ave
★ Chicago, IL 60604
312-322-8524 InvRe
312-322-8599 fax #
800-851-4229 admr
www.bwauto.com

Buy fees: no cost
$50-120,000/yr(52)
DIP: $500
part. DR/cash-only
sfkg-free/p. sale-$15 + 12¢/sh
rec common
gifting free

Boston Beer Co Inc (N-SAM) (div/yr: $0.00) [S&P ranking: B +] food/beverage-craft beer
brewer
75 Arlington St, 5th floor   Buy fees: 12¢/sh-cash*
Boston, MA 02116 $50-10,000/mo EFT*(52)
 888-877-2890 admr   DIP: $500 + $10 + 12¢/sh**   ★
 617-368-5500 fax #   sfkg-free/p. sale-$25 + 12¢/sh
 617-368-5000 co #   common
www.samadams.com or www.bostonbeer.com   gifting free
NOTE: **or $50/mo EFT/*plus $5 check/$3 EFT fee/co does not pay dividends

Boston Properties Inc (N-BXP) (div/yr: $ 2.60) REIT
111 Huntington Ave   Buy fees: no cost-orig iss
Boston, MA 02199   3% disc-div   ✂
 888-485-2389 admr $100-25,000/qtr EFT(4)
 617-236-3300 InvRe   DIP: $100   **%**
e-mail: investor_relations@bostonproperties.   part. DR/cash-only
www.bostonproperties.com   sfkg-free/p. sale-$15 + fees   ★
                                               rec comm
NOTE: co does not pay div

Bowater Inc (N-BOW) (div/yr: $ 0.80) [S&P ranking: B-] mfg-paper
P O Box 1028/55 E Camperdown Way   Buy fees: no cost
Greenville, SC 29602 $100-5,000/mo*(12)
 864-271-7733 InvRe   or UK res £75-3,500/mo   ✂
 864-282-9482 fax #   part. DR/cash-only
 800-845-6002 admr   common
www.bowater.com

Bowne & Co Inc (N-BNE) (div/yr: $ 0.22) [S&P ranking: B-] svcs-legal/financial/corp printer
345 Hudson St   Buy fees: no cost   ✂
New York, NY 10014-4589 $50-100,000/yr EFT(52)
 800-524-4458 admr   DIP: $500   ★
 212-229-7392 fax #   p. sale-$15 + 12¢/sh
 212-924-5500 co #   common/no residency restrict.
e-mail: bowne@bowne.com
www.bowne.com

Brady Corp (N-BRC) (div/yr: $ 0.44) [S&P ranking: B +] mfg-adhesives & coatings
P O Box 571   Buy fees: no cost
Milwaukee, WI 53201-0571 $100-15,000/qtr EFT(12)   ✂
 800-468-9716 admr   Class A common
 414-438-6910 fax #
 414-358-6600 Treas
e-mail: investor@bradycorp.com
www.bradycorp.com

Brandywine Realty Trust (N-BDN) (div/yr: $ 1.76) [S&P ranking: B] REIT-office/industrial prop-
erties
401 Plymouth Rd Ste 500   Buy fees: no cost
Plymouth Meeting, PA 19462   0-5% disc-div/cash**
 800-317-4445 admr $100-10,000/mo EFT*(12)   ✂
 610-325-5622 fax #   part. DR/cash-only
 610-325-4907 InvRe   p. sale-avail   **%**
e-mail: chris.marr@brandywinerealty.com   div deposit/gifting avail
brandywinerealty.com
NOTE: *req waiver for cash pymts $10,000/**on orig issue shs

Briggs & Stratton Corp (N-BGG) (div/yr: $ 0.68) [S&P ranking: B +] mfg-gas engines
P O Box 702   Buy fees: no cost
Milwaukee, WI 53201-0702 $25-5,000/qtr(12)
✄ 800-622-6757 admr   sfkg-free/p. sale-$10 + fees
  414-259-5773 fax #   rec common/no residency restrict.
  414-259-5496 ShRel
  www.briggsandstratton.com

Bristol-Myers Squibb Co (N-BMY) (div/yr: $ 1.12) [S&P ranking: A-] drug/pharm industry
345 Park Ave   Buy fees: 4% svc chg *
New York, NY 10154-0037 $105-10,025/mo(52)
800-356-2026 admr   sfkg-free/p. sale-$15 + bkg
212-546-9552 fax #   rec comm 50 sh min/no residency restrict.
212-546-3309 StkSv
www.bms.com/investors
NOTE: *up to $5 for div, to $25 for cash pymt/$15 term fee

Brown Shoe Co Inc (N-BWS) (div/yr: $ 0.40) [S&P ranking: B] retail/wholesale - shoes
8300 Maryland Ave/P O Box 29   Buy fees: no cost
✄ St Louis, MO 63166-0029 $25-1,000/month(12)
  800-446-2617 admr   cash-only option
  314-854-4274 fax #   sfkg-free/p. sale-avail
  314-854-4000 ShRel   rec common/no residency restrict.
  e-mail: info@brownshoe.com
  www.brownshoe.com

Brown-Forman Corp (N-BF.A) (div/yr: $ 0.98) [S&P ranking: A] beverages-liquor(Jack
Daniels/wine/Lenox dinnerware
c/o National City Bank   Buy fees: no svc chg
P O Box 94946 $50-3,000/qtr(12)
Cleveland, OH 44101-4946   cash-only option
800-622-6257 admr   common A & B*
502-774-7876 fax #   div deposit
502-774-7690 StkSv
e-mail: brown-forman@bf.com
www.brown-forman.com
NOTE: *Each class of common div purchases same class of stock

Brunswick Corp (N-BC) (div/yr: $ 0.60) [S&P ranking: B] consumer prod-recreation equip
1 N Field Ct   Buy fees: no cost
✄ Lake Forest, IL 60045-4811 $10-2,000/month(12)
  847-735-4293 ShSvc   sfkg-free/p. sale-avail
  847-735-4671 fax #   rec common/no residency restrict.
  847-735-4294
  e-mail: services@bruncorp.com
  www.brunswick.com

Brush Engineered Materials Inc (N-BW) (div/yr: $0.00) [S&P ranking: C] metals/mining
17876 St Clair Ave   Buy fees: no cost
✄ Cleveland, OH 44110 $25-5,000/qtr(12)
  800-246-5761 admr   sfkg-free/p. sale-$10 + 12¢/sh
  216-481-2523 fax #   rec common
  216-486-4200 Treas
  e-mail: contact_corporate@bemic.com
  www.beminc.com
  NOTE: co does not pay div

Burlington Northern Santa Fe Corp (N-BNI) (div/yr: $ 0.68) [S&P ranking: A-] trans-railroad
c/o EquiServe Trust Co NA
PO Box 2598 #4675
Jersey City, NJ 07303-2598
 800-526-5678 admr
 817-352-7669 fax #
 817-352-6856 InvRe
e-mail: investor.relations@bnsf.com
www.bnsf.com

$50-60,000/yr(12)
sfkg-free/p. sale-avail
rec common
div deposit

C

CBL & Associates Properties Inc (N-CBL) (div/yr: $ 3.25) [S&P ranking: A] REIT-regional malls
2030 Hamilton Place Blvd #500
Chattanooga, TN 37421-6511
 800-568-3476 admr
 423-855-0001 co #
e-mail: info@cblproperties.com
www.cblproperties.com

Buy fees: no cost
$100-5,000/qtr(12)
part. DR/cash-only
sfkg-free/p. sale-5% to $10
common

CBRL Group Inc (NDQ-CBRL) (div/yr: $ 0.48) [S&P ranking: B +] food-chain restaurants/stores-Cracker Barrel
P O Box 787
Lebanon, TN 37088-0787
 800-568-3476 CorpSecy
 615-444-5533 CorpSecy
e-mail: investorrelations@cbrl.com
www.cbrl.com

Buy fees: no cost
US$100-5,000/qtr(4)
partial DR option
sfkg-free/p. sale-avail
rec common

CH Energy Group Inc (N-CHG) (div/yr: $ 2.16) [S&P ranking: A-] utility-gas/electric
c/o EquiServe Trust Co NA
P O Box 2598 # 4675
Jersey City, NJ 07303-2598
 800-428-9578 admr
 845-486-5879 fax #
 845-486-5204 ShSvc
www.chenergygroup.com

Buy fees: no cost
to $150,000/yr EFT(12)
DIP: $100
part. DR/cash-only
sfkg-free/p. sale-daily sale
rec common/no residency restrict.

★

CIGNA Corp (N-CI) (div/yr: $ 0.10) [S&P ranking: B +] insurance
1601 Chestnut St
Philadelphia, PA 19192-2378
 800-317-4445 admr
 215-761-5583 fax #
 215-761-3517 co #
www.cigna.com

Buy fees: no cost
$10-5,000/month(12)
part. DR/cash-only
rec common

CLARCOR Inc (N-CLC) (div/yr: $ 0.51) [S&P ranking: A] mfg-svcs-diversified
840 Crescent Centre Dr Ste 600
Franklin, TN 37067-4687
 800-446-2617 admr
 615-771-3100 CorpSecy
www.clarcor.com

Buy fees: no cost
$25-3,000/month(12)
rec common

CLECO Corp (N-CNL) (div/yr: $ 0.90) [S&P ranking: B +] utility-electric
c/o EquiServe Trust Co NA
P O Box 2598 # 4675
Jersey City, NJ 07303-2598
 800-253-2652 InvRe
 318-484-7777 fax #
 318-484-7687 InvRe
www.cleco.com

Buy fees: no cost
$25-5,000/month(12)
part. DR/cash-only
sfkg-free/p. sale-avail
rec comm/pref

CMS Energy Corp (N-CMS) (div/yr: $0.00) [S&P ranking: C] utility-elec/gas
One Energy Plaza   Buy fees: no cost
Jackson, MI 49201-2236 $25-250,000/yr EFT(52)
✂ 517-788-1867 DRP   DIP: $250 or $50 EFT/mo for 5 mos
517-788-1859 fax #   part. DR/cash-only
★ 517-788-1868 InvSv   sfkg-free/p. sale-5¢/sh
e-mail: invest@cmsenergy.com   comm/pref(Cons Energy)*/no res restrict.
www.cmsenergy.com/shareholder   div deposit/gifting avail

CNF Inc (N-CNF) (div/yr: $ 0.40) [S&P ranking: B-] transportation-freight forwarding-Emery
3240 Hillview Ave   Buy fees: 5% to $3 + 10¢/sh
Palo Alto, CA 94304 $25-60,000/yr(12)
866-517-4584 admr   cash-only option
650-813-0160 fax #   sfkg-free/p. sale-$15 + 10¢/sh
650-494-2900 InvRe   rec common
e-mail: cnfinvest@cnf.com   gifting free
www.cnf.com

CPI Corp (N-CPY) (div/yr: $ 0.64) [S&P ranking: B-] misc-portrait studios
✂ 1706 Washington Ave   Buy fees: no cost
St Louis, MO 63103-1790 $10-10,000/qtr(12)
800-669-9699 ShrSv   partial DR option
314-231-4233 fax #   sfkg-avail/p. sale-$5 + bkg fee
314-231-1575 legal   rec common
www.cpicorp.com

CRT Properties Inc (N-CRO) (div/yr: $ 1.40) [S&P ranking: B] REIT-office properties
225 NE Mizner Blvd Ste 200   Buy fees: no cost
✂ Boca Raton, FL 33432   no cash plan
800-468-9716 admr   partial DR option
561-394-7712 fax #   common
561-395-9666 co #   div deposit
e-mail: invrel@crtproperties.com
www.crtproperties.com

CSX Corp (N-CSX) (div/yr: $ 0.40) [S&P ranking: B-] trans/int'l-railroad/trucking
✂ 500 Water St C160   Buy fees: no cost
Jacksonville, FL 32202 $50-10,000/mo EFT(52)
★ 800-521-5571 admr   DIP: $500 + $10
904-366-4248 fax #   partial DR option
904-359-3256 ShrSv   sfkg-free/p. sale-$10 + 15¢/sh
e-mail: CSXShareholders@csx.com   rec comm/no residency restrict.
www.csx.com   gifting free

CTS Corp (N-CTS) (div/yr: $ 0.12) [S&P ranking: B +] mfg-wireless electronic components
✂ 905 West Blvd N   Buy fees: no cost-div*
Elkhart, IN 46514-1899 $500-10,000/mo*EFT(12)
★ 866-326-1180 admr   DIP: $1,000 + $10
574-29460516 fax #   part. DR/cash-only
574-293-7511 legal   sfkg-free/p. sale-$15 + 10¢/sh
e-mail: kdiller@ctscorp.com   common
www.ctscorp.com
NOTE: *cash pymt-$5 by check/$2 EFT pymt + 5¢/sh /waiver may be obtained for more than $10,000 and a discount for the waiver amt may be given

CVS CORP (N-CVS) (div/yr: $ 0.29) [S&P ranking: B] retail-drugstores/apparel
One CVS Dr   Buy fees: no cost*-div
✂ Woonsocket, RI 02895 $100-250,000/yr EFT
877-287-7526 admr   DIP: $100 + $7.50 + 10¢/sh
★ 401-765-1500 co #   p. sale-$10 + 10¢/sh
e-mail: investorinfo@cvs.com   common
www.cvs.com
NOTE: *cash pymt fee: $2.50 check/$1.00 EFT + 10¢/sh

Cabot Corp (N-CBT) (div/yr: $ 0.64) [S&P ranking: B-] mfg-chemicals
2 Seaport Ln Ste 1300
Boston, MA 02210-2019
  617-342-6244 admr
  617-342-6242 fax #
  617-345-0100 InvRe
  www.cabot-corp.com

Buy fees: no cost
$10-10,000/qtr(4)
part. DR/cash-only
sfkg-free
rec common

Cadmus Communications Corp (NDQ-CDMS) (div/yr: $ 0.25) [S&P ranking: B-] svcs-printing
& graphic arts
c/o First Union Nat'l Bank-NC
2 First Union Plz CMG5
Charlotte, NC 28388
  804-287-5680 CorpSecy
  804-287-6267 fax #
  704-374-2697 admr
  www.cadmus.com

Buy fees: no svc chg
$25-3,000/qtr(4)
sfkg-free
rec common
div deposit

Calgon Carbon Corp (N-CCC) (div/yr: $ 0.12) [S&P ranking: B-] mfg-activated carbons
400 Calgon Carbon Dr
Pittsburgh, PA 15205-1133
  412-787-6795 InvRe
  412-787-6713 fax #
  800-317-4445 admr
  e-mail: ccc-info@calgoncarbon.com
  www.calgoncarbon.com

Buy fees: no cost-div*
$50-350,000/yr EFT*(52)
DIP: $250 or $50/mo EFT
partial DR option
sfkg-free/p. sale-$15 + 12¢/sh
rec common
gifting free

NOTE: *EFT fee $2 + 3¢/sh or $5 + 3¢/sh by check

California Water Service Group (N-CWT) (div/yr: $ 1.14) [S&P ranking: B +] utility-water
1720 N First St
San Jose, CA 95112-4598
  800-426-5523 admr
  408-367-8430 fax #
  408-367-8200 treas
  www.calwater.com

Buy fees: no cost
$100-24,000/mo EFT(52)
DIP: $500
partial DR option
sfkg-free
common/no residency restrict.
div deposit

Callaway Golf Co (N-ELY) (div/yr: $ 0.28) [S&P ranking: B-] rec/ent-designs & mfg golf clubs-
"Big Bertha"
2180 Rutherford Rd
Carlsbad, CA 92008-8815
  760-931-1771 ShrRe
  760-931-8013 fax #
  800-368-7068 admr
  e-mail: invrelations@callawaygolf.com
  www.callawaygolf.com

Buy fees: no cost
$50-5,000/qtr(12)
part. DR/cash-only
sfkg-free
common

Campbell Soup Co (N-CPB) (div/yr: $ 0.68) [S&P ranking: B +] food-process/distr
Campbell Place
Camden, NJ 08103-1799
  800-446-2617 admr
  856-342-3878 fax #
  201-324-0498 admr
  www.campbellsoups.com

Buy fees: 3%or $3 + 3¢/sh
$50-350,000/yr*EFT(52)
DIP: $500** + $18 + 3¢/sh
part. DR/cash-only
sfkg-free/p. sale-$15 + 12¢/sh
rec common/no residency restrict.

NOTE: **or $50/mo EFT for 10 months/*$5 + 3¢/sh fees for cash pymts (EFT fee $2 +
3¢/sh; min $25/mo)/IRA-$35 ann fee/$35 fee + int on loan

Canadian Imperial Bank of Commerce (N-BCM) (div/yr: $ 2.60) [S&P ranking: B +] banking/financial svcs-CDN

c/o CIBC Mellon Trust Co | Buy fees: no cost
P O Box 7010 Adelaide St Postal Sta | C$100-50,000/yr*(12)
Toronto, ONT M5C 2W9, Canada | p. sale-avail
416-643-5500 InvRe | comm/Japan res not elig*
416-980-5028 fax #
800-387-0825 admr
www.cibc.com
NOTE: *US residents elig for stock div option only

Canadian Oil Sands Trust (OTC-COSWF) (div/yr: $0.00) energy trust-CANADA
350 7th Ave SW 2500 1st Canadian Ct | Buy fees: no cost
Calgary, ALB T2P 3N9, Canada | 5% disc-distribution
800-663-9097 admr | $1000-100,000/qtr(4)
403-218-6201 fax # | holder-1 sh min/Cdn residents*
403-218-6200 InvRe
e-mail: investor_relations@cos-trust.com
www.cos-trust.com
NOTE: trades on Toronto Exch as COS.UN/*US residents elig for cash option only

Capital One Financial Corp (N-COF) (div/yr: $ 0.11) [S&P ranking: A +] fin svcs-credit card issuer/svcs
1680 Capital One Dr | Buy fees: no cost
McLean, VA 22102 | $50-10,000/mo* EFT(12)
800-446-2617 admr | part. DR/cash-only
703-720-2221 fax # | sfkg-free/p. sale-$15 + 12¢/sh
703-720-2289 AsoGC | common/no residency restrict.
e-mail: investor.relations@capitalone.com
www.capitalone.com
NOTE: *cash pymts >$10,000, subj to req for waiver, may receive a discount; $1 EFT fee

Caraustar Industries Inc (NDQ-CSAR) (div/yr: $0.00) [S&P ranking: C] mfg-recycled paperboard & packaging products
P O Box 115 | Buy fees: no cost-orig iss
Austell, GA 30168 | $50-300,000/yr(12)
800-524-4458 admr | DIP: $250 + 10¢/sh
770-799-5832 fax # | part. DR/cash-only
770-948-3101 CorpSecy | sfkg-free/p. sale-$5 + 10¢/sh
e-mail: csarinvestor@caraustar.com | common
www.caraustar.com
NOTE: co does not pay div

Carlisle Cos Inc (N-CSL) (div/yr: $ 0.92) [S&P ranking: A +] mfg-diversified rubber/plastics
250 S Clinton St | Buy fees: no cost
Syracuse, NY 13202-1258 | $10-3,000/qtr(4)
212-608-8440 admr | common/no residency restrict.
315-474-2008 fax #
315-682-1423 CorpSecy
e-mail: info@carlisle.com
www.carlisle.com

Carnival Corp (N-CCL) (div/yr: $ 0.80) [S&P ranking: A +] rec/enter-cruise ships-PANAMA
3655 NW 87th Ave | Buy fees: no cost
Miami, FL 33178-2428 | no cash plan
800-568-3476 admr | partial DR option
305-406-4758 fax # | p. sale-avail
305-599-2600 GenCo | rec common
www.carnivalcorp.com
NOTE: div not taxed by Panama

Carpenter Technology Corp (N-CRS) (div/yr: $ 0.40) [S&P ranking: B-] mfg-steel
c/o American Stock Transfer & Trust
P O Box 922 Wall St Sta
New York, NY 10269-0560
  800-278-4353 admr
  610-208-3068 fax #
  610-208-3011 StkRe
  e-mail: csheetz@cartec.com
  www.cartech.com
NOTE: $2.50 fee + 10¢/sh for cash pymts
Buy fees: no cost*-div
$25-20,000/pymtEFT(52)
DIP: $250 + $2.50 + 10¢/sh
part. DR/cash-only
sfkg-$7.50/p. sale-$7.50 + 10¢/sh
rec common/no residency restrict.
div deposit/gifting free

CarrAmerica Realty Corp (N-CRE) (div/yr: $ 2) [S&P ranking: B +] REIT
1850 K St N W Ste 500
Washington, DC 20006
  202-729-7500 co #
  202-737-2346 fax #
  800-417-2277 admr
  www.carramerica.com
Buy fees: no cost
$25-25,000/yr(12)
part. DR/cash-only
p. sale-5% + bkg fee
common

Cascade Financial Corp (NDQ-CASB) (div/yr: $ 0.32) [S&P ranking: B +] banks/banking
2828 Colby Ave
Everett, WA 98201
  800-839-2983 admr
  425-339-5500 InvRe
  www.cascadebank.com
Buy fees: 6¢/sh-div*
$25-250,000/yr EFT*
DIP: $250 + $15 + 6¢/sh
part. DR/cash-only
p. sale-$15 + 12¢/sh
no residency restrict.
div deposit
NOTE: *cash pymt fees: 6¢/sh + $2 EFT/$5 check

Cascade Natural Gas Corp (N-CGC) (div/yr: $ 0.96) [S&P ranking: B +] utility-gas
222 Fairview Ave N
Seattle, WA 98109
  206-381-6744 StkDp
  206-624-7215 fax #
  888-269-8845 admr
  e-mail: mgrant@cngc.com
  www.cnge.com
NOTE: res cust may buy initial shs from co $250 min
Buy fees: no cost
$50-20,000/yr(12)
part. DR/cash-only
sfkg-free/p. sale-avail
rec comm/no residency restrict.
gifting avail

Casey's General Stores Inc (NDQ-CASY) (div/yr: $ 0.16) [S&P ranking: A-] retail-convenience stores/gas stations
1 Convenience Blvd
Ankeny, IA 50021-9437
  515-965-6100
  515-965-6160 fax #
  800-884-4225 admr
  www.caseys.com
Buy fees: no cost
$50-10,000/qtr EFT(12)
sfkg-free/p. sale-$5 + bkg fee
rec common
gifting $5

Cash America International Inc (N-CSH) (div/yr: $ 0.03) [S&P ranking: B] fin svcs-pawn shops/payday advance/check cash svcs
1600 W 7th St
Fort Worth, TX 76102
  800-635-9270 admr
  817-570-1699 fax #
  817-335-1100 InvRe
  e-mail: investor_relations@cashamerica.com
  www.cashamerica.com
Buy fees: no cost
$50-120,000/yr EFT
DIP: $250 or 5 $50/mo EFT
part. DR/cash-only
p. sale-$15 + 12¢/sh
no residency restrict.
div deposit

Castle (A M) & Co (A-CAS) (div/yr: $ 0.06) [S&P ranking: C] distr-carbon, stainless steel, alloy metals

✂ 3400 N Wolf Rd   Buy fees: no cost
Franklin Park, IL 60131-1319 $100-10,000/qtr(4)
847-455-7111 InvRe   cash-only option
847-455-7136 fax #   common
718-921-8208 admr
www.amcastle.com

Caterpillar Inc (N-CAT) (div/yr: $ 1.64) [S&P ranking: B +] mfg-machinery
100 NE Adams St   Buy fees: $2.50 + 3¢/sh
★ Peoria, IL 61629-7310 $25-no max EFT*(52)
866-203-6622 admr   DIP: $250 + $15 + 3¢/sh
309-675-6620 fax #   sfkg-free/p. sale-$15 + 12¢/sh
309-675-4619 CorpSecy   rec common
e-mail: catir@cat.com   div deposit
www.cat.com
NOTE: *$1-1.75 EFT fee

Cedar Fair LP (N-FUN) (div/yr: $ 1.84) entertainment-owns & operates amusement parks
One Cedar Point Dr $50-5,000/qtr(12)
Sandusky, OH 44870-5259   sfkg-free/p. sale-avail
419-626-2227 co #   rec units-min 50
419-627-2260 fax #
419-627-2233 admr
e-mail: investing@cedarfair.com
www.cedarfair.com

Cendant Corp (N-CD) (div/yr: $ 0.44) [S&P ranking: B] svcs-real estate/travel svcs
9 W 57th St   Buy fees: 5%to$3 + 6¢/sh-div*
★ New York, NY 10019 $25-250,000/yr EFT*
800-589-9469 admr   DIP: $250 + $15 + 6¢/sh**
212-413-1800 InvRe   part. DR/cash-only
www.cendant.com   p. sale-$15 + 12¢/sh
                                             no residency restrict.
                                             div deposit
NOTE: *cash pymt fees: 6¢/sh + $2 EFT/$5 check/**or $50/month

✂ **CenterPoint Properties Trust SBI** (N-CNT) (div/yr: $ 1.71) [S&P ranking: A] REIT
1808 Swift Dr   Buy fees: no cost
Oak Brook, IL 60523-1501 $25-100,000/yr(4)
630-586-8000 co #   part. DR/cash-only
630-586-8010 fax #   sfkg-free/p. sale-avail*
800-446-2617 admr   common
e-mail: info@center-prop.com
www.centerpoint-prop.com
NOTE: *partial sales by phone (bkg fees imposed)

Centerpoint Energy Inc (N-CNP) (div/yr: $ 0.40) [S&P ranking: B] utility-elec/gas transmission/sales hldg co
✂ P O Box 4505   Buy fees: no cost-orig iss
Houston, TX 77210-4505 $50-120,000/yr EFT(52)
★ 800-231-6406 InvSv   DIP: $250
713-207-3169 fax #   part. DR/cash-only
713-207-3060 in TX   sfkg-free/p. sale-avail
e-mail: info@centerpointenergy.com   comm/no residency restrict.
www.centerpointenergy.com   div deposit/gifting avail

Central Vermont Public Service Corp (N-CV) (div/yr: $ 0.92) [S&P ranking: B] utility-electric
77 Grove St
Rutland, VT 05701-3400
 800-937-5449 admr
 802-747-1913 fax #
 800-354-2877 ShrSv
 www.cvps.com

Buy fees: no cost-orig iss
$100-5,000/mo EFT(12)
DIP: $250
part. DR/cash-only
sfkg-free/p. sale-avail
rec comm/pref/USA for init pur
div deposit/gifting avail

✂
★

CenturyTel Inc (N-CTL) (div/yr: $ 0.24) [S&P ranking: A] telecommunications
P O Box 4065
Monroe, LA 71211-4065
 800-833-1188 admr
 318-388-9562 fax #
 318-388-9000 co #
 e-mail: christian.drost@centurytel.com
 www.centurytel.com

Buy fees: no cost
$25-150,000/yr(52)
partial DR option
sfkg-free/p. sale-avail
rec common
div deposit

✂

Ceridian Corp (N-CEN) (div/yr: $0.00) [S&P ranking: B-] tech svcs-data processing/hosting
3311 Old Shakopee Rd
Minneapolis, MN 55425-1640
 800-524-4458 admr
 952-853-8100
 e-mail: investor.relations@ceridian.com
 www.ceridian.com
NOTE: co does not pay div/*$200 initial pymt for rec shareholders

Buy fees: $2.50 + 10¢/sh
$100-25,000/inv(240)
DIP: $500
sfkg-free/p. sale-$10 + 10¢/sh
rec comm*-1 sh min

★

Chase Corp (A-CCF) (div/yr: $ 0.35) [S&P ranking: B +] mfg-specialty chemicals/electronic mfg svcs
26 Summer St
Bridgewater, MA 02324
 877-253-6849 admr
 508-697-6419 fax #
 508-279-1789 InvRe
 www.chasecorp.com

NOTE: *cash purch fee-$2.50 + 10¢/sh

Buy fees: 2%to$2.50 + 10¢/sh
$25-10,000/wk*(52)
DIP: $250 + 10¢/sh
part. DR/cash-only
sfkg-$7.50/p. sale-$15 + 10¢/sh
common
div deposit/gifting free

★

Chemed Inc (N-CHE) (div/yr: $ 0.48) [S&P ranking: B-] svcs-residential & comm bldg svcs/home health
255 E 5th St
Cincinnati, OH 45202-4726
 800-468-9716 admr
 513-762-6590 fax #
 513-762-6463 InvRe
 e-mail: investorinfo@chemed.com
 www.rotorooter.com
NOTE: $5 fee for certificates/frmly: Roto Rooter, returned to Chemed name May 04

Buy fees: no cost
$50-5,000/mo EFT*(12)
cash-only option
sfkg-$5/p. sale-$5 + bkg
rec comm 25 sh min/no residency restrict.
div deposit

✂

Chemical Financial Corp (NDQ-CHFC) (div/yr: $ 1.06) [S&P ranking: A] banking
P O Box 569
Midland, MI 48640-0569
 800-261-0598 admr
 989-839-5255 fax #
 989-839-5350 InvRe
 www.chemicalbankmi.com

Buy fees: no cost
$40-40,000/yr EFT(52)
DIP: $50
part. DR/cash-only
sfkg-free/p. sale-$12.50 + 7c
common/U S residents
gifting avail

✂
★

Chesapeake Corp (N-CSK) (div/yr: $ 0.88) [S&P ranking: B-] mfg-packaging
1021 E Cary St, Box 2350   Buy fees: no cost
Richmond, VA 23218-2350 $10-5,000/qtr(12)
312-588-4991 admr   sfkg-avail
804-697-1192 fax #   rec common/no residency restrict.
804-697-1166 SpSec
www.cskcorp.com

Chesapeake Utilities Corp (N-CPK) (div/yr: $ 1.12) [S&P ranking: B] energy-nat gas
distr&trans/propane distr/info svcs
P O Box 615   Buy fees: no cost
Dover, DE 19903-0615 $50-15,000/qtr(12)
800-736-3001 admr   part. DR/cash-only
302-734-6750 fax #   sfkg-free/p. sale-avail
888-742-5275 InvRe   comm-min 1 sh
www.chpk.com   div deposit

ChevronTexaco Corp (N-CVX) (div/yr: $ 1.60) [S&P ranking: B +] energy-petroleum
6001 Bollinger Canyon Rd   Buy fees: 5% to $3 + 5¢/sh*
San Ramon, CA 94582 $50-100,000/yr*EFT(52)
800-368-8357 admr   DIP: $250 + $10 fee + 5¢/sh
925-842-5690 InvRe   part. DR/cash-only
e-mail: invest@chevrontexaco.com   sfkg-free/p. sale-$15 + 10¢/sh
www.chevrontexaco.com   rec common
    div deposit/gifting free
NOTE: *cash pymt fees: EFT $2 + 5¢/sh or by check $4 + 5¢/sh

Chiquita Brands International Inc (N-CQB) (div/yr: $ 0.20) food-fresh fruit & vegetable
distr/food processor
250 E 5th St   Buy fees: no cost
Cincinnati, OH 45202-5190   no cash plan
800-368-3417 admr   p. sale-$5 + costs
513-287-8270 fax #   rec comm 100 sh min/no residency re-
513-784-6366 InvRe   strict.
www.chiquita.com
NOTE: certificates issued once a quarter

Chittenden Corp (N-CHZ) (div/yr: $ 0.72) [S&P ranking: B +] banks/banking
2 Burlington Sq   Buy fees: no cost
Burlington, VT 05401 $25-10,000/qtr(4)
800-969-3386 admr   sfkg-free/p. sale-5% to $10
802-660-1320 fax #   rec common
802-660-1412 ShrRe   div deposit
e-mail: efortin@chittenden.com
www.chittenden.com

Chubb Corp (N-CB) (div/yr: $ 1.72) [S&P ranking: B +] insurance/property-casualty
P O Box 1615/15 Mountain View   Buy fees: 5% to $3.00
Warren, NJ 07061-1615 $10-60,000/yr EFT*(12)
908-903-3841 ShSvc   part. DR/cash-only
908-903-2003 fax #   sfkg-free/p. sale-$10 + 12¢/sh
800-317-4445 admr   common/no residency restrict.
e-mail: info@chubb.com
www.chubb.com
NOTE: TTY: 201/222-4955/*$1 EFT fee + svc + bkg fees

Church & Dwight Co Inc (N-CHD) (div/yr: $ 0.24) [S&P ranking: A] mfg-sodium bicarbonate-
Arm & Hammer brand
469 N Harrison St   Buy fees: no cost   ✂
Princeton, NJ 08543-5297 $250-5,000/qtr(4)
 609-683-5900 ShSvc   partial DR option
 609-683-5092 fax #   sfkg-free
 800-851-9677 admr   common
 www.churchdwight.com

Cincinnati Bell Inc (N-CBB) (div/yr: $0.00) [S&P ranking: B-] telecommunications
PO Box 2301/201 E 4th St Rm 700   Buy fees: no cost   ✂
Cincinnati, OH 45201-2301 $25-5,000/mo(12)
 800-31725122 admr   cash-only option
 513-241-0715 fax #   common
 513-397-0373 InvRe
 www.cincinnatibell.com
NOTE: co does not pay div

Cincinnati Financial Corp (NDQ-CINF) (div/yr: $ 1.22) [S&P ranking: A-] insurance-property-
casualty/lif ins/asset mgmt
P O Box 145496   Buy fees: 5% to$3 + 8¢/sh*
Cincinnati, OH 45250-5496 $25-10,000/mo* EFT(24)
 800-317-2512 admr   cash-only option
 513-870-2066 fax #   sfkg-avail/p. sale-$10 + 8¢/sh
 516-870-2639 InvRe   common/US res only
 e-mail: investor_inquiries@cinfin.com
 www.cinfin.com
NOTE: *cash purch fee-$3 + 8¢/sh/must make 4 pymts/yr (div or cash)

Cinergy Corp (N-CIN) (div/yr: $ 1.92) [S&P ranking: B +] utility-electric
c/o National City Bank   Buy fees: no cost
P O Box 94946 $25-100,000/yr EFT(12)   ✂
Cleveland, OH 44101-4945   DIP: $245
 800-325-2945 admr   part. DR/cash-only   ★
 800-262-3000 InvRe   sfkg-free/p. sale-avail
 e-mail: shareholders@cinergy.com   comm/pref*/no residency restrict.
 www.cinergy.com   div deposit/gifting avail
NOTE: *PSI merged w *Cincinnati Gas & Elec (pref div purchases common) /to merge
with Duke Energy

Citizens Banking Corp (MI) (NDQ-CBCF) (div/yr: $ 1.14) [S&P ranking: B +] banks/banking
328 S Saginaw St   Buy fees: $2.50 + 10¢/sh
Flint, MI 48502-2003 $100-10,000/mo(240)
 877-627-7020 admr   DIP: $100
 810-257-2570 fax #   partial DR option   ★
 810-257-2506 InvRe   sfkg-$7.50
 e-mail: investorrelations@cbcf-net.com   rec common/US & terr res
 www.citizensonline.com   div deposit

Citizens Communications Co (N-CZN) (div/yr: $ 2.75) [S&P ranking: B-] telecomm-phone svc
in rural/small communities
P O Box 3801   Buy fees: no cost-orig iss*   ✂
Stamford, CT 06905 $100-25,000/qtr*(12)
 800-248-8845 InvRe   sfkg-free/p. sale-$15 + 2¢/sh
 203-322-7186 fax #   common
 203-614-5600   gifting avail
 e-mail: citizens@czn.com
 www.czn.net
NOTE: *nontaxable stock div/$6 + 2¢/sh for market purchases/co does not pay div

Cleveland-Cliffs Inc (N-CLF) (div/yr: $ 0.20) [S&P ranking: B-] metals/mining-iron ore
1100 Superior Ave, 15th flr   Buy fees: no cost
Cleveland, OH 44114-2589 $20-30,000/yr EFT(12)
  800-214-0739 InvRe   sfkg-free/p. sale-avail
  216-694-6741 fax #   rec common
  800-446-2617 admr   div deposit
  201-222-4955 TTY
www.cleveland-cliffs.com
NOTE: blanket request for certificates may be made for full shares

Clorox Co (N-CLX) (div/yr: $ 1.12) [S&P ranking: A] consumer prod-household prod
c/o EquiServe Trust Co NA   Buy fees: no cost
P O Box 2598 # 4675 $10-60,000/yr EFT($1 EFT fee)(12)
Jersey City, NJ 07303-2598   part. DR/cash-only
  510-271-7000 SpSec   sfkg-free/p. sale-avail
  510-271-1696 fax #   rec common
  781-575-2726 admr
e-mail: investor_relations@clorox.com
www.clorox.com

Coca-Cola Bottling Co Consolidated (NDQ-COKE) (div/yr: $ 1) [S&P ranking: B +] distr-soft drinks
c/o Wachovia Bank NA $10-1,000/month(4)
1525 West W T Harris Blvd 3C3   sfkg-free
Charlotte, NC 28288-1153   common
  704-557-4400 co #   div deposit
  704-557-4451 fax #
  704-557-4038 Treas
e-mail: investor_relations@ccbcc.com
www.cokeconsolidated.com

Coca-Cola Co (N-KO) (div/yr: $ 1.12) [S&P ranking: B +] beverages-soft drink
P O Box 1734   Buy fees: no cost
Atlanta, GA 30301-1734 $10-125,000/yr EFT ($1 EFT fee)(12)
  888-265-3747 admr   part. DR/cash-only
  404-676-6792 fax #   sfkg-free/p. sale-$10 + 12¢/sh
  404-676-2777 co #   rec common/no residency restrict.
www.coca-cola.com   div deposit

Coca-Cola Enterprises Inc (N-CCE) (div/yr: $ 0.16) [S&P ranking: B] svc-bottling
P O Box 723040   Buy fees: no cost
Atlanta, GA 31139-0440 $10-100,000/yr EFT(250)
  800-418-4223 admr   part. DR/cash-only
  770-989-3788 fax #   sfkg-free/p. sale-$10 + 10¢/sh
  770-989-3796 ShrRe   rec common
www.cokecce.com   div deposit

Codorus Valley Bancorp Inc (NDQ-CVLY) (div/yr: $ 0.48) [S&P ranking: A-] banks/banking
PO Box 2887, 105 Leader Heights Rd $100-3,000/qtr
York, PA 17405-2887   rec common (owners of 4% of stock not
  800-468-9716 admr   elig)
  717-747-1519 InvRe

Colgate-Palmolive Co (N-CL) (div/yr: $ 1.16) [S&P ranking: A +] consumer prod-home prod
300 Park Ave   Buy fees: no cost
New York, NY 10022-7499 $20-60,000/yr EFT ($1 EFT fee) (12)
  800-519-3111 admr   part. DR/cash-only
  212-310-2475 fax #   sfkg-free/p. sale-avail
  212-310-2575 InvRe   rec comm
e-mail: investor_relations@colpal.com
www.colgate.com

Colonial BancGroup (AL) (N-CNB) (div/yr: $ 0.61) [S&P ranking: A-] banking
P O Box 1108/Colonial Fin Ctr
Montgomery, AL 36101-1108
334-240-5105 InvRe
334-240-5147 fax #
888-843-0622 admr
www.colonialbank.com

Buy fees: no cost
$10-120,000/yr(12)
partial DR option
sfkg-free/p. sale-avail
common
div deposit

Colonial Properties Trust (N-CLP) (div/yr: $ 2.70) [S&P ranking: A-] REIT
2101 6th Ave North Ste 750
Birmingham, AL 35203
800-730-6001 admr
205-250-8890 fax #
205-250-8700 InvRe
www.colonialprop.com

Buy fees: no cost
5% disc-div/cash
$200-25,000/yr(12)
part. DR/cash-only
sfkg-free/p. sale-avail
rec comm *

NOTE: *as well as unitholders of Colonial Realty Ltd Ptrship

Columbus McKinnon Corp (NDQ-CMCO) (div/yr: $0.00) mfg-design/mfg materials handling products
140 John James Audubon Pkwy
Amherst, NY 14228-1197
888-200-3161 admr
716-689-5694 fax #
716-689-5409 co #
www.cmworks.com

Buy fees: 2%to$2.50 + 10¢/sh
$25-10,000/day*EFT
part. DR/cash-only
sfkg-$7.50/p. sale-$15 + 10¢/sh
common
gifting free

NOTE: *cash purch fee-$2.50 + 10¢/sh/co does not pay div

Comerica Inc (N-CMA) (div/yr: $ 2.20) [S&P ranking: A] banking
c/o Wells Fargo Bank NA
616 N Concord-Exchange
S St Paul, MN 55075
800-292-1300 admr
313-965-4648 fax #
313-222-6317 InvRe
www.comerica.com

Buy fees: no cost
$10-3,000/qtr(4)
sfkg-free/p. sale-$10 + 5¢/sh
rec common/US residents

Commerce Bancorp Inc (NJ) (N-CBH) (div/yr: $ 0.44) [S&P ranking: A +] banking
1701 Route 70 East
Cherry Hill, NJ 08034-5400
888-470-5884 admr
856-751-1147 fax #
856-751-9000 AsstSecy
www.commerceonline.com

3% disc-div/cash
$100-10,000/mo(12)
partial DR option
sfkg-free
comm/NJ, PA residents*

NOTE: *other state residents may qualify, inquire of company

Commercial Federal Corp (N-CFB) (div/yr: $ 0.54) [S&P ranking: B +] banks/banking
13220 California St
Omaha, NE 68154-5227
402-554-9200 InvRe
402-390-5392 fax #
800-468-9716 admr
e-mail: investorrelations@commercialfed.com
www.comfedbank.com

Buy fees: no cost
$50-10,000/qtr EFT(12)
sfkg-avail/p. sale-avail
rec common

Commercial Net Lease Realty Inc (N-NNN) (div/yr: $ 1.30) [S&P ranking: B +] REIT
450 S Orange Ave Ste 900
Orlando, FL 32801
800-829-8432 admr
407-650-1044 fax #
407-265-7348 InvRe
e-mail: carolejones@nnnreit.com
www.nnnreit.com

Buy fees: no cost
no cash plan
partial DR option
sfkg-free
common

Community Bank System Inc (NY) (N-CBU) (div/yr: $ 0.72) [S&P ranking: A-] banking

5790 Widewaters Parkway
DeWitt, NY 13214-1850
✂ 315-445-7313 InvRe
315-445-2997 fax #
★ 800-937-5449 admr
www.communitybankna.com

Buy fees: no cost
$25-10,000/mo EFT(52)
DIP: $250 + $2.50 + 10¢/sh
part. DR/cash-only
sfkg-free/p. sale-$7.50 + 10¢/sh
rec comm-1 sh min
div deposit/gifting free

Community Banks Inc (PA) (NDQ-CMTY) (div/yr: $ 0.68) [S&P ranking: A] banks/banking

750 E Park Dr
✂ Harrisburg, PA 17111
866-255-2580 admr
% 717-920-1683 fax #
717-920-5811 co #
www.communitybanks.com

Buy fees: no cost-orig iss
5% disc-div/cash
$100-5,000/qtr EFT(4)
partial DR option
sfkg-free
rec common
div deposit

Compass Bancshares Inc (NDQ-CBSS) (div/yr: $ 1.40) [S&P ranking: A+] banking

P O Box 10566
Birmingham, AL 35296-0001
800-509-5586 admr
205-297-3043 fax #
205-933-3331 InvRe
www.compassweb.com

Buy fees: $1-2.50 + bkg fee
$25-5,000/mo(12)
cash-only option
sfkg-free
common

Computer Associates International Inc (N-CA) (div/yr: $ 0.08) [S&P ranking: B-] mfg-computer software

1 Computer Associates Plaza
Islandia, NY 11788-7000
516-342-5224 co #
800-244-7155 admr
e-mail: cainvestor@ca.com
www.cai.com

uy fees: $1.50 + bkg fee
$25-3,000/mo(12)
cash-only option
sfkg-$7.50
rec comm-50 shs min

ConAgra Foods Inc (N-CAG) (div/yr: $ 1.09) [S&P ranking: A] food-diversified products

✂ One ConAgra Dr
Omaha, NE 68102-5001
402-595-4000 AsstSecy
402-595-4707 fax #
800-214-0349 admr
www.conagra.com

Buy fees: no cost
$50-50,000/yr EFT(24)
partial DR option
sfkg-free/p. sale-$10 + 15¢/sh
rec comm/no residency restrict.
div deposit

Connecticut Water Service Inc (NDQ-CTWS) (div/yr: $ 0.84) [S&P ranking: A-] utility-water

✂ 93 W Main St
Clinton, CT 06413-1600
800-428-3985 x3015
860-669-5579 fax #
860-669-8630 CorpSecy
e-mail: mdiacri@ctwater.com
www.ctwater.com

Buy fees: no cost
$25-1,000/mo EFT(12)
partial DR option
p. sale-$10 + bkg
rec common
div deposit

NOTE: partial reinvestment limited to 50% or more of shares/IRA 800-525-8188

ConocoPhillips (N-COP) (div/yr: $ 2.48) [S&P ranking: B] energy-petroleum

c/o Mellon Investor Services LLC
✂ P O Box 24850 Church St Sta
South Hackensack, NJ 07606-1938
★ 918-661-0130 ShrSv
918-661-6279 fax #
800-356-0066 admr
www.conocophillips.com

Buy fees: no cost
$50-10,000/mo EFT(52)
DIP: $500 + $10
sfkg-free/p. sale-$15 + 5¢/sh
rec common
div deposit

Consolidated Edison Inc (N-ED) (div/yr: $ 2.28) [S&P ranking: B +] utility-elec/gas
4 Irving Pl Rm 249 S
New York, NY 10003
800-522-5522 InvSv
212-475-0734 fax #
212-780-8596 InvSv
e-mail: corpcomm@coned.com
www.coned.com

Buy fees: no cost-div/$2 fee for cash purch
$100-24,000/yr(52)
partial DR option
sfkg-free/p. sale-$2 + 10¢/sh
rec comm-50 shs min/no residency restrict.
gifting avail

Constellation Energy Group Inc (N-CEG) (div/yr: $ 1.34) [S&P ranking: B] utility-elec/gas
P O Box 1642 - Shareholder Svcs
Baltimore, MD 21203-1642
800-258-0499 ShrSv
410-234-5034 fax #
800-492-2861 in MD
www.constellationenergy.com

Buy fees: 2.5 ¢/sh
$25-100,000/yr(12)
part. DR/cash-only
sfkg-free/p. sale-$5 + 2.5¢/sh
common/no residency restrict.
div deposit

Cooper Industries Ltd (N-CBE) (div/yr: $ 1.48) [S&P ranking: B +] mfg-electrical, tools, hard-ware-BERMUDA
P O Box 4446
Houston, TX 77210-4446
781-575-2725 admr
713-209-8985 fax #
713-209-8673 ShrRe
e-mail: info@cooperindustries.com
www.cooperindustries.com

Buy fees: no cost
$25-24,000/yr EFT(12)
part. DR/cash-only
p. sale-$15 + 12¢/sh
rec common Cl A/no residency restrict.

NOTE: *EFT fee $2.50/investment, one-time (online) EFT pymt or auto monthly

Cooper Tire & Rubber Co (N-CTB) (div/yr: $ 0.42) [S&P ranking: B +] mfg-tires
701 Lima Ave
Findlay, OH 45840
419-423-1321 InvRe
419-420-6029 fax #
800-837-2755 admr
e-mail: cooperinfo@coopertire.com
www.coopertire.com

Buy fees: 5% to $3-div/$3 - cash purch
$100-10,000/yr*(12)
p. sale-$3 + bkg
rec common

Corn Products International Inc (N-CPO) (div/yr: $ 0.28) [S&P ranking: B +] food-corn refiners, spun off from Bestfoods 1997
5 Westbrook Corporate Center
Westchester, IL 60154
800-524-4458 admr
708-551-2700 fax #
708-551-2600 CorpSecy
e-mail: ir@cornproducts.com
www.cornproducts.com

Buy fees: 5% to $3 + bkg-div*
$100-350,000/yr EFT(12)
partial DR option
sfkg-free/p. sale-$15 + 10¢/sh
rec common
div deposit/gifting free

NOTE: *cash pymt fee ($5 check/$2 EFT) + 3¢/sh

Corning Inc (N-GLW) (div/yr: $0.00) [S&P ranking: C] mfg-glass
One Riverfront Plaza
Corning, NY 14831-0001
800-255-0461 admr
607-974-8551 fax #
607-974-9000 CorpSecy
e-mail: info@corning.com
www.corning.com

Buy fees: no cost
$10-5,000/mo EFT(12)
sfkg-free/p. sale-avail
common

NOTE: omitted dividend 7/01

Corporate Office Properties Trust (N-OFC) (div/yr: $ 1.02) [S&P ranking: B +] REIT
8815 Centre Park Dr Ste 400.   Buy fees: no cost
Columbia, MD 21045-2272 $50-25,000/qtr(12)
✂ 800-468-9716 admr   sfkg-free
   410-740-1174 fax #   common
   410-730-9092 CorpSecy   div deposit
   e-mail: ir@copt.com
   www.copt.com

Costco Wholesale Corp (NDQ-COST) (div/yr: $ 0.46) [S&P ranking: B +] retail-membership
warehouse stores
999 Lake Dr   Buy fees: 5%to$3 + 3¢/sh-di*
Issaquah, WA 98027 $25-$250,000/yr EFT
★ 800-249-8982 admr   DIP: $250 + $15 + 3¢/sh**
   425-313-6593 fax #   part. DR/cash-only
   425-313-8203 CFO   sfkg-free/p. sale-$15 + 12¢/sh
   e-mail: investor@costco.com   common/no residency restrict.
   www.costco.com/common   div deposit/gifting free
   NOTE: *no cost for DR on less than 100shs/*cash pymt fees: 6¢/sh + $2-3.50 EFT/$5
   check/**or $25/mo for 10 months

Countrywide Financial Corp (N-CFC) (div/yr: $ 0.60) [S&P ranking: A-] fin svcs-mortgage
bankg/insurance/loan closing svc
✂ 4500 Park Granada Blvd CH 19   Buy fees: no cost
   Calabasas, CA 91302   0-5% disc-orig issue
   800-524-4458 admr $100-3,000/mo*(12)
   818-225-4051 fax #   part. DR/cash-only
   818-225-3550 InvRe   p. sale-avail
   e-mail: ir@countrywide.com   common
   www.countrywide.com
   NOTE: *request for waiver of upper limit call 818-225-3550

Crane Co (N-CR) (div/yr: $ 0.40) [S&P ranking: B] mfg-engineered products
c/o EquiServe Trust Co NA   Buy fees: no cost
✂ P O Box 2598 # 4675 $10-5,000/month(12)
   Jersey City, NJ 07303-2598   part. DR/cash-only
   203-363-7300 co #   sfkg-free/p. sale-avail
   203-363-7295 fax #   common
   888-272-6327 admr
   e-mail: investor@craneco.com
   www.craneco.com

Crompton Corp (N-CK) (div/yr: $ 0.20) [S&P ranking: B-] mfg-specialty chem/process eq &
controls
✂ 199 Benson Rd   Buy fees: no cost
   Middlebury, CT 06749 $30-3,000/qtr(12)
   800-288-9541 admr   sfkg-$5
   203-573-2430 fax #   rec comm 50 sh min
   203-573-2213 InvRe
   www.cromptoncorp.com

Crown Holdings Inc (N-CCK) (div/yr: $0.00) [S&P ranking: C] mfg-metal/plastic packaging
One Crown Way   Buy fees: no cost*
✂ Philadelphia, PA 19154-4599 $25-25,000 yr EFT*(12)
   215-698-5100 co #   part. DR/cash-only
   215-698-7050 fax #   p. sale-bkg fee
   800-317-4445 admr   common
   e-mail: public relations@crowncork.com
   www.crowncork.com
   NOTE: *$1 fee for EFT pyments/co does not pay div

Cummins Inc (N-CMI) (div/yr: $ 1.20) [S&P ranking: B-] mfg-diesel engines
c/o Wells Fargo Bank NA
P O Box 64856
St Paul, MN 55164-0856
 800-468-9716 admr
 812-377-4937 fax #
 812-377-3121 InvRe
 e-mail: investor_relations@cummins.com
 www.cummins.com

Buy fees: no cost
$10-24,000/yr EFT(12)
sfkg-free/p. sale-avail
rec common/no residency restrict.

✂

Curtiss-Wright Corp (N-CW) (div/yr: $ 0.36) [S&P ranking: A-] mfg-aerospace/process equip
4 Becker Farm Rd
Roseland, NJ 07068-1739
 877-854-0844 admr
 974-597-4710 InvRe
 e-mail: adeignan@curtisswright.com
 www.curtisswright.com

$100-10,000/mo EFT(52)
DIP: $2,000 + $5 + 12¢/sh
part. DR/cash-only
sfkg-free/p. sale-$15 + 12¢/sh
common 20 sh min
div deposit/gifting free

★

D

DPL Inc (N-DPL) (div/yr: $ 0.96) [S&P ranking: B +] utility-elect holding co
1065 Woodman Dr
Dayton, OH 45432
 800-322-9244 InvRe
 937-259-7147 fax #
 800-736-3001 admr
 www.dplinc.com

Buy fees: no cost
$25-1,000/qtr(4)
part. DR/cash-only
sfkg-free/p. sale-avail
rec comm/pref*/no residency restrict.
div deposit

✂

NOTE: *Dayton Power & Light pref buys DPL comm

DTE Energy (N-DTE) (div/yr: $ 2.06) [S&P ranking: B +] utility-electric
2000 Second Ave Rm 833WCB
Detroit, MI 48232
 866-388-8558 admr
 313-235-9470 fax #
 313-235-8772 ShSvc
 e-mail: shareholdersvcs@dteenergy.com
 www.dteenergy.com

Buy fees: $1 + 3¢/sh-div*
$50-100,000/yr EFT(12)
DIP: $250
part. DR/cash-only
p. sale-$10 + 3¢/sh
rec comm/no residency restrict.
div deposit

★

NOTE: *$1 + 3¢/sh cash pymt/$3/mo EFT fee

Dana Corp (N-DCN) (div/yr: $ 0.48) [S&P ranking: B-] mfg-vehicular/industrial parts
P O Box 1000
Toledo, OH 43697-1000
 866-350-3262 admr
 419-535-4827 fax #
 419-535-4635 ShSvc
 www.dana.com

Buy fees: no cost
$25-2,000/month(52)
sfkg-$3
rec common/no residency restrict.

✂

NOTE: 800/537-8823 24-hour answering svc, in OH 800/472-8810

Darden Restaurants Inc (N-DRI) (div/yr: $ 0.08) [S&P ranking: A-] food/beverage-Red Lob-
ster/Olive Garden restaurants
5900 Lake Ellenor Dr
Orlando, FL 32809-3330
 800-241-8518 admr
 407-245-6459 fax #
 407-235-6458 InvRe
 e-mail: irinfo@darden.com
 www.darden.com

Buy fees: $1-5 + 10¢/sh*
$50-25,000/qtr(52)
DIP: $1,000 + $10 + 10¢/sh
partial DR option
sfkg-free/p. sale-$15
rec comm-50 sh min/no residency restrict.

★

NOTE: *DR fee 5%($1 min/$5 max) + 10¢/sh; cash purch-$5 + 10¢/sh

Deere & Co (N-DE) (div/yr: $ 1.24) [S&P ranking: B] mfg-farm equip
One John Deere Place
Moline, IL 61265-8098
 800-727-7033 admr
 309-765-5671 fax #
★ 309-765-4539 StkRe
e-mail: stockholder@deere.com
www.JohnDeere.com

Buy fees: 5% to $3
$100-10,000/mo EFT*(52)
DIP: $500 + $7.50 + 5¢/sh
part. DR/cash-only
sfkg-$3/p. sale-$10 + 5¢/sh
rec common/no residency restrict.

NOTE: *cash pymt fees: $3 check/$1 EFT + 5¢/sh

Del Monte Foods Co (N-DLM) (div/yr: $0.00) food/bev-processed fruits & vegetables
P O Box 193575
San Francisco, CA 94119-3575
★ 866-582-1370 admr
 415-247-3000 InvRe

Buy fees: 5%to$5 + 10¢/sh*
$50-100,000/yr EFT(12)
DIP: $200 + $10
part. DR/cash-only
sfkg-$10/p. sale-$10 + 10¢/sh
rec common
gifting $5

NOTE: *cash pymt fees: 10¢/sh + $5/co does not pay div

Delhaize SA (Etablissements) (N-DEG) (div/yr: $ 2.73) food-supermarkets-Food Lion-BEL-GIUM
c/o Bank of New York
P O Box 11258 Church St Sta
New York, NY 10286-0125
★ 888-269-2377 admr
 704-637-2581 fax #
 704-633-8250 x2529
e-mail: investor@delhaizegroup.com
www.delhaizegroup.com

Buy fees: 5% to $5 + 10¢/sh*
$50-100,000/yr*EFT(52)
DIP: $200 + $10 + 3 ¢/sh
part. DR/cash-only
sfkg-$10/p. sale-$10 + 10¢/sh
ADR
div deposit/gifting $5

NOTE: *$5 fee + 10¢/sh for cash purchases

Delphi Corp (N-DPH) (div/yr: $ 0.12) mfg-automotive components
5725 Delphi Dr
Troy, MI 48098
★ 800-818-6599 admr
 248-813-2495 InvRe
www.delphi.com

Buy fees: div-5% to $3 + 4¢/sh*
$50-350,000/yr*(52)
DIP: $500 + $10
sfkg-avail/p. sale-$15 + 7¢/sh
common

NOTE: *$5 + 4 ¢/sh for cash pymt

Delta Air Lines Inc (N-DAL) (div/yr: $0.00) [S&P ranking: C] trans-airline
1030 Delta Blvd
✂ Atlanta, GA 30311
 800-259-2345 admr
★ 404-715-2391 StkRe
www.delta.com

Buy fees: no cost-div*
$50-100,000/yr EFT(52)
DIP: $250 + $10 + 3¢/sh**
partial DR option
sfkg-free/p. sale-$10 + 10¢/sh
rec common/U S res only
gifting free

NOTE: *cash pymt fees:3¢/sh + $2 check or $1 EFT/**or $50/mo EFT for 5 months/co does not pay div

Delta Natural Gas Co Inc (NDQ-DGAS) (div/yr: $ 1.18) energy-natural gas distr & transmission
3617 Lexington Rd
✂ Winchester, KY 40391-9797
 312-588-4990 admr
 859-744-6552 fax #
 859-744-6171 CpSvc
e-mail: delta@mis.net
www.deltagas.com

Buy fees: no cost
$25-50,000/yr(12)
partial DR option
rec common
div deposit/gifting avail

Diebold Inc (N-DBD) (div/yr: $ 0.82) [S&P ranking: A] mfg-fin transaction systems/security products

P O Box 3077/5995 Mayfair Rd	Buy fees: no cost-div
North Canton, OH 44720-8077	$50-10,000/mo EFT*(52)
800-432-0140 admr	DIP: $500 + $7.50 + 10¢/sh
330-490-3794 fax #	sfkg-free/p. sale-$10 + 10¢/sh
330-490-6638 InvRe	rec common

e-mail: stockinfo@diebold.com
www.diebold.com
NOTE: *$1 EFT fee, $1 cash-option fee + 10¢/sh

✂ ★

Dofasco Inc (T-DFS.C) (div/yr: $0.00) [S&P ranking: B +] mfg-steel-CDN

PO Box 2460-1330 Burlington St E	C$50-50,000/yr + (4)
Hamilton, ONT L8N 3J5, Canada	common/Canadian res only
800-387-0825 admr	div deposit
905-548-4249 fax #	
905-544-3761 x6905	

e-mail: corpsec@dofasco.ca
www.dofasco.ca

Dollar General Corp (N-DG) (div/yr: $ 0.16) [S&P ranking: A +] retail-low-price merchandise

100 Mission Ridge # 500	Buy fees: no cost-div*
Goodlettsville, TN 37072	to $7,500/mo EFT(12)
800-368-5948 admr	DIP: $50 + $5
615-855-4000 InvRe	partial DR option
www.dollargeneral.com	sfkg-avail/p. sale-$10

NOTE: *cash pymt fees: 75¢ EFT/$1 check

✂ ★

Dominion Resources Inc (N-D) (div/yr: $ 2.68) [S&P ranking: B +] utility-electric

P O Box 26532	Buy fees: no cost-div*
Richmond, VA 23261	$40-100,000/qtr EFT(24)
800-552-4034 InvSv	DIP: $350 or $40/mo-EFT*
804-771-6768 fax #	part. DR/cash-only
804-775-2500 InvSv	sfkg-free/p. sale-10¢/sh
e-mail: shareholder_services@dom.com	rec comm-5 shs min
www.dom.com	div deposit/gifting avail**

NOTE: *$1.00 fee for cash purch/**or cash by mail/**trans of sh to another acct (5 shs min)/online transactions at website

✂ ★

Donaldson Co Inc (N-DCI) (div/yr: $ 0.24) [S&P ranking: A +] mfg-filtration products

c/o Wells Fargo Bank Minnesota NA	Buy fees: no cost
P O Box 738	$10-1,000/month(12)
South St Paul, MN 55075-0738	sfkg-free
800-468-9716 admr	rec common
651-450-4085 fax #	
952-887-3131 CorpSecy	
www.donaldson.com	

✂

Donegal Group Inc (NDQ-DGIC) (div/yr: $ 0.40) [S&P ranking: B +] insur-property/casualty

P O Box 302	Buy fees: no cost
Marietta, PA 17547-0302	$25-12,000/yr EFT(12)
800-317-4445 admr	partial DR option
717-426-1931 CorpSecy	sfkg-avail/p. sale-$15 + 12¢/sh
www.donegalgroup.com	common-Cl A & B*/no residency restrict.
	gifting avail

NOTE: *reinvest div & cash pymts purchase Cl A shs

✂

Donnelley (R R) & Sons Co (N-RRD) (div/yr: $ 1.04) [S&P ranking: B] svcs-printing
77 W Wacker Dr   Buy fees: no cost
Chicago, IL 60601-1696 $10-60,000/yr(12)
✂ 800-317-4445 admr   part. DR/cash-only
312-326-7156 fax #   sfkg-free/p. sale-avail
312-326-8313 InvRe   rec common
e-mail: investor.info@rrd.com   div deposit
www.rrdonnelley.com

Dow Chemical Co (N-DOW) (div/yr: $ 1.34) [S&P ranking: B] mfg-chemicals
2030 Dow Center   Buy fees: 10¢/sh
Midland, MI 48674 $25-120,000/yr EFT(52)
800-369-5606 admr   part. DR/cash-only
989-636-1830 fax #   sfkg-free/p. sale-$5 + 10¢/sh
989-636-1463 InvRe   rec com-1 sh min/no residency restrict.
e-mail: ir@dow.com   div deposit/gifting free
www.dow.com

Dow Jones & Co Inc (N-DJ) (div/yr: $ 1) [S&P ranking: B] publishing
✂ 4300 Rt 1 North   Buy fees: no cost
South Brunswick, NJ 08852 $100-10,000/month(12)
★ 609-520-4000 InvRe   DIP: $1,000 + $5
800-851-4228 admr   part. DR/cash-only
e-mail: investorrelations@dowjones.com   sfkg-free/p. sale-$15 + 12¢/sh
www.dj.com   rec comm & comm B

du Pont de Nemours (E I) & Co (N-DD) (div/yr: $ 1.48) [S&P ranking: B] mfg-chemicals, spe-
cialty & life sciences products
c/o EquiServe Trust Co NA $20-5,000/mo(12)
P O Box 2598   sfkg-free/p. sale-avail
Jersey City, NJ 07308-2598   rec comm/pref
302-774-1000 co #
888-983-8766 admr
e-mail: info@dupont.com
www.dupont.com

Duke Energy Corp (N-DUK) (div/yr: $ 1.10) [S&P ranking: B +] utility-electric
✂ P O Box 1005   Buy fees: no cost
Charlotte, NC 28201-1005 $50-100,000/mo EFT*(52)
★ 800-488-3853 InvRe   DIP: $250
704-382-3814 fax #   part. DR/cash-only
704-382-3853 InvRe   sfkg-free^/p. sale-5¢/sh
e-mail: investduk@duke-energy.com   comm/pref/no residency restrict.
www.duke-energy.com/investors   div deposit
NOTE: *EFT min $25/month/^safekeeping avail only for common stock

Duke Realty Corp (N-DRE) (div/yr: $ 1.86) [S&P ranking: A-] REIT
✂ 600 E 96th St Ste 100   Buy fees: no cost
Indianapolis, IN 46240 $50-10,000/mo* EFT(24)
★ 317-808-6005 InvRe   DIP: $250
317-808-6770 fax #   partial DR option
800-278-4353 admr   sfkg-free/p. sale-bkg fee
e-mail: ir@dukerealty.com   common
www.dukerealty.com
NOTE: *monthly EFT-$25 min & waiver may be obtained for cash purchases >$10,000

Duquesne Light Holdings Inc (N-DQE) (div/yr: $ 1) [S&P ranking: B] utility-electric
P O Box 68 - Dividend Reinvest Buy fees: 5¢/sh
Pittsburgh, PA 15230-0068 $10-60,000/yr EFT(12)
 800-247-0400 ShRel DIP: $100 + $5 fee
 412-393-1263 fax # partial DR option   ★
 412-393-6167 ShRel sfkg-free/p. sale-7¢/sh
 e-mail: share@duqlight.com comm/pref*/US residents only
 www.dqe.com gifting avail
NOTE: *pref of Duquesne Light purchases DQE common/frmly: DQE Inc 10/1/03

E

EMC Insurance Group Inc (NDQ-EMCI) (div/yr: $ 0.60) [S&P ranking: B-] insur holding co
PO Box 712 - 717 Mulberry St Buy fees: no cost   ✄
Des Moines, IA 50303-0712 $50-5,000/mo(12)
 800-884-4225 admr part. DR/cash-only
 515-280-2515 InvRe sfkg-free/p. sale-$5 + bkg
 e-mail: emcins.group@emcins.com rec common
 div deposit

ESB Financial Corp (NDQ-ESBF) (div/yr: $ 0.40) [S&P ranking: A-] S&L/savings bank
600 Lawrence Ave Buy fees: no cost   ✄
Ellwood City, PA 16117 $25-25,000/qtr(4)
 800-368-5948 admr sfkg-$5
 724-758-0576 fax # rec common
 724-758-5584 InvRe
 wwwesbbank.com
NOTE: $5 fee for certificate issuance

Eastern Co (A-EML) (div/yr: $ 0.44) mfg-security products & locks
112 Bridge St/P O Box 460 Buy fees: no cost
Naugatuck, CT 06770-2903 $25-10,000/week(52)
 877-611-7981 admr DIP: $250 + $5*   ✄
 203-723-8653 fax # part. DR/cash-only
 203-729-2255 InvRe sfkg-$7.50/p. sale-$15 + 10¢/sh ★
 e-mail: ir@easterncompany.com rec common
 www.easterncompany.com
NOTE: *online initial purchase from bank acct at www.investpower.com

Eastman Chemical Co (N-EMN) (div/yr: $ 1.76) [S&P ranking: B-] mfg-chemicals-plastic/fiber products
100 N Eastman Rd Buy fees: $2.50 + 10¢/sh
Kingsport, TN 37660-5075 $25-60,000/yr EFT(52)
 800-323-EAST co # DIP: $250
 423-229-2000 adm part. DR/cash-only   ★
 www.eastman.com sfkg-$7.50/p. sale-4¢/sh
 rec common/US residents
 div deposit

Eastman Kodak Co (N-EK) (div/yr: $ 0.50) [S&P ranking: B-] mfg-photo products
c/o BankBoston N A Buy fees: no cost   ✄
PO Box 8023 $50-120,000/yr(52)
Boston, MA 02266-8023 DIP: $150
 800-253-6057 admr part. DR/cash-only   ★
 585-724-1089 fax # sfkg-free/p. sale-$10 + 10¢/sh
 585-724-5492 InvRe rec comm 1 sh min
 www.kodak.com/go/shares

Eaton Corp (N-ETN) (div/yr: $ 1.24) [S&P ranking: B +] mfg-industrial engineered products
✄ Eaton Center
  Cleveland, OH 44114-2584
  800-446-2667 admr
  216-523-4907 fax #
  888-328-6647 InvRe
  www.eaton.com
      Buy fees: no cost*
      $10-60,000/yr EFT ($1 EFT fee) (12)
      part. DR/cash-only
      sfkg-free/p. sale-avail
      common

Ecolab Inc (N-ECL) (div/yr: $ 0.35) [S&P ranking: A] svcs-specialty chemicals
✄ 370 N Wabasha St
  St Paul, MN 55102-1390
  800-322-8325 admr
  651-293-2573 fax #
  651-293-2573 AsstSecy
  e-mail: investor.info@ecolab.com
  www.ecolab.com/investor
      Buy fees: no cost
      $10-60,000/yr(12)
      part. DR/cash-only
      sfkg-free/p. sale-$15 + 10¢/sh
      rec common

Edison International (N-EIX) (div/yr: $ 1) [S&P ranking: B] utility hldg co-elec util/land dev & fin svc
  P O Box 400 Shareholder Svcs
✄ Rosemead, CA 91770-0400
  800-347-8625 ShSvc
  626-302-1937 CorpSecy
  e-mail: heidi.townshend@edisonintl.com
  www.edisoninvestor.com
      Buy fees: no cost
      $25-10,000/mo(12)
      part. DR/cash-only
      sfkg-free/p. sale-avail
      rec common/no residency restrict.

El Paso Corp (N-EP) (div/yr: $ 0.16) energy-exploration/devlop/distr natural gas
  P O Box 2511
✄ Houston, TX 77252-2511
  877-453-1503 admr
  713-420-4099 fax #
  713-420-5429 ShRel
  e-mail: shareholderleations@elpaso.com
  www.elpaso.com
      Buy fees: no cost
      $50-10,000/mo EFT(24)
      cash-only option
      sfkg-free/p. sale-$10 + 15¢/sh
      rec common

Electronic Data Systems Corp (N-EDS) (div/yr: $ 0.20) [S&P ranking: B] svcs-computer systems
  c/o American Stock Transfer & Trust
  P O Box 922, Wall St Sta
★ New York, NY 10269-0560
  877-253-6851 admr
  972-605-6662 fax #
  972-604-5486 InvRe
  e-mail: info@eds.com
  www.eds.com
      Buy fees: 2% to $2.50 + 10¢/sh*
      $25-10,000/mo EFT(250)
      DIP: $250 + $2.50 + 10¢/sh
      cash-only option
      sfkg-$7.50/p. sale-$15 + 10¢/sh
      common
      div deposit
  NOTE: *cash pymt fee $2.50 + 10¢/sh/online transactions avail

Emerson Electric Co (N-EMR) (div/yr: $ 1.66) [S&P ranking: A] mfg-indus instrument
✄ 8000 W Florissant Ave
  St Louis, MO 63136-8506
★ 888-213-0970 admr
  314-553-1213 fax #
  314-553-2197 InvRe
  www.gotoemerson.com
      Buy fees: no cost
      $25-250,000/yr EFT(52)
      DIP: $250 + $15
      part. DR/cash-only
      sfkg-free/p. sale-$15 + 12¢/sh
      rec common/no residency restrict.
      div deposit/gifting free

✄ **Empire District Electric Co** (N-EDE) (div/yr: $ 1.28) [S&P ranking: B] utility-electric
  602 Joplin St
% Joplin, MO 64802
  800-468-9716 admr
  417-625-5173 fax #
  417-625-6166 ShRe
  www.empiredistrict.com
      Buy fees: no cost-div*
      3% disc-div(orig is)
      $50-125,000/yr EFT*(52)
      part. DR/cash-only
      sfkg-free/p. sale-$10 + 10¢/sh
      rec common
      div deposit/gifting free
  NOTE: *cash pymt fees: $1.45 check/$1 EFT

Energen Corp (N-EGN) (div/yr: $ 0.80) [S&P ranking: A] energy-natural gas, oil
605 Richard Arrington Jr Blvd North   Buy fees: no cost
Birmingham, AL 35203-2707 $25-250,000/yr EFT(52)
800-654-3206 InvRe   DIP: $250 or $25/mo EFT for 10 mos*
205-326-1811 fax #   part. DR/cash-only
888-764-5603 admr   sfkg-free/p. sale-$15 + 12¢/sh
e-mail: mspeed@energen.com   common
www.energen.com   div deposit

Energy East Corp (N-EAS) (div/yr: $ 1.10) [S&P ranking: B +] utility-elec/gas
52 Farm View Dr   Buy fees: no cost
New Gloucester, ME 04260-4457 $25-100,000/yr(12)
800-542-7480 admr   DIP: CT/MA/ME/NY res-$25 min
207-688-4354 fax #   part. DR/cash-only
207-688-4336 InvRe   sfkg-free/p. sale-avail
www.energyeast.com   rec comm 1 share/no residency restrict.

Energy West Inc (NDQ-EWST) (div/yr: $ 0.14) [S&P ranking: B-] utility-natural gas/liquid propane distr
P O Box 2229   Buy fees: no cost
Great Falls, MT 59403-2229   no cash plan
877-588-4258 admr   p. sale-avail
406-791-7560 fax #   common
800-570-5688 ShrSv
e-mail: jshogan@ewst.com
www.ewst.com

EnergySouth Inc (NDQ-ENSI) (div/yr: $ 1.80) utility-gas
P O Box 2607   Buy fees: no cost
Mobile, AL 36652-2248 $25-5,000/qtr(12)
251-450-4638 Treas   part. DR/cash-only
251-478-5817 fax #   p. sale-avail
800-736-3001 admr   rec common/no residency restrict.
www.energysouth.com   div deposit

Enesco Group Inc (N-ENC) (div/yr: $0.00) [S&P ranking: C] retail-whsle/direct sales- gift items
225 Windsor Dr   Buy fees: no cost
Itasca, IL 60143 $10-5,000/qtr(4)
800-436-3726 admr   sfkg-free
630-875-5846 fax #   common
630-875-5856 Treas
www.enesco.com   NOTE: co does not pay div

Engelhard Corp (N-EC) (div/yr: $ 0.48) [S&P ranking: B +] mfg-specialty chem/envt tech/engineered materials
101 Wood Ave South   Buy fees: no cost
Iselin, NJ 08830-0770 $10-3,000/month(12)
732-205-6106 InvRe   rec common
732-321-5079 fax #
800-526-0801 InvRe
e-mail: investor.relations@engelhard.com
www.engelhard.com

Entergy Corp (N-ETR) (div/yr: $ 2.16) [S&P ranking: B +] utility-holding co/electric
P O Box 61000   Buy fees: no svc chg   **%**
New Orleans, LA 70161   0-3% on cash*
800-292-9960 ShrSv $100-3,000/mo EFT(12)
504-576-5000 fax #   DIP: $1,000
800-333-4368 admr   part. DR/cash-only
www.entergy.com   sfkg-$10/p. sale-avail
                                          common/US & terr res
NOTE: waiver of $3,000 limit & disc may be made by fax request

Entertainment Properties Trust (N-EPR) (div/yr: $ 2.50) REIT-entertaint/leisure properties
✂ 30 W Pershing Rd Ste 201   Buy fees: no cost-orig iss
Kansas City, MO 64108 $50-100,000/yr EFT(12)
★ 816-472-1700 InvRe   DIP: $200
816-472-5794 fax #   part. DR/cash-only
800-884-4225 admr   sfkg-free
e-mail: info@eprkc.com   common/U S citizen only
www.eprkc.com   gifting free

Equifax Inc (N-EFX) (div/yr: $ 0.12) [S&P ranking: B +] svcs-administrative
P O Box 4081/1550 Peachtree St   Buy fees: no cost-div
✂ Atlanta, GA 30302-4081 $50-10,000/mo EFT*(52)
404-885-8412 AsstSecy   DIP: $500 + $5 + 7¢/sh
★ 800-568-3476 admr   cash-only option
e-mail: corpsec@equifax.com   sfkg-free/p. sale-$15 + 7¢/sh
www.equifax.com   rec common
                                              div deposit/gifting free
NOTE: *$5 + 7¢/sh cash pymt fee, EFT on qtrly basis

Equitable Resources Inc (N-EQT) (div/yr: $ 1.68) [S&P ranking: A-] energy marketing
One Oxford Centre, Ste 3300   Buy fees: no cost
✂ Pittsburgh, PA 15219-1407 $25-5,000/mo(12)
800-589-9026 admr   sfkg-$7.50/p. sale-avail
412-553-7781 fax #   rec common
412-553-5891 AsstSecy
www.eqt.com

Equity Office Properties Trust (N-EOP) (div/yr: $ 2.00) REIT
2 North Riverside Plaza $25-25,000/mo(12)
Chicago, IL 60606   DIP: $250
★ 888-752-4831 admr   part. DR/cash-only
312-559-5259 fax #   sfkg-free/p. sale-$15 + 12¢/sh
312-466-3462 CorpSecy   rec common
www.equityoffice.com

Equity One Inc (N-EQY) (div/yr: $ 1.16) REIT-neighborhood shopping centers
✂ 1696 N E Miami Gardens Dr   Buy fees: no cost
% North Miami Beach, FL 33179   5% disc-div/cash
877-253-6850 admr $100-10,000/mo(12)
305-947-1734 fax #   part. DR/cash-only
305-947-1664 CorpSecy   sfkg-free/p. sale-$15 + 10¢/sh
e-mail: agallagher@equityone.net   comm-100 sh min*
www.equityone.net
NOTE: *min 100 shs to reinvest div, no min for cash option feature

Equity Residential (N-EQR) (div/yr: $ 1.73) [S&P ranking: B +] REIT
✂ 2 N Riverside Plaza Ste 400   Buy fees: no cost-orig iss
% Chicago, IL 60606-2609   0-5% disc-cash**
800-733-5001 admr $250-5,000/mo*(12)
312-454-0614 fax #   part. DR/cash-only
888-879-6356 InvRe   p. sale-$10 + 15¢/sh
e-mail: mmckenna@eqrworld.com   comm/pref/LP units
www.equityresidential.com
NOTE: *waiver for amts over $5,000 may be granted/**discount determined each mo

Essex Property Trust Inc (N-ESS) (div/yr: $ 3.24) [S&P ranking: A-] REIT
✂ 925 East Meadow Dr   Buy fees: no cost-div/$5 cash pymt fee
Palo Alto, CA 94303 $100-20,000/mo*EFT(52)
312-360-5354 admr   partial DR option
650-494-8743 fax #   p. sale-$10 + 15¢/sh
650-494-1656 InvRe
www.essexproperties.com

Estee Lauder Cos Inc (N-EL) (div/yr: $ 0.40) [S&P ranking: A-] consumer products-women's
cosmetics
767 5th Ave   Buy fees: no cost-div*   ✄
New York, NY 10153 $100-10,000/mo*EFT
800-860-6235 admr   DIP: $250 + $10 + 12¢/sh   ★
212-672-4204 ShrRe   part. DR/cash-only
e-mail: irdept@estee.com   p. sale-$15 + 12¢/sh
www.elcompanies.com   no residency restrict.
                                     div deposit
NOTE: *cash pymt fees:12¢/sh + $3 EFT/$5 check

Exelon Corp (N-EXC) (div/yr: $ 1.60) [S&P ranking: B +] utility-electric
P O Box A-3005 - Secretary's Office Buy fees: no svc chg   ✄
Chicago, IL 60690-3005 $25-60,000/yr EFT(12)
866-530-8108 admr   part. DR/cash-only
312-394-7251 fax #   sfkg-free/p. sale-avail
312-394-8811 InvRe   rec common/no residency restrict.
www.exeloncorp.com   div deposit

ExxonMobil Corp (N-XOM) (div/yr: $ 1.16) [S&P ranking: A-] energy-petroleum
c/o EquiServe Trust   Buy fees: no cost
P O Box 43008 $50-200,000/yr EFT(52)   ✄
Providence, RI 02940-3008   DIP: $250
800-252-1800 admr   part. DR/cash-only   ★
781-828-8813 fax #   sfkg-free/p. sale-$5 + 5¢/sh
972-444-1000 InvRe   rec common/no residency restrict.
www.exxonmobil.com   div deposit/gifting free

F

FBL Financial Group Inc (N-FFG) (div/yr: $ 0.42) [S&P ranking: B +] insurance holding co
5400 University Ave   Buy fees: no cost-div*
West Des Moines, IA 50266 $50-150,000/yr EFT*(52)
515-226-6780 InvRd   DIP: $250 + $10   ✄
515-226-6966 fax #   part. DR/cash-only
866-892-5627 admr   sfkg-free/p. sale-$15 + 12¢/sh   ★
e-mail: invrelations@fbfs.com   common/no residency restrict.
www.fblfinancial.com   gifting $10
NOTE: *fees for cash pymts $5/$3.50/$2 by ck/EFT/auto + 3¢/sh

FNB Corp (PA) (N-FNB) (div/yr: $ 0.92) [S&P ranking: B +] banks/banking
1 FNB Blvd   Buy fees: no cost
Hermitage, PA 15901 $50-10,000/qtr(52)
888-441-4362 admr   DIP: $1,000   ✄
721-981-6000 InvRe   p. sale-$10 + fee
                                     common   ★

FPL Group Inc (N-FPL) (div/yr: $ 1.42) [S&P ranking: A-] utility holding co
P O Box 14000   Buy fees: no cost
Juno Beach, FL 33408-0420 $100-100,000/yr EFT(4)   ✄
800-222-4511 InvSv   part. DR/cash-only
561-694-6331 fax #   sfkg-free/p. sale-avail
888-218-4392 admr   comm/no residency restrict.
e-mail: dinah_washam@fpl.com   div deposit
www.fpl.com

Fannie Mae (N-FNM) (div/yr: $ 1.04) fin svcs-mortgages
c/o EquiServe Trust Co NA   Buy fees: no cost-div**
P O Box 2598 $25-250,000/yr EFT(12)
✂ Jersey City, NJ 07303-2598   DIP: $250* + $15 + 3¢/sh
  202-752-7115 InvRe   partial DR option
★ 800-910-8277 admr   sfkg-free/p. sale-$15 + 12¢/sh
  e-mail: investor_relations@fanniemae.com rec common
  www.fanniemae.com
NOTE: *$100 min for minors/**$5 cash purch fee ($2 EFT) + bkg comm if more than
$2,500/program for children has different fee structure/phone sales/formal name: Fed-
eral National Mortgage Assn

FedEx Corp (N-FDX) (div/yr: $ 0.28) [S&P ranking: B +] trans-air/ground package delivery
942 S Shady Grove Ave   Buy fees: 5% to$3 + 3¢/sh*
Memphis, TN 38120-4117 $100-250,000/yr EFT(104)
★ 800-446-2617 admr   DIP: $1,000 + +$15 + 3¢/sh
  901-818-7200 InvRe   part. DR/cash-only
  e-mail: ir@fedex.com   sfkg-free/p. sale-$15 + 9¢/sh
  www.fedex.com or eip.equiserve.com   common
                                           div deposit/gifting free

NOTE: *cash pymt fees: 3¢/sh + $2 EFT/$5 check

Federal Realty Investment Trust (N-FRT) (div/yr: $ 2.02) [S&P ranking: A-] REIT-shopping ctrs
✂ 1626 E Jefferson St   Buy fees: no cost
  Rockville, MD 20852-4041 $25-10,000/mo EFT(24)
★ 877-611-8039 admr   DIP: $250
  301-998-3713 fax #   part. DR/cash-only
  301-998-8100 InvRe   sfkg-free/p. sale-avail
  e-mail: ir@federalrealty.com   rec common-1 sh min
  www.federalrealty.com   div deposit

Federal Signal Corp (N-FSS) (div/yr: $ 0.24) [S&P ranking: B] mfg-diversified
  1415 W 22nd St   Buy fees: no cost
✂ Oak Brook, IL 60523-2004 $100-60,000/yr EFT*(12)
  800-622-6757 admr   DIP: $100
★ 630-954-2030 fax #   part. DR/cash-only
  630-954-2000 co #   sfkg-free/p. sale-$15 + 12¢/sh
  www.federalsignal.com   rec comm-50 sh min/no residency restrict.
                                           gifting free

NOTE: *$2 EFT fee/purchases & sales by phone or internet possible

Ferro Corp (N-FOE) (div/yr: $ 0.58) [S&P ranking: B] mfg-chemicals
  1000 Lakeside Ave   Buy fees: no cost
✂ Cleveland, OH 44114-1183 $10-3,000/mo(12)
  800-622-6757 admr   part. DR/cash-only
  216-641-8580 co #   sfkg-free/p. sale-avail
  www.ferro.com   rec common

✂ **Fifth Third Bancorp** (NDQ-FITB) (div/yr: $ 1.40) [S&P ranking: A +] banking
  38 Fountain Plz - Trust #0085   Buy fees: no cost
  Cincinnati, OH 45263-0001 $25-1,000/month(12)
  513-579-5132 CorpTrust   cash-only option
  513-579-6246 fax #   common
  513-744-8577 co #
  www.53.com/bancorp

First American Corp (N-FAF) (div/yr: $ 0.72) [S&P ranking: B +] insurance-title insurance
1 First American Way
Santa Ana, CA 92707-4642
  800-468-9716 admr
  607-278-6914 fax #
  800-854-3643 InvRe
  www.firstam.com
NOTE: *on sales of less than $25,000

Buy fees: no cost
$50-5,000/qtr EFT(52)
DIP: $250 + $10
p. sale-$10 + 15¢/sh*
rec common
gifting $10

✂
★

First Charter Corp (NDQ-FCTR) (div/yr: $ 0.76) [S&P ranking: B] banks/banking
P O Box 37937
Charlotte, NC 28237-7937
  800-368-5948 admr
  800-422-5650 InvRe
  www.firstcharter.com

Buy fees: no cost-orig iss
$25-3,000/qtr EFT(12)
partial DR option
sfkg-free/p. sale-$15 + bkg
rec comm - min 1 sh
div deposit

✂

First Commonwealth Financial Corp (N-FCF) (div/yr: $ 0.66) [S&P ranking: B +] banking
22 N 6th St
Indiana, PA 15701
  724-349-7220 InvRe
  724-349-6427 fax #
  800-524-4458 admr
  www.fcfbank.com

Buy fees: no cost
10% disc-div
$50-120,000/yr EFT ($1 EFT fee)(52)
DIP: $500 + $7.50
part. DR/cash-only
sfkg-free/p. sale-$10 + 10¢/sh
rec common
div deposit/gifting free

✂
%
★

First Financial Holdings Inc (NDQ-FFCH) (div/yr: $ 0.92) [S&P ranking: A] S&L-savings banks
P O Box 118068/34 Broad St
Charleston, SC 29401
  800-368-5948 admr
  843-529-5929 fax #
  843-529-5933 InvRe
  e-mail: investorrelatons@firstfinacialholdings.com
  www.firstfinancialholdings.com

Buy fees: no cost
$100-5,000/mo EFT(52)
DIP: $250
partial DR option
sfkg-$3.50/p. sale-$3.50 + fee
rec comm-1 sh min
div deposit

✂
★

First Horizon National Corp (N-FHN) (div/yr: $ 1.72) [S&P ranking: A +] banks/banking
165 Madison Ave
Memphis, TN 38103
  877-536-3558 admr
  901-523-4444 InvRe

NOTE: frmly: First Tennessee

Buy fees: no cost
$25-10,000/qtr EFT(12)
part. DR/cash-only
sfkg-free/p. sale-$10 + 10¢/sh
rec common

✂

First Indiana Corp (NDQ-FINB) (div/yr: $ 0.72) [S&P ranking: A-] banks/banking
135 N Pennsylvania St
Indianapolis, IN 46204
  800-622-6757 admr
  317-269-1200 co #
  e-mail: investorrleations@firstindiana.com
  www.firstindiana.com

Buy fees: no cost
$100-5,000/qtr(4)
sfkg-free/p. sale-avail
common

✂

First Merchants Corp (IN) (NDQ-FRME) (div/yr: $ 0.92) [S&P ranking: A] banks/banking
P O Box 792
Muncie, IN 47308-0792
  765-741-7278 co #
  765-741-7283 fax #
  800/262-4261 Trust
  e-mail: dharris@firstmerchants.com
  www.firstmerchants.com
NOTE: *res of AZ, AR, CA, GA, ME, MN, NV, NY, OR, PA, UT, WI not eligible

Buy fees: no cost
$100-2,500/qtr(12)
cash-only option
rec comm*

✂

First Midwest Bancorp Inc (NDQ-FMBI) (div/yr: $ 0.96) [S&P ranking: A] banking
300 Park Blvd Ste 400
Itasca, IL 60143-0459
✂ 800-526-0801 admr
630-875-7360 fax #
630-875-7345 CorpSecy
e-mail: investor.relations@firstmidwest.com
www.firstmidwest.com

Buy fees: no cost
$100-5,000/qtr EFT(12)
part. DR/cash-only
sfkg-free/p. sale-avail
common
div deposit

First United Corp (MD) (NDQ-FUNC) (div/yr: $ 0.74) [S&P ranking: A] banks/banking
19 S Second St
✂ Oakland, MD 21550
800-230-2574 admr
301-334-5784 fax #
301-387-6893 Trust
www.mybankfirstunited.com

Buy fees: no cost
$50-10,000/qtr
part. DR/cash-only
p. sale-free
no residency restrict.
div deposit

FirstEnergy Corp (N-FE) (div/yr: $ 1.65) [S&P ranking: B +] utility-electric
76 S Main St
★ Akron, OH 44308-1890
800-736-3402 ShrSv
330-384-3866 fax #
330-384-5510 co #
www.firstenergycorp.com

Buy fees: no svc chg 9¢/sh
$25-100,000/yr EFT(24)
DIP: $250
part. DR/cash-only
sfkg-free/p. sale-avail
rec comm/pref*/no residency restrict.
div deposit

NOTE: *pref of Ohio Edison/Toledo Edison/Cleveland Elec/Jersey Central/div may be paid to shrholder on shs in plan

FirstMerit Corp (NDQ-FMER) (div/yr: $ 1.08) [S&P ranking: B +] banking
✂ 121 S Main St Ste 200
Akron, OH 44308-1440
330-384-7347 CpTrs
800-261-0406 admr
www.firstmerit.com

Buy fees: no cost
$25-5,000/qtr(4)
sfkg-free
rec common/no residency restrict.

Florida Public Utilities Co (A-FPU) (div/yr: $ 0.60) utility
P O Box 3395
✂ West Palm Beach, FL 33402-3395
800-937-5449 admr
561-833-8562 fax #
561-838-1729 CSecy
www.fpuc.com

Buy fees: no cost
$25-2,000/qtr(4)
part. DR/cash-only
p. sale-avail
rec common
div deposit

Foot Locker Inc (N-FL) (div/yr: $ 0.30) [S&P ranking: B-] retail-stores
112 W 34th St
✂ New York, NY 10120
866-857-2216 admr
212-720-4116 fax #
212-720-4477 AsstSecy
e-mail: sclarke@venatorgroup.com
www.footlocker-inc.com

Buy fees: no cost
$20-60,000/yr(12)
part. DR/cash-only
sfkg-free
rec common

Foothill Independent Bancorp (NDQ-FOOT) (div/yr: $ 0.52) [S&P ranking: A-] banks/banking
✂ 510 E Grand Ave
Glendora, CA 91741
626-963-8551 InvRe
626/914-5373 fax #
800-368-5948 admr
e-mail: info@foothillbank.com
www.foothillbank.com

Buy fees: no cost
$100-10,000/qtr(12)
part. DR/cash-only
sfkg-$5
common

Ford Motor Co (N-F) (div/yr: $ 0.40) [S&P ranking: B] mfg-auto
c/o EquiServe Trust Co NA
PO Box 43081
Providence, RI 02940-3081
　800-279-1237 admr
　201-222-4177 fax #
　800-555-5259 co #
　e-mail: stockinfo@ford.com
　www.ford.com

Buy fees: 5%to$5 + 3¢/sh*
$50-250,000/yr EFT*(52)
DIP: $1,000 + $13 + 3¢/sh^
part. DR/cash-only
sfkg-free/p. sale-$15 + 12¢/sh
rec common

★

NOTE: ^or $100/mo for 10 mo for DIP/*$1 EFT fee or $5 check + 3¢/sh/IRA $35 ann fee/loans on stock/line of credit on stock-$35 + interest

Fortune Brands Inc (N-FO) (div/yr: $ 1.32) [S&P ranking: B] consumer prod-leisure/home/office/distilled spirit
300 Tower Parkway
Lincolnshire, IL 60069-3640
　800-225-2719 ShRel
　847-484-4110 fax #
　847-484-4400 ShRel
　e-mail: investorrelations@fortunebrands.com
　www.fortunebrands.com

Buy fees: no cost
$50-15,000/qtr EFT(12)
part. DR/cash-only
sfkg-free/p. sale-avail
rec common/no residency restrict.
div deposit/gifting avail

✂

Franklin Resources Inc (N-BEN) (div/yr: $ 0.40) [S&P ranking: A-] fin svcs-mutual fund advisors & svcs
P O Box 7777
San Mateo, CA 94403-7777
　800-524-4458 admr
　650-525-7675 fax #
　650-525-8900 x28900 IR
　e-mail: aweinfeld@frk.com
　www.franklintempleton.com

Buy fees: no cost
$100-50,000/month(12)
cash-only option
sfkg-$7.50/p. sale-$3 + 5¢/sh
common

✂

Freddie Mac (N-FRE) (div/yr: $ 1.40) [S&P ranking: A] fin svcs-residential mortgages
8200 Jones Branch Dr
McLean, VA 22102-3107
　800-519-3111 admr
　571-382-4732 CorpSecy
　www.freddiemac.com

Buy fees: no cost-div*
$25-250,000/yr*EFT
DIP: $250 + $15 + 3¢/sh
part. DR/cash-only
sfkg-free/p. sale-$15 + 12¢/sh
common
gifting free

✂

★

NOTE: *$2 + 3¢/sh EFT/$5 + 3¢/sh-check

Freescale Semiconductor Inc (N-FSL) (div/yr: $0.00) mfg-semicons for auto/networking/wireless indust
6501 William Cannon Dr West
Ustin, TX 78735
　800-230-2574 admr
　512-895-8962 InvRe
　e-mail: investors@freescale.com
　www.freescale.com

Buy fees: 6¢/sh + $5check*
$50-250,000/yr*EFT(52)
DIP: $500 + $15 +6¢/sh
sfkg-free/p. sale-$15 + 12¢/sh
common/no residency restrict.
gifting free

★

NOTE: *cash pymt fees: 6¢/sh + $2 auto EFT/$3.50 single EFT/$5 check/co does not pay div/ spun off from Motorola 7/04

Fuller (H B) Co (N-FUL) (div/yr: $ 0.49) [S&P ranking: B] mfg-industrial adhesives
P O Box 64683
St Paul, MN 55164-0683
　800-468-9716 admr
　800-214-2523 CpRel
　www.hbfull.com

Buy fees: no cost
3% disc-div
$25-6,000/mo EFT(12)
part. DR/cash-only
sfkg-free/p. sale-avail
common/no residency restrict.
div deposit/gifting avail

✂

%

Fulton Financial Corp (NDQ-FULT) (div/yr: $ 0.58) [S&P ranking: A] banking
P O Box 3215   Buy fees: no cost-orig iss
Lancaster, PA 17604 $25-5,000/month(12)
800-626-0255 CpTrust   partial DR option
717-295-2534 fax #   sfkg-free/p. sale-$35 + 10¢/sh
717-291-2546 CpTrust   rec common
www.fult.com

G

GATX Corp (N-GMT) (div/yr: $ 0.80) [S&P ranking: A-] fin svcs/leasing
500 W Monroe St   Buy fees: no cost
Chicago, IL 60661-3676 $25-36,000/yr(12)
866-767-6259 admr   sfkg-free/p. sale-avail
312-621-6647 fax #   common/no residency restrict.
312-621-6603 AsstSecy
e-mail: ir@gatx.com
www.gatx.com

Gannett Co Inc (N-GCI) (div/yr: $ 1.08) [S&P ranking: A] publishing
7950 Jones Branch Dr   Buy fees: no cost
McLean, VA 22107-0001 $10-5,000/mo EFT(12)
703-854-6960 co #   part. DR/cash-only
800-778-3299 admr   sfkg-free/p. sale-avail
www.gannett.com   rec comm-min 1 sh/no resid restrict.

GenCorp Inc (N-GY) (div/yr: $0.00) [S&P ranking: B] mfg-aerospace/real estate
P O Box 537012   Buy fees: no cost
Sacramento, CA 95853-7012 $50-120,000/yr EFT(52)
★ 800-524-4458 admr   DIP: $500 + $7.50
916-351-8665 fax #   sfkg-$5/p. sale-$5 + 10¢/sh
916-351-8515 ShSvc   rec common
www.gencorp.com   gifting $5
NOTE: co omitted div

General Electric Co (N-GE) (div/yr: $ 0.88) [S&P ranking: A +] mfg-indus equip/cons prod
c/o Bank of New York   Buy fees: no cost-div*
P O Box 19552 $10-10,000/wk EFT*(52)
Newark, NJ 07195-0552   DIP: $250 + $7.50
★ 800-786-2543 admr   part. DR/cash-only
518-218-2951 StkDp   sfkg-free/p. sale-$10 + 15¢/sh
www.ge.com   rec com -1 sh min/no residency restrict.
                                      div deposit/gifting free
NOTE: *cash purch fees: $3 check/$1 EFT

General Growth Properties Inc (N-GGP) (div/yr: $ 1.44) [S&P ranking: A-] REIT-regional malls
110 N Wacker Dr   Buy fees: no cost
Chicago, IL 60606-1511 $50-50,000/mo EFT(12)
312-960-5048 InvRe   DIP: $200 (or $50/mo) + $15
★ 312-960-5463 fax #   part. DR/cash-only
800-526-0801 admr   sfkg-free/p. sale-$15 + 12¢/sh (phone sales)
www.generalgrowth.com   common
                                      gifting free

General Mills Inc (N-GIS) (div/yr: $ 1.34) [S&P ranking: B +] food-cereals, prepared foods
P O Box 1113   Buy fees: no cost
Minneapolis, MN 55440-1113 $10-3,000/qtr EFT(12)
800-670-4763 admr   partial DR option
763-764-5011 fax #   sfkg-free
763-764-3617 CorpSecy   rec common
www.genmills.com

General Motors Corp (N-GM) (div/yr: $ 2) [S&P ranking: B] mfg-automobiles/trucks
c/o EquiServe
P O Box 8036 - G M Corp
Boston, MA 02266-8036
313-667-1432 ShSvc
800-331-9922 admr
www.gm.com

Buy fees: no cost
$25-150,000/yr*EFT(52)
part. DR/cash-only
sfkg-free/p. sale-$15+bkg
rec comm-min 1 sh
div deposit/gifting free

NOTE: *maximum of $100,000 div reinvest/account access via internet

Genuine Parts Co (N-GPC) (div/yr: $ 1.25) [S&P ranking: A] distr-automotive parts
2999 Circle 75 Parkway
Atlanta, GA 30339-3050
800-568-3476 admr
770-953-1700 ShSvc
www.genpt.com

$10-3,000/qtr(12+)
sfkg-free
rec common

NOTE: +monthly if aggregate amt will purchase 100 sh lot

Georgia-Pacific Corp (N-GP) (div/yr: $ 0.70) [S&P ranking: B-] mfg-paper/bldg products
P O Box 105605
Atlanta, GA 30348-5605
800-519-3111 admr
404-584-1461 fax #
· 404-652-4893 CorpSecy
www.gp.com

Buy fees: no brkg fee
$25-5,000/mo EFT(12)
part. DR/cash-only
sfkg-free/p. sale-avail
rec common
div deposit

German American Bancorp (NDQ-GABC) (div/yr: $ 0.56) banks/banking
P O Box 810
Jasper, IN 47547-0810
812-482-1314 ShrRe
800-884-4225 admr

Buy fees: no cost
$100-100,000/yr EFT(12)
DIP: $100
part. DR/cash-only
p. sale-$5+bkg fee
common-1 sh min
gifting free

Gillette Co (N-G) (div/yr: $ 0.65) [S&P ranking: A-] consumer prod-personal care
Prudential Tower Blg
Boston, MA 02199-3799
888-218-2841 admr
617-421-7968 fax #
617-421-7000 CorpSecy
www.gillette.com

$58-120,000/yr EFT(52)
DIP: $1,000 + $10 + 8¢/sh
cash-only option
sfkg-free*/p. sale-$10+ 8¢/sh
rec common

NOTE: *shares must be deposited 60 days before sale

Glacier Bancorp Inc (NDQ-GBCI) (div/yr: $ 0.72) [S&P ranking: A+] banks/banking
49 Commons Loop
Kalispell, MT 59901-2679
877-390-3076 admr
406-751-4729 fax #
406-751-4702 InvRe
e-mail: jstrosahl@glacierbankcorp.com
www.glacierbancorp.com

Buy fees: 2%/$2.50+10¢/sh*
$25-10,000/dayEFT*(250)
DIP: $250 + $2.50 + 10¢/sh
sfkg-$7.50/p. sale-$15+10¢/sh
rec common
div deposit/gifting free

NOTE: *$2.50 + 10¢/sh per cash investment, monthly EFT

Gladstone Capital Corp (NDQ-GLAD) (div/yr: $ 1.56) fin svcs-loans to small businesses
1616 Anderson Rd Ste 208
McLean, VA 22102
800-524-4458 admr
703-286-7000 ShrRe
www.GladstoneCapital.com

Buy fees: no svc fee
no cash plan
p. sale-avail
rec comm

Gladstone Commercial Corp (NDQ-GOOD) (div/yr: $ 0.96) REIT
1616 Anderson Rd Ste 208
McLean, VA 22102
800-524-4458 admr
703-286-7000 ShrRe
www.GladstoneCommercial.com

Buy fees: no svc fee
no cash plan
partial DR option
p. sale-avail
rec comm

GlaxoSmithKline plc (N-GSK) (div/yr: $ 1.53) drug/pharmaceuticals-UK
c/o Bank of New York
P O Box 11258 Church St Sta
New York, NY 10286
★ 800-524-4458 admr
215-751-7002 InvRe
www.gsk.com

Buy fees: 5%/$5 + 10¢/sh*
$20-100,000/yr EFT(52)
DIP: $200 + $10
part. DR/cash-only
sfkg-$10/p. sale-$10 + 10¢/sh
rec ADR/US residents only
div deposit

NOTE: *cash pymt fee-$5 + $10¢/sh/$5 electronic sh trans

Glenborough Realty Trust Inc (N-GLB) (div/yr: $ 1.40) [S&P ranking: B] REIT
400 S El Camino Real Ste 1100
✄ San Mateo, CA 94402-1708
650-343-9300 co #
★ 650-343-7438 fax #
800/368-5948 admr
e-mail: shareholderservices@glenborough.com
www.glenborough.com

Buy fees: no cost
$100-10,000/mo EFT(12)
DIP: $250
partial DR option
sfkg-free/p. sale-bkg fee
common

Glimcher Realty Trust (N-GRT) (div/yr: $ 1.92) REIT-regional/community shopping centers
20 S Third St
% Columbus, OH 43215-3602
800-738-4931 admr
★ 614-621-9321 fax #
614-621-9000 co #

0-5% disc-div/cash*
$100-3,000/qtr(12)
DIP: $100 + $10
partial DR option
p. sale-$10 + 10¢/sh
common/no residency restrict.

NOTE: *disc avail only on orig issue shs

Golden Enterprises Inc (NDQ-GLDC) (div/yr: $ 0.03) [S&P ranking: B-] food-snack foods
✄ 2140 11th Ave South, Ste 208
Birmingham, AL 35205-2840
205-933-9300 co #
205-458-9310 fax #
212-815-3896 admr
www.goldenflake.com

Buy fees: no cost
no cash plan
p. sale-avail
common

Goodrich Corp (N-GR) (div/yr: $ 0.80) [S&P ranking: B] mfg-aerospace
✄ 2730 W Tyvola Rd
Charlotte, NC 28217
704-423-5517 InvRe
704-423-5512 fax #
800-524-4458 admr
e-mail: investor.relations@goodrich.com
www.goodrich.com

Buy fees: no cost
$25-1,000/month(12)
cash-only option
sfkg-free
rec common/no residency restrict.

Goodyear Tire & Rubber Co (The) (N-GT) (div/yr: $0.00) [S&P ranking: B-] mfg-rubber tires
c/o EquiServe Trust Co NA
P O Box 2598 # 4675
★ Jersey City, NJ 07303-2598
800-317-4445 admr
330-796-3751 InvRe
www.goodyear.com

Buy fees: div-$1 + 3¢/sh
$25-150,000/yr*EFT(52)
DIP: $250 + $10 + 3¢/sh
part. DR/cash-only
sfkg-free/p. sale-$15 + 15¢/sh
rec common/no residency restrict.
gifting free

NOTE: *3¢/sh bkg fee only on cash purch & EFT/co omitted div

DIVIDEND REINVESTMENT PLANS

G

Gorman-Rupp Co (The) (A-GRC) (div/yr: $ 3.17) [S&P ranking: A-] mfg-pumps
P O Box 1217
Mansfield, OH 44901-1217
800-622-6757 admr
419-755-1233 fax #
419-755-1011 co #
e-mail: demmens@gormanrupp.com
www.gormanrupp.com
Buy fees: no cost
$50-5,000/month(52)
DIP: $500 + $100 fee
part. DR/cash-only
p. sale-$10 + bkg
rec common
div deposit

Grace (W R) & Co (N-GRA) (div/yr: $0.00) [S&P ranking: D] mfg-specialty chemicals
c/o Mellon Investor Svcs
P O Box 750
Pittsburgh, PA 15230
410-531-4194 InvRe
800-648-8392 admr
www.grace.com
NOTE: omitted dividends 3/98, in Chp 11
Buy fees: no cost
$100-100,000/yr(12)
sfkg-free/p. sale-$15 + 12¢/sh
rec comm 50 sh min/no residency restrict.

Graco Inc (N-GGG) (div/yr: $ 0.52) [S&P ranking: A-] mfg-pump & spray equip
P O Box 1441
Minneapolis, MN 55440-1441
800-468-9716 admr
612-623-6942 fax #
612-623-6659 InvRe
www.graco.com
NOTE: blanket req for full shares in book entry registration
Buy fees: no cost
$25/mo-1,000/qtr(12)
sfkg-free
common
div deposit

Granite Construction Inc (N-GVA) (div/yr: $ 0.40) [S&P ranking: A-] svcs-public works construction
585 W Beach Street
Watsonville, CA 95076
800-368-5948 admr
831-761-7871 fax #
831-724-1011 InvRe
www.graniteconstruction.com
Buy fees: no cost-div rein
$100-10,000/mo(12)
DIP: $3,000 +$5 + 12¢/sh
part. DR/cash-only
sfkg-free/p. sale-$15 + 12¢/sh
comm-25 shs min (for DR)
div deposit/gifting free

Gray Television Inc (N-GTN) (div/yr: $ 0.12) entertainment-TV stations/newspapers
4370 Peachtree Rd N E
Atlanta, GA 30319
888-835-2869 admr
404-504-9828 InvRe
Buy fees: no cost
$100-10,000/mo(52)
DIP: $250 + $5 + 12¢/sh
partial DR option
sfkg-free*/p. sale-$15 + 12¢/sh
common Cl A & B**
div deposit/gifting free
NOTE: *safekeeping for Cl B shs only/**div & cash invest in Cl B shs

Great Plains Energy Inc (N-GXP) (div/yr: $ 1.66) [S&P ranking: B] utility-electric
P O Box 418679
Kansas City, MO 64141-9679
800-245-5275 ShrRe
816-556-2367 fax #
816-860-7891 admr
e-mail: todd.kobayashi@kcpl.com
www.greatplainsenergy.com
frmly: Kansas City Power & Light
Buy fees: no svc chg
$100-5,000/mo EFT(12)
DIP: $500 + $5 + 5¢/sh
part. DR/cash-only
sfkg-free/p. sale-$10 + 10¢/sh
comm-1 sh min
div deposit

Greater Bay Bancorp (CA) (NDQ-GBBK) (div/yr: $ 0.60) [S&P ranking: A-] banks/banking
2860 West Bayshore Rd
Palo Alto, CA 94303
800-468-9716 admr
650-813-8200 ShSvc
Buy fees: no cost
$50-1,000/mo(12)
partial DR option
sfkg-avail/p. sale-$10 + 15¢/sh
rec comm-25 shs min

✂ ★ **Green Mountain Power Corp** (N-GMP) (div/yr: $ 1) [S&P ranking: B] utility-electric
163 Acorn Ln
Colchester, VT 05446
800-851-9677 admr
802-655-8419 fax #
802-655-8420 CorpSecy
www.greenmoutainpower.biz

Buy fees: no cost
$50-40,000/yr(12)
DIP: Vt res $50
part. DR/cash-only
sfkg-free/p. sale-avail
rec comm 1 sh min/no residency restrict.

★ **Guidant Corp** (N-GDT) (div/yr: $ 0.40) [S&P ranking: B] healthcare-mfg medical devices
c/o EquiServe Trust Co NA
P O Box 43081
Providence, RI 02940-3081
888-756-3638 admr
317-971-2257 fax #
317-971-2000 co #
www.guidant.com

Buy fees: div-5% to $3+3¢/sh
$50 min EFT*(104)
DIP: $250 + $5 + 3¢/sh**
part. DR/cash-only
sfkg-free/p. sale-$15+12¢/sh
rec common
div deposit

NOTE: *cash/online pymt-$5 + 3¢/sh fee;EFT $2.50+3¢/sh/**or $50/mo for 5 months

H

✂ **HMN Financial Inc** (NDQ-HMNF) (div/yr: $ 0.88) [S&P ranking: B +] S&L/savings banks
1016 Civic Center Dr NW
Rochester, MN 55903-6057
800-468-9716 admr
507-346-1111 fax #
507-535-1200 InvRe
www.justcallhome.com

Buy fees: no cost
$50-5,000/mo EFT
sfkg-free
common

✂ **HRPT Properties Trust** (N-HRP) (div/yr: $ 0.84) [S&P ranking: B] REIT
400 Centre St
Newton, MA 02458-2076
800-468-9716 admr
617-969-5730 fax #
617-332-3990 admr

Buy fees: no cost
up to $10,000/qtr(4)
rec common

NOTE: frmly: Health & Retirement Properties Trust

✂ **Hancock Holding Co** (NDQ-HBHC) (div/yr: $ 0.66) [S&P ranking: A-] banks/banking
P O Box 4019 - Trust Dept
Gulfport, MS 39502
228-868-4605 Trust
www.hancockbank.com

Buy fees: no cost-div*
$50-5,000/qtr(4)
part. DR/cash-only
rec common

NOTE: *bkg fee on market-purchased shares

Hanson plc (N-HAN) (div/yr: $ 1.71) mfg-bldg materials-UK
1350 Campus Parkwy, Ste 302
Neptune, NJ 07753
877-248-4237 admr
732-919-2310 InvRe
e-mail: pdefelice@hanson.com
www.hansonplc.com

Buy fees: bkg fee*
$50-60,000/yr*(12)
part. DR/cash-only
sfkg-free/p. sale-$3 + bkg
rec ADR/US & CDN res only

NOTE: *$2.50 + bkg fee for cash purchases

✂ ★ **Harland (John H) Co** (N-JH) (div/yr: $ 0.50) [S&P ranking: B] misc-check printing/data svcs
P O Box 105250
Atlanta, GA 30348-5250
800-829-8432 admr
770-593-5619 fax #
770-593-5617 CorpSecy
www.harland.net

Buy fees: no cost-div/$5-cash
$50-250,000/yr EFT(52)
DIP: $500 + $10 + 10¢/sh
part. DR/cash-only
p. sale-$15+10¢/sh
rec common
gifting free

Harley-Davidson Inc (N-HDI) (div/yr: $ 0.50) [S&P ranking: A +] mfg-motorcycles
3700 W Juneau Ave   Buy fees: no cost-div*
Milwaukee, WI 53208 $30-100,000/yr EFT*(52)
 414-343-8002 InvRe   DIP: $500 + $10
 866-360-5339 admr   sfkg-free/p. sale-$10 + 10¢/sh
 www.harley-davidson.com   rec common
                                      gifting free
NOTE: *cash pymt fee $5 + 10¢/sh (EFT fee $1.50 + 10¢/sh)

Harleysville Group Inc (NDQ-HGIC) (div/yr: $ 0.68) [S&P ranking: B] insurance-prop-
erty/casualty
355 Maple Ave   Buy fees: no cost
Harleysville, PA 19438-2297 $100-25,000/yr(4)
 215-456-5026 StkRe   partial DR option
 215-256-5601 fax #   p. sale-avail
 800-523-6344 admr   common
 www.harleysvillegroup.com   gifting avail

Harrah's Entertainment Inc (N-HET) (div/yr: $ 1.32) [S&P ranking: B] enter-casinos
One Harrah's Ct   Buy fees: 10%to$3 + 10¢/sh-*
Las Vegas, NV 89119 $50-120,000/yr EFT*(52)
 800-524-4458 admr   DIP: $200 + $10
 702-407-6383 fax #   partial DR option
 702-407-6381 InvRe   sfkg-free/p. sale-$15 + 10¢/sh
 e-mail: investors@harrahs.com   gifting free
 http://investor.harrahs.com
NOTE: *div/cash pymt fees: 10¢/sh + $3 EFT/$5 check

Harris Corp (N-HRS) (div/yr: $ 0.24) [S&P ranking: B-] mfg-communications eq
1025 W NASA Blvd   Buy fees: no cost
Melbourne, FL 32919-0001 $10-5,000/qtr(12)
 321-727-9100 CorpSecy   common/no residency restrict.
 321-727-9636 fax #
 888-261-6777 admr
 www.harris.com

Harsco Corp (N-HSC) (div/yr: $ 1.20) [S&P ranking: B +] misc-diversified indus svcs/mfg
PO Box 8888 - 350 Poplar Church Rd   Buy fees: no cost
Camp Hill, PA 17001-8888 $10 or more/pymt(12)
 717-763-7064 co #   sfkg-$5
 717-763-6424 fax #   rec common/no residency restrict.
 800-526-0801 admr   div deposit
 e-mail: info@harsco.com
 www.harsco.com

Hartford Financial Services Group Inc (The) (N-HIG) (div/yr: $ 1.16) [S&P ranking: B] insur-
ance
690 Asylum Ave   Buy fees: no cost
Hartford, CT 06115 $50-5,000/month(52)
 800-254-2823 admr   sfkg-free/p. sale-avail
 860-547-2552 fax #   common
 860-547-2403 InvRe   gifting avail
 www.thehartford.com

Hartmarx Corp (N-HMX) (div/yr: $0.00) [S&P ranking: B-] consumer prod-apparel
101 No Wacker Dr   Buy fees: no cost
Chicago, IL 60606-7389 $25-1,000/month(12)
 312-372-6300 co #   cash-only option
 800-446-2617 admr   common
 www.hartmarx.com
NOTE: omitted div 1/92

Hawaiian Electric Industries Inc (N-HE) (div/yr: $ 1.24) [S&P ranking: B +] utility holding co
P O Box 730   Buy fees: 50¢/qtr + 3¢/sh*
Honolulu, HI 96808-0730 $25-120,000/yr EFT(24)
  808-532-5841 StkTr   DIP: $250
★ 808-532-5868 fax #   part. DR/cash-only
  808-543-5662 co #   sfkg-free/p. sale-$15 + bkg
  e-mail: invest@hei.com   rec comm/pref**/no residency restrict.
  www.hei.com   div deposit
  NOTE: *no bkg fee on orig issue shs/**legal age

Hawkins Inc (NDQ-HWKN) (div/yr: $ 0.36)
3100 E Hennepin Ave   Buy fees: no cost
Minneapolis, MN 55413 $200-5,000/qtr(4)
✂ 800-468-9716 admr   sfkg-avail/p. sale-avail
  612-331-6910 co #
  e-mail: ir@hawkinsinc.com
  www.hawkinschemical.com

Health Care Property Investors Inc (N-HCP) (div/yr: $ 1.68) [S&P ranking: B] REIT-hospi-
tals/assisted living/nursing homes
  3760 Kilroy Airport Way Ste 300   Buy fees: no cost
✂ Long Beach, CA 90806-2473   0-1% disc-orig issue
  866-857-2227 admr $100-10,000/mo EFT(12)
% 562-733-5104 InvRe   DIP: $750
  e-mail: investorrelations@hcpi.com   partial DR option
★ www.hcpi.com   p. sale-avail
                                                common
                                                gifting avail

Health Care REIT Inc (N-HCN) (div/yr: $ 2.48) [S&P ranking: A-] REIT
  c/o Mellon Investor Services LLC   Buy fees: no cost
✂ P O Box 750   4% disc-div/cash
  South Hackensack, NJ 07606-1938 $50-5,000/qtr*(4)
% 888-216-7206 admr   part. DR/cash-only
  419-247-2826 fax #   sfkg-avail
  419-247-2800 co #   common
  www.hereit.com
  NOTE: *all accounts in behalf of an individual are aggregated for max limit

Healthcare Realty Trust Inc (N-HR) (div/yr: $ 2.62) [S&P ranking: A-] REIT
  c/o EquiServe   Buy fees: no cost
  P O Box 43010   5% disc-div
✂ Providence, RI 02940-3010 $25-60,000/yr EFT(12)
  800-730-6001 admr   part. DR/cash-only
% 615-269-8461 fax #   sfkg-free/p. sale-avail
  615-269-8175 InvRe   rec comm-1 sh min
  e-mail: hrinfo@healthcarerealty.com   div deposit
  www.healthcarerealty.com

Heinz (H J) Co (N-HNZ) (div/yr: $ 1.14) [S&P ranking: B] food-processor
  c/o Mellon Investor Services LLC   Buy fees: no cost
  P O Box 750 $50-10,000/mo EFT(52)
✂ South Hackensack, NJ 07606-1938   DIP: $250
  800-253-3399 admr   partial DR option
★ 412-456-5700 co #   sfkg-free
  www.heinz.com   rec common/no residency restrict.
                                                div deposit

Henry (Jack) & Associates Inc (NDQ-JKHY) (div/yr: $ 0.18) [S&P ranking: A +] svcs-data processing for banks & credit unions
P O Box 807
Monett, MO 65708-0807
 816-860-3753 admr
 417-235-4281 fax #
 417-235-6652 co #
 www.jackhenry.com

Buy fees: no svc chg
no cash plan
partial DR option
p. sale-avail
common

Hercules Inc (N-HPC) (div/yr: $0.00) [S&P ranking: B-] mfg-chemicals
c/o Mellon Investor Services LLC
P O Box 750
South Hackensack, NJ 07606-1938
 302-594-5000 co #
 302-594-7315 fax #
 800-237-9980 admr
 www.herc.com
NOTE: *$5 + bkg fee for cash pymts/omitted div 11/15/00

Buy fees: no cost-div*
$50-2,000/month(12)
part. DR/cash-only
sfkg-$3/p. sale-$15 + bkg fee
rec common

Hershey Foods Corp (N-HSY) (div/yr: $ 0.88) [S&P ranking: A-] food-chocolate
P O Box 810
Hershey, PA 17033-0810
 800-851-4216 admr
 800-539-0261 InvRe
 www.hersheys.com
NOTE: *cash pumt fees: 6¢/sh + $2 EFT/$5 check

Buy fees: no cost-div*
$25-250,000/yr EFT*(52)
DIP: $250 + $15 + 6¢/sh
part. DR/cash-only
sfkg-free/p. sale-$15 + 12¢/sh
rec comm/no residency restrict.
div deposit/gifting free

Hewlett-Packard Co (N-HPQ) (div/yr: $ 0.32) [S&P ranking: A-] mfg-computer/off equipment
3000 Hanover St - Shareholder Rcds
Palo Alto, CA 94304
 800-286-5977 admr
 650-857-4837 fax #
 650-857-1501 InvRe
 www.hp.com
NOTE: *cash pymt fees:8¢/sh + $2.50 by check/$1.25 EFT/EFT-mo or qrtly pynmts.

Buy fees: 5%/$2.50* + 8¢/sh
$50-10,000/mo EFT*(12)
sfkg-free/p. sale-$10 + 8¢/sh
rec comm-10 sh min

Hibernia Corp (N-HIB) (div/yr: $ 0.80) [S&P ranking: A-] banking
P O Box 61540/313 Carondelet
New Orleans, LA 70161-1540
 800-245-4388 admr
 504-533-2367 fax #
 504-533-3411 AsstSecy
 www.hiberniabank.com

Buy fees: no cost
5% disc-div
$100-3,000/month(12)
part. DR/cash-only
sfkg-free/p. sale-avail
common/no residency restrict.

Hickory Tech Corp (NDQ-HTCO) (div/yr: $ 0.48) [S&P ranking: B] telecomm-svc in Minn & Iowa
221 East Hickory St
Mankato, MN 56002-3248
 800-468-9716 admr
 507-387-3355 ShrRe

Buy fees: no cost
no cash plan
partial DR option
sfkg-free/p. sale-avail
rec common

Highwoods Properties Inc (N-HIW) (div/yr: $ 1.70) [S&P ranking: B +] REIT
3100 Smoketree Ct Ste 600
Raleigh, NC 27604-1051
 800-829-8432 admr
 919-876-6929 fax #
 919-431-1529 InvRe
 e-mail: HIW-IR@highwoods.com
 www.highwoods.com

Buy fees: no cost
0-5% disc-div
$25-10,000/mo(12)
part. DR/cash-only
p. sale-avail
common/no residency restrict.
div deposit

H

Directory of Companies Offering

Hillenbrand Industries (N-HB) (div/yr: $ 1.12) [S&P ranking: B +] mfg-burial caskets/hospital equip
700 State Rt 46 E
Batesville, IN 47006-8835
 800-716-3607 admr
 812-934-7371 fax #
 812-934-8400 InvRe
 e-mail: wendy.wilson@hillenbrand.com
 www.hillenbrand.com
Buy fees: no cost-div*
$100-50,000/yr EFT(52)
DIP: $250
part. DR/cash-only
sfkg-free/p. sale-$10 + 10¢/sh
common
gifting $5
NOTE: *cash pymt fees: $5 by check, $2.50 EFT + 10¢/sh / not open to instituitional investors

Home Depot Inc (The) (N-HD) (div/yr: $ 0.40) [S&P ranking: A +] retail-building materials/home improvement
2455 Paces Ferry Rd NW
Atlanta, GA 30339-4024
 800-577-0177 admr
 770-433-8211 AsstSecy
 www.HomeDepot.com
$25-100,000/yr EFT(104)
DIP: $250
part. DR/cash-only
sfkg-free/p. sale-$10
rec common

Home Properties Inc (N-HME) (div/yr: $ 2.52) REIT-residential
850 Clinton Sq
Rochester, NY 14604
 800-230-2574 admr
 585-232-3147 fax #
 585-246-4140 ShrSv
 e-mail: yvonnew@homeproperties.com
 www.homeproperties.com
Buy fees: no cost
$50-1,000*/mo EFT(12)
DIP: $1,000
part. DR/cash-only
sfkg-free/p. sale-$15 + 12¢/sh
common
div deposit
NOTE: $50 initial pymt for residents of HME properties/*co approval for > $5,000

Honeywell International Inc (N-HON) (div/yr: $ 0.83) [S&P ranking: B] mfg-high technology
P O Box 50000
Morristown, NJ 07962
 800-937-5449 admr
 973-455-2142 ShRel
 www.honeywell.com
 NOTE: frmly: AlliedSignal
Buy fees: no cost
$25-120,000/yr(12)
part. DR/cash-only
sfkg-$7/p. sale-avail
rec common

Hooper Holmes Inc (A-HH) (div/yr: $ 0.06) [S&P ranking: B] insurance-medical underwriting info to ins cos
170 Mt Airy Rd
Basking Ridge, NJ 07920-2016
 800-368-5948 admr
 908-953-6304 fax #
 908-953-6337 InvRe
 e-mail: hholmes@hooperholmes.com
 www.hooperholmes.com
no cash plan
sfkg-avail/p. sale-$15

Horizon Financial Corp (WA) (NDQ-HRZB) (div/yr: $ 0.54) [S&P ranking: B +] banks/banking
P O Box 580/1500 Cornwall Ave
Bellingham, WA 98227
 800-278-4353 admr
 360-733-7019 fax #
 360-733-3050 InvRe
 e-mail: info@horizonbank.com
 www.horizonbank.com
Buy fees: no cost
$125-3,000/qtr(4)
part. DR/cash-only
sfkg-free/p. sale-svc + bkg fees
rec common

DIVIDEND REINVESTMENT PLANS H

Hormel Foods Corp (N-HRL) (div/yr: $ 0.52) [S&P ranking: A] food-meat
1 Hormel Place
Austin, MN 55912-3680
 877-536-3559 admr
 507-437-5135 fax #
 507-437-5220 GC
 www.hormel.com
Buy fees: no cost
$25-20,000/qtr EFT(12)
sfkg-free
rec common
NOTE: a blanket request for certificates of full shares may be made

Hospitality Properties Trust (N-HPT) (div/yr: $ 2.88) [S&P ranking: A-] REIT
400 Centre St
Newton, MA 02458
 866-877-6331 admr
 617-969-5730 fax #
 617-964-8369 InvRe
Buy fees: no cost
to $10,000/qtr EFT(4)
sfkg-avail

Hubbell Inc (N-HUB/A) (div/yr: $ 1.32) [S&P ranking: B +] mfg-elec equip
c/o Mellon Investor Services LLC
P O Box 3338
South Hackensack, NJ 07606-1938
 800-851-9677 admr
 203-799-4333 fax #
 203-799-4100 co #
 www.hubbell.com/
Buy fees: no cost
$100-5,000/qtr(12)
part. DR/cash-only
sfkg-$3/p. sale-avail
rec common Cl A & B
NOTE: each class reinvests in same class shs

Hudson United Bancorp Inc (N-HU) (div/yr: $ 1.48) [S&P ranking: B +] banking
1000 MacArthur Blvd
Mahwah, NJ 07430
 718-921-8206 admr
 718-236-4588 fax #
 201-236-2641 co #
 www.hudsonunitedbancorp.com
$10-20,000/qtr(12)
sfkg-free/p. sale-avail
common

Hudson's Bay Co (T-HBC) (div/yr: $0.00) retail-CDN
401 Bay St Ste 500
Toronto, Ont M5H 2Y4, Canada
 800-387-0825 admr
 416-861-4720 fax #
 416-861-4593 CorpSecy
 e-mail: james.ingram@hbc.com
 www.hbc.com
Buy fees: no cost
no cash plan
partial DR option
rec common/US res not elig
NOTE: co does not pay div

Huffy Corp (NDQ-HUFCQ) (div/yr: $0.00) [S&P ranking: C] consumer prod-mfg / retail svcs
225 Byers Rd
Miamisburg, OH 45342
 937-866-6251 co #
 937-865-5470 fax #
 800-246-5761 admr
 www.huffy.com
Buy fees: no cost
$50-100,000/yr EFT(52)
DIP: $500 + $10 + 10¢/sh
sfkg-free/p. sale-$10 + 10¢/sh
common 1 sh min/no residency restrict.
NOTE: *$10¢/sh on cash pymts/div omitted '99

Huntington Bancshares Inc (NDQ-HBAN) (div/yr: $ 0.80) [S&P ranking: B +] banking/insur-ance
41 S High St - HC0935
Columbus, OH 43287
 800-725-0674 admr
 614-480-5284 fax #
 614-480-5676 InvRe
 www.huntington.com
Buy fees: no cost
$200-10,000/qtr EFT(4)
partial DR option
sfkg-free*/p. sale-avail
common 1 sh min/no residency restrict.
div deposit/gifting avail
NOTE: *option of book-entry not in DRP

IDACorp (N-IDA) (div/yr: $ 1.20) [S&P ranking: B] utility-hydroelectric
P O Box 70
Boise, ID 83707-0070
★ 800-565-7890 ShrSv
208-388-6955 fax #
208-388-2634 co #
e-mail: barbsmith@idahopower.com
www.idacorpinc.com
NOTE: sales by phone/online

Buy fees: 4¢/sh
$10-15,000/qtr EFT(4)
DIP: $200 + $10
part. DR/cash-only
sfkg-free/p. sale-10¢/sh
common - 1sh min/no residency restrict.
gifting avail

IDEX Corp (N-IEX) (div/yr: $ 0.48) [S&P ranking: B +] mfg-industrial products
✂ 630 Dundee Rd Ste 400
Northbrook, IL 60062-2745
800-622-6757 admr
847-498-3940 fax #
847-498-7070 CorpSecy
e-mail: dlennox@idexcorp.com
www.idexcorp.com

Buy fees: no cost
$50-5,000/qtr(12)
partial DR option
p. sale-$10
rec common-1 sh min

IKON Office Solutions Inc (N-IKN) (div/yr: $ 0.16) [S&P ranking: B-] distr-office equip
70 Valley Stream Pkwy
Malvern, PA 19355
610-296-8000 AsstSecy
610-401-7964 fax #
800-622-6757 admr
www.ikon.com

Buy fees: no svc chg
$25-5,000/month(12)
part. DR/cash-only
sfkg-free/p. sale-$2
common

iStar Financial Inc (N-SFI) (div/yr: $ 5.93) [S&P ranking: B] REIT-commercial properties
✂ 1114 Ave of the Americas, 27th Flr
New York, NY 10036
% 800-317-4445
212-930-9494 fax #
★ 212-930-9400 co #

Buy fees: no cost
0-3% disc-div/cash
$100-10,000/mo(12)
DIP: $100
part. DR/cash-only
sfkg-free/p. sale-avail
div deposit/gifting avail

ITT Industries Inc (N-ITT) (div/yr: $ 0.72) [S&P ranking: B] mfg-defense elec/fluid technology
4 W Red Oak Ln
✂ White Plains, NY 10604
800-254-2823 admr
★ 914-696-2960 fax #
914-641-2033 InvRe
www.itt.com

Buy fees: no cost
$50-120,000/yr EFT(52)
DIP: $500 + $7.50
sfkg-free/p. sale-$5 + 10¢/sh
rec common/no residency restrict.
gifting $5

Illinois Tool Works Inc (N-ITW) (div/yr: $ 1.12) [S&P ranking: A +] mfg-diversified
3600 W Lake Ave
Glenview, IL 60025-5811
✂ 888-829-7424 adnr
847-724-7500 InvRe
www.tw.com

Buy fees: no cost*
$100-10,000/mo EFT ($1.50 EFT fee) (12)
sfkg-free/p. sale-avail
common

Imperial Chemical Industries plc (N-ICI) (div/yr: $ 0.54) [S&P ranking: B-] mfg-chemicals-UK
10 Findeme Ave
Bridgewater, NJ 08807
800-749-1687 admr
★ 908-203-2922 US IR
www.ici.com

Buy fees: 5% to $2.50
$50-100,000/yr EFT (52)
DIP: $250 + $15
part. DR/cash-only
sfkg-free/p. sale-$5 + 12¢/sh (daily sales)
ADR

Imperial Oil Ltd (A-IMO) (div/yr: $ 0.86) energy-petroleum-CDN
111 St Clair Ave W
Toronto, ONT M5W 1K3, Canada
800-387-0825 admr
416-968-4095 fax #
416-968-5387 ShrSv
www.imperialoil.ca
Buy fees: no svc chg/2¢/sh bkg fee
C$50-5000/qtr(4)
part. DR/cash-only
common/no residency restrict.

Independent Bank Corp (Mich) (NDQ-IBCP) (div/yr: $ 0.76) [S&P ranking: A] banking
230 West Main St
Ionia, MI 48846-1617
800-257-1617 admr
616-527-5833 fax #
616-527-9450 InvRe
e-mail: info@ibcp.com
www.ibcp.com
Buy fees: no cost
$50-10,000/qtr EFT(4)
part. DR/cash-only
rec common/Michigan res *

IndyMac Bancorp (N-NDE) (div/yr: $ 1.70) [S&P ranking: B +] fin svcs-internet mortgage bank
155 N Lake Ave
Pasadena, CA 91101
800-814-0291 admr
626-535-5901 InvRe
www.indymacbank.com
Buy fees: no cost
US$50-10,000/mo*(52)
DIP: $250 or 5 $50 EFT
p. sale-$15 + 12¢/sh
common
NOTE: must accept all documents (ann rpts, etc) online/*waiver may be available for amts greater than $10,000

Ingersoll-Rand Co (N-IR) (div/yr: $ 1) [S&P ranking: A] mfg-const eq/mach
200 Chestnut Ridge Rd
Woodcliff Lake, NJ 07675-7703
800-524-4458 admr
201-573-3448 fax #
201-573-0123 InvRe
www.ingersoll-rand.com
Buy fees: no cost
$10-3,000/qtr(12)
rec common

Insteel Industries Inc (NDQ-IIIN) (div/yr: $0.00) mfg-wire & wire products
c/o Wachovia Bank
2 First Union Center
Charlotte, NC 28288-1154
704-383-5183 admr
336-786-2144 fax #
336-786-2141 x3008
e-mail: gkniskern@insteel.com
www.insteel.com
Buy fees: no cost
$10 or more/mo(12)
rec common

Intel Corp (NDQ-INTC) (div/yr: $ 0.32) [S&P ranking: A] mfg-semiconductor memory chips
2200 Mission College Blvd
Santa Clara, CA 95052-8119
800-298-0146 admr**
408-765-1679 InvRe
www.intel.com
Buy fees: no cost
$25-15,000/mo EFT (mo/qtr)*(12)
sfkg-free/p. sale-avail
common
div deposit

Interchange Financial Services Corp (NDQ-IFCJ) (div/yr: $ 0.36) [S&P ranking: A] banking
Park 80 West/Plaza 2
Saddle Brook, NJ 07663
800-509-5586 admr
201-843-3945 fax #
201-703-2265 ShRel
e-mail: ghutter@interchangebank.com
www.interchangebank.com
25/mo or more (EFT from ISB acct) (12)
DIP: $100
common
gifting avail

International Business Machines Corp (N-IBM) (div/yr: $ 0.80) [S&P ranking: B +] mfg-computers/off eq
c/o EquiServe Trust Co NA
P O Box 2598 # 4675
★ Jersey City, NJ 07303-2598
 914-499-1900 StkRe
 914-765-7037 fax #
 888-426-6700 admr
 e-mail: ibm@equiserve.com
 www.ibm.com
NOTE: *$50/mo EFT for 10 months/cash pymt fee ($1 EFT/$5 by check)

Buy fees: 2% to $3-div
$50-250,000/qtr EFT(52)
DIP: $500 + $15 fee or*
partial DR option
sfkg-free/p. sale-$15 + 10¢/sh
rec comm 1 sh min/no residency restrict.
div deposit/gifting avail

International Flavors & Fragances (N-IFF) (div/yr: $ 0.70) [S&P ranking: B] mfg-flavors & fragrance products
521 W 57th St
✂ New York, NY 10019-2960
 800-829-8432 admr
 212-765-5500 Legal
 www.iff.com

Buy fees: no cost
$25-5,000/month(12)
sfkg-free
rec common

International Paper Co (N-IP) (div/yr: $ 1) [S&P ranking: B-] mfg-paper
400 Atlantic St
Stamford, CT 06921
★ 800-678-8715 admr
 203-541-8218 fax #
 203-541-8494 AsstSecy
 www.internationalpaper.com

Buy fees: 12¢/sh
$50-20,000/yr EFT(12)
DIP: $500 + $5
part. DR/cash-only
sfkg-free/p. sale-$15 + 12¢/sh
comm-25 shs min/no residency restrict.
div deposit/gifting free

NOTE: 6 mo wait to re-enter after termination

Interpublic Group of Cos Inc (N-IPG) (div/yr: $0.00) [S&P ranking: C] misc-advertising
c/o EquiServe Trust Co NA
P O Box 2598 # 4675
Jersey City, NJ 07303-2598
 800-519-3111 admr
 212-399-8101
 www.interpublic.com
NOTE: co does not pay div

Buy fees: 5% to $2.50 + bkg fee
$10-3,000/qtr(4)
sfkg-free
rec common

Interstate Bakeries Corp (OTC-IBCIQ) (div/yr: $0.00) [S&P ranking: D] food-bakery
12 E Armour Blvd
Kansas City, MO 64111
 816-502-4000 co #
 800-884-4225 admr
NOTE: co not paying div /Chp 11 9/22/04

$50-3,000/qtr(4)
sfkg-free/p. sale-$2
common

Invacare Corp (N-IVC) (div/yr: $ 0.05) [S&P ranking: B +] mfg/distr-wheelchairs/medical products & supplies
✂ PO Box 4028
Elyria, OH 44036-2125
 800-622-6757 admr
 440-365-6936 fax #
 440-329-6001 InvRe
 e-mail: rgudbranson@invacare.com
 www.invacare.com

Buy fees: no cost
$10-5,000/mo(12)
part. DR/cash-only
sfkg-free/p. sale-no sale fee
rec common & Cl B

Investors Financial Services Corp (NDQ-IFIN) (div/yr: $ 0.08) [S&P ranking: A-] banks/bank-
ing-svcs to financial asset mgrs
200 Clarendon St   Buy fees: no cost-div*
Boston, MA 02116 $100-1 mil EFT*(52)
 201-324-0313 admr   DIP: $250
 617-330-6700 InvRe   sfkg-free/p. sale-$15
 e-mail: investor_relations@ibtco.com gifting free
 www.ibtco.com
NOTE: *cash pymt fees: $2 EFT (min $50)/$5 check

J

J P Morgan Chase & Co (N-JPM) (div/yr: $ 1.36) [S&P ranking: B] banking
270 Park Ave   Buy fees: no cost
New York, NY 10017-2070   no cash plan
 800-758-4651 admr   partial DR option for common only
 212-270-4040 CorpSecy   sfkg-free
 www.jpmorganchase.com   comm/pref
                                      div deposit

Janus Capital Group Inc (N-JNS) (div/yr: $ 0.04) fin svcs-investment advisor-Janus funds
100 Filmore St   Buy fees: no svc fees
Denver, CO 80206 $50-5,000/qtr(12)
 303-691-3905 co #   partial DR option
 800-525-3717   sfkg-free/p. sale-bkg fee
                                      common
                                      gifting avail

Jefferson-Pilot Corp (N-JP) (div/yr: $ 1.67) [S&P ranking: A+] insurance/TV
c/o Wachovia Bank NA   Buy fees: no cost
1525 W W T Harris Blvd 3C3 $20-2,000/month(12)
Charlotte, NC 28262-8522   sfkg-free
 800-829-8432 admr   rec common/no residency restrict.
 336-691-3283 fax #   div deposit
 336-691-3382 CorpSecy
 e-mail: investor.relations@jpfinancial.com
 www.jpfinancial.com

Johnson & Johnson (N-JNJ) (div/yr: $ 1.14) [S&P ranking: A+] health care products
1 Johnson & Johnson Plaza   Buy fees: no cost
New Brunswick, NJ 08933-0001 $25-50,000/yr EFT*(12)
 800-328-9033 admr   part. DR/cash-only
 732-524-0400   sfkg-free/p. sale-$15 + 12¢/sh
 www.jnj.com   rec common
                                      div deposit
NOTE: *$1/transaction by EFT/telephone sales

Johnson Controls Inc (N-JCI) (div/yr: $ 1) [S&P ranking: A+] mfg-comm blg automation, auto
seats/batteries
P O Box 591   Buy fees: 4%to$2 + 3¢/sh*
Milwaukee, WI 53201-0591 $50-5,000/mo EFT*(52)
 800-524-6220 admr   DIP: $250 + $10
 414-524-2828 fax #   partial DR option
 414-524-2363 ShSvc   sfkg-free/p. sale-$10 + 10¢/sh
 e-mail: arlene.gumm@jci.com   rec comm/pref/no residency restrict.
 www.johnsoncontrols.com   div deposit
NOTE: *$2 + 3¢/sh cash pymt fee($1 + 3¢/sh EFT)

Kaman Corp (NDQ-KAMNA) (div/yr: $ 0.44) [S&P ranking: B] mfg-diversified
✂ c/o Mellon Investor Svcs
   P O Box 750
★ Pittsburgh, PA 15230-0750
   860-243-6307 InvRe
   800-227-0291 admr
   www.kaman.com

               Buy fees: no cost-div*
               $50-5,000/mo EFT*(52)
               DIP: $250 + $5/$3(EFT)
               partial DR option
               sfkg-free/p. sale-$15 + 12¢/sh
               rec comm Cl A-10 sh/no residency restrict.
               div deposit

   NOTE: *cash pymt $5 fee/$3 EFT

Keithley Instruments Inc (N-KEI) (div/yr: $ 0.15) [S&P ranking: B] mfg-electronic test equip
✂ 28775 Aurora Rd
   Solon, OH 44139-1891
★ 440-498-2627 co #
   440-248-6168 fax #
   800/622-6757 admr
   e-mail: investor_relations@keithley.com
   www.keithley.com

               Buy fees: no cost
               $50-10,000/mo(12)
               DIP: $250
               part. DR/cash-only
               sfkg-free/p. sale-avail
               rec common

Kellogg Co (N-K) (div/yr: $ 1.01) [S&P ranking: B +] food-cereals
✂ c/o Wells Fargo Bank Minnesota NA
   P O Box 64856
   St Paul, MN 55164-0856
   877-910-5385 admr
   269-660-4178 fax #
   269-961-2830 InvRe
   www.kelloggcompany.com

               Buy fees: no cost
               $25-25,000/yr EFT(12)
               partial DR option
               sfkg-free
               rec common/no residency restrict.

Kellwood Co (N-KWD) (div/yr: $ 0.64) [S&P ranking: B +] consumer prod-apparel mfg
   P O Box 14374
✂ St Louis, MO 63178
   314-576-3350 co #
★ 314-576-3388 fax #
   800-937-5449 admr
   e-mail: andee.althoff@kellwood.com
   www.kellwood.com

               Buy fees: no cost
               $25-3,000/month(12)
               DIP: $100
               part. DR/cash-only
               sfkg-free/p. sale-$5 + bkg fee
               rec common

Kelly Services Inc (NDQ-KELY.A) (div/yr: $ 0.40) [S&P ranking: A-] svcs-temporary help agency
✂ 999 W Big Beaver Rd
   Troy, MI 48084-4782
★ 866-249-4586 admr
   248-362-4444 InvRe

               Buy fees: no cost
               $25-100,000/yr(52)
               DIP: $250 + $5
               part. DR/cash-only
               sfkg-free/p. sale-$15 + 12¢/sh
               rec comm Cl A
               div deposit/gifting free

Kennametal Inc (N-KMT) (div/yr: $ 0.68) [S&P ranking: B] mfg-metal fabricating
✂ P O Box 231
   Latrobe, PA 15650-0231
   412-236-8173 admr
   724-539-3839 fax #
   724-539-5204 CorpSecy
   www.kennametal.com

               Buy fees: no cost
               5% disc-div
               $25-4,000/qtr(4)
               part. DR/cash-only
               sfkg-free/p. sale-avail
               common/no residency restrict.

Kerr-McGee Corp (N-KMG) (div/yr: $ 1.80) [S&P ranking: B] energy-petroleum-exp/dev
✂ Kerr-McGee Center/PO Box 25861
   Oklahoma City, OK 73125
★ 877-860-5820 admr
   405-270-2863 fax #
   800-786-2556 StkRe
   e-mail: jbyrne@kmg.com
   www.kerr-mcgee.com

               Buy fees: no cost
               $10-1,000/month(12)
               DIP: $750
               p. sale-free
               rec common/no residency restrict.
               gifting avail

KeyCorp (N-KEY) (div/yr: $ 1.30) [S&P ranking: A-] banking/financial svcs
127 Public Sq 01-127-1113
Cleveland, OH 44114-1113
216-689-0519 fax #
216-689-0520 InvRe
201-222-4955 TDD
www.keybank.com

Buy fees: no cost
$10-10,000/month(12)
part. DR/cash-only
sfkg-free/p. sale-$10 + 5¢/sh
rec common/no residency restrict.
div deposit

800-539-7216 admr

✂

KeySpan Corp (N-KSE) (div/yr: $ 1.82) [S&P ranking: B] utility-electric /gas
One Metro Tech Center
Brooklyn, NY 11201
718-403-3196 InvRe
800-482-3638 admr
201-222-4955 TDD
e-mail: financial@keyspanenergy.com
http://investor.keyspanenergy.com
NOTE: B/O may participate only in DR

Buy fees: no cost-orig iss
$25-150,000/yr EFT(52)
DIP: $250
part. DR/cash-only
sfkg-free/p. sale-$5 + 5¢/sh
rec comm
div deposit/gifting free

✂

★

Kilroy Realty Corp (N-KRC) (div/yr: $ 2.04) [S&P ranking: B +] REIT-office properties in Calif
12200 W Olympic Blvd Ste 200
Los Angeles, CA 90064-1044
800-816-7506 admr
310-481-6580 fax #
310-481-8484 InvRe
www.kilroyrealty.com

Buy fees: no cost
**
$100-5,000/mo EFT(12)
DIP: $750
part. DR/cash-only
sfkg-avail/p. sale-$15-12¢/sh
no residency restrict.
div deposit/gifting for minors

NOTE: **2% discount may be given to purchases over $5,000

✂

★

Kimberly-Clark Corp (N-KMB) (div/yr: $ 1.80) [S&P ranking: A-] consumer prod-home papers
P O Box 619100
Dallas, TX 75261-9100
800-730-4001 admr
972-281-1519 fax #
972-281-1521 AsstSecy
www.kimberly-clark.com

Buy fees: no cost
$25-3,000/qtr EFT(8)
partial DR option
sfkg-free/p. sale-$1-10 + bkg fee
rec common
div deposit

✂

Kimco Realty Corp (N-KIM) (div/yr: $ 2.44) [S&P ranking: A +] REIT - shopping centers
P O Box 5020
New Hyde Park, NY 10042-0020
866-557-8695 admr
516-869-7250 fax #
516-869-7197 InvRe
e-mail: kimco@kimcorealty.com
www.kimcorealty.com
NOTE: *$5(check)/$2(EFT) + 5¢/sh for cash pymt

Buy fees: no cost-div*
$50-250,000/yr EFT*(52)
DIP: $100 + $10 + 5¢/sh
part. DR/cash-only
sfkg-avail/p. sale-$15 + 10¢/sh
comm/pref
gifting avail

✂

★

Kinder Morgan Inc (N-KMI) (div/yr: $ 2.80) [S&P ranking: B] energy-natural gas-develop/distr
500 Dallas Ste 1000
Houston, TX 77002
713-369-9460 InvRe
800-730-4001 admr
www.kindermorgan.com
NOTE: *cash pymt fees: $2 EFT/$5 check

Buy fees: no cost-div*
$25-no max
DIP: $250 + $13
p. sale-$15
div deposit

✂

★

Knape & Vogt Manufacturing Co (NDQ-KNAP) (div/yr: $ 0.17) [S&P ranking: B-] mfg-hard-war/storage prod for indust & home decor

✄ ★
c/o Computershare Trust Co Inc
P O Box A3309
Chicago, IL 60690
  800-962-4284 admr
  616-459-3311 InvRe
  e-mail: investor@kv.com
  www.knapeandvogt.com

Buy fees: no cost
$100-10,000/yr EFT(52)
DIP: $100
cash-only option
sfkg-free*/p. sale-$10 + 10¢/sh
rec comm & Cl B

NOTE: *only Cl A shares may be deposited for safekeeping

Knight-Ridder Inc (N-KRI) (div/yr: $ 1.38) [S&P ranking: A-] publishing

✄
c/o Bank of New York
P O Box 11258 Church St Sta
New York, NY 10286-1258
  800-524-4458 admr
  408-938-0255 fax #
  408/938-7700 ShSvc
  www.kri.com

Buy fees: no cost
$25-10,000/month(52)
common
div deposit

Kraft Foods Inc (N-KFT) (div/yr: $ 0.82) food/bev-mfg/mktg/distr of foods products

★
c/o EquiServe Trust Co
P O Box 43069
Providence, RI 02940-3069
  866-655-7238 admr
  847-998-2000 InvRe
  www.kraft.com

Buy fees: 5% to $3 + bkg fee
$50-250,000/yr EFT
DIP: $500 + $13 + bkg fee
sfkg-avail/p. sale-$15 + bkgfee
rec comm 1 sh min/no residency restrict.
div deposit

NOTE: cash pymt fees: $2.50 EFT/$5 check

L

LESCO Inc (NDQ-LSCO) (div/yr: $0.00) mfg/svcs-lawn care products to turf care industry

✄
1301 E 9th St Ste 1300
Cleveland, OH 44114-1849
  800-622-6757 admr
  216-706-5163 fax #
  216-706-9250 InvRe
  e-mail: dbrattoli@lesco.com
  www.lesco.com

Buy fees: no cost
$25-5,000/mo(12)
p. sale-$5 + bkg
rec common

NOTE: co does not pay div

LSB Bancshares (NDQ-LXBK) (div/yr: $ 0.68) [S&P ranking: A-] banks/banking

✄ ★
One LSB Plaza
Lexington, NC 27292
  866-367-6351 admr
  336-248-6500 CpAcc
  e-mail: info@isbnc.com
  www.isbnc.com

Buy fees: no cost*
$50-350,000/yr*EFT
DIP: $250 + $10
sfkg-avail/p. sale-$15
rec common-1 sh min

NOTE: *cash pymt fees: $2 EFT/$5 check

LTC Properties Inc (N-LTC) (div/yr: $ 1.32) [S&P ranking: B-] REIT-health care facilities

✄
22917 Pacific Coast Hwy Ste 350
Malibu, CA 90265-6409
  312-360-5294 admr
  805-981-8663 fax #
  805 981-8655 CFO
  www.ltcproperties.com

Buy fees: no cost-div
$25-1,000/month(12)
partial DR option
common

La-Z-Boy Inc (N-LZB) (div/yr: $ 0.44) [S&P ranking: A-] consumer prod-furniture
1284 N Telegraph Rd   Buy fees: no cost
Monroe, MI 48162-3390 $25-1,000/month(12)
718-921-8200 admr   cash-only option
734-457-2005 fax #   sfkg-$7.50/p. sale-$15
734-241-4414 co #   rec common
e-mail: investorrelations@la-z-boy.com
www.lazboy.com

LaSalle Hotel Properties (N-LHO) (div/yr: $ 0.96) REIT-lodging
3 Bethesda Metro Center Ste 1200   Buy fees: no cost
Bethesda, MD 20814 $100-5,000/mo(12)
877-360-7251 admr   sfkg-avail
301-941-1553 fax #   common
301-941-1500 InvRe
www.lasallehotels.com

Laclede Group Inc (N-LG) (div/yr: $ 1.38) [S&P ranking: B +] utility-gas
720 Olive St   Buy fees: no cost
St Louis, MO 63101-2338 $100-30,000/yr(12)
800-884-4225 admr   part. DR/cash-only
314-421-1979 fax #   sfkg-free
314-342-0503 CorpSecy   common/no residency restrict.
www.thelacledegroup.com

Lafarge North America Inc (N-LAF) (div/yr: $ 0.88) [S&P ranking: A] mfg-cement/aggre-
gates/concrete/gypsum/wallboard
12950 Worldgate Dr Ste 500   Buy fees: no cost
Herndon, VA 20170-6001   5% disc-div*
703-480-3600 CorpSecy   no cash plan
800-633-4236 CorpSecy   rec common/no residency restrict.
www.lafargenorthamerica.com
NOTE: *or stock dividend

Lancaster Colony Corp (NDQ-LANC) (div/yr: $ 1) [S&P ranking: A] misc-food/glassware/can-
dles/auto prod
37 W Broad St   Buy fees: no cost
Columbus, OH 43215-4177 $50-20,000/yr(12)
614-224-7141 CorpSecy   partial DR option
614-469-8219 fax #   sfkg-free/p. sale-avail
800-278-4353 admr   rec common
www.lancastercolony.com

Lance Inc (NDQ-LNCE) (div/yr: $ 0.64) [S&P ranking: B] food-snack products
c/o Wachovia Bank N A   Buy fees: no cost-div*
1525 W W T Harris Blvd 3C3 $10-1,000/month*(12)
Charlotte, NC 28288-1153   p. sale-avail
800-829-8432 admr   common
704-554-5562 fax #
704-554-1421 AsstSecy
www.lance.com
NOTE: *4% up to $2.50 cash option fee

Lear Corp (N-LEA) (div/yr: $ 1) [S&P ranking: B +] mfg-auto/truck seats
P O Box 5008   Buy fees: no bkg fee
Southfield, MI 48086-5008 $50-150,000/yr*(12)
248-447-1500 InvRe   DIP: $250 + $2 fee
248-447-1722 fax #   sfkg-$5/p. sale-$5 + 7¢/sh
800-524-4458 admr   rec common
e-mail: investor@lear.com
www.lear.com
NOTE: *$2 fee for cash pymts/trans of sh to another acct/co does not pay div

Lehman Brothers Holdings Inc (N-LEH) (div/yr: $ 0.80) [S&P ranking: A] fin svcs-investment banking

745 7th Ave	Buy fees: no cost
New York, NY 10019	$50-175,000/yr(52)
800-824-5707 admr	DIP: $500 + $7.50
646-758-2652 fax #	partial DR option
212-526-8381 InvRe	sfkg-free/p. sale-$10 + 10¢/sh
e-mail: inquiry@lehman.com	common
www.lehman.com	

Libbey Inc (N-LBY) (div/yr: $ 0.40) [S&P ranking: B] mfg-consumer glassware

300 Madison Ave	Buy fees: no cost
Toledo, OH 43604	$20-25,000/yr*(52)
419-325-2100 co #	DIP: $100 + $7.50 + 7¢/sh
800-524-4458 admr	partial DR option
www.libbey.com	sfkg-$5/p. sale-$5 + 7¢/sh
	common
	gifting $5

NOTE: *limit of $5,000/investment

Lilly (Eli) & Co (N-LLY) (div/yr: $ 1.52) [S&P ranking: B +] drug/pharm industry

Lilly Corporate Center	Buy fees: 3%to$3 + 3¢/sh-div*
Indianapolis, IN 46285-9600	$50-150,000/yr EFT(52)
800-833-8699 admr	DIP: $1,000 + $15
317-276-6993 ShSvc	part. DR/cash-only
www.lilly.com	sfkg-free/p. sale-$10 + 12¢/sh
	common
	div deposit/gifting avail

NOTE: *cash pymt fees 3¢/sh + $2 EFT; $5 check

Limited Brands Inc (N-LTD) (div/yr: $ 0.60) [S&P ranking: B +] retail-specialty stores

Two Limited Pkwy, PO Box 16000	Buy fees: no cost
Columbus, OH 43216-6000	$30-6,000/qtr(8)
800-829-8432 admr	common
614-479-7000 co #	
www.limited.com	

Lincoln National Corp (N-LNC) (div/yr: $ 1.46) [S&P ranking: B +] insurance

1500 Market St, Ste 3900	Buy fees: no cost
Philadelphia, PA 19102-2112	$25-5,000/month(12)
617-575-2900 admr	part. DR/cash-only
215-448-1413 CorpSecy	sfkg-free
e-mail: investorrelations@lnc.com	comm/pref
www.lfgnc.com	

Liz Claiborne Inc (N-LIZ) (div/yr: $ 0.23) [S&P ranking: A] consumer prod-apparel mfg/retail

c/o EquiServe Trust Co NA	Buy fees: no cost
P O Box 2598 # 4675	$25/mo-60,000/yr EFT ($1 mo fee) (12)
Jersey City, NJ 07303-2598	part. DR/cash-only
800-446-2617 admr	sfkg-free/p. sale-avail
201-295-7840 InvRe	common
e-mail: investor_relations@liz.com	
www.lizclaiborne.com	

Lockheed Martin Corp (N-LMT) (div/yr: $ 1) [S&P ranking: B-] mfg-aerospace

6801 Rockledge Dr	Buy fees: no cost
Bethesda, MD 20817-1836	$50-no max EFT(12)
800-548-7701 ShrSv	DIP: $250
301-897-6255 ShrSv	part. DR/cash-only
201-222-4955 TDD	sfkg-free/p. sale-$10 + 12¢/sh
e-mail: george.g.martinson@lmco.com	common/no residency restrict.
www.lockheedmartin.com	div deposit/gifting free

Long Island Financial Corp (NDQ-LICB) (div/yr: $ 0.42) banks/banking
One Suffolk Sq   Buy fees: no cost*
Islandia, NY 11749 $100-3,500/mo*EFT(12)
800-362-3705   partial DR option
631-348-0888 CorpSecy   sfkg-avail/p. sale-$15 + 12¢/sh
www.licb.com   div deposit/gifting avail
NOTE: *cash pymt fees: 12¢/sh + $2 auto EFT/$3.50 single EFT/$5 check

Longs Drug Stores Corp (N-LDG) (div/yr: $ 0.56) [S&P ranking: B +] retail-drug store chain
141 N Civic Dr   Buy fees: $1.25 + 5¢/sh-div*
Walnut Creek, CA 94596 $25-5,000/qtr EFT(52)
800-468-9716 admr   DIP: $500 + $10 + 5¢/sh
925-937-1170 InvRe   partial DR option
e-mail: investor_relations@longs.com   sfkg-free/p. sale-$10 + 10¢/sh
www.longs.com   gifting avail
NOTE: *cash pymt fees: 5¢/sh + $1.25 EFT/$2.25 check

Louisiana-Pacific Corp (N-LPX) (div/yr: $ 0.40) [S&P ranking: B-] mfg-building products
414 Union St Ste 2000   Buy fees: no cost
Nashville, TN 37219-1711 $25-12,000/yr EFT(12)
800-756-8200 admr   sfkg-free/p. sale-$12 + fee
503-821-5105 fax #   rec common/no residency restrict.
503-821-5113 ShSvc   div deposit
www.lpcorp.com

Lowe's Cos Inc (N-LOW) (div/yr: $ 0.16) [S&P ranking: A +] retail-bldg /home improvement
c/o EquiServe Trust Co   Buy fees: 5%to $2.50 + 5¢/sh
P O Box 8040 MS 45-01-20 $25-250,000/yr EFT(52)
Boston, MA 02266-8040   DIP: $250
888-345-6937 admr   part. DR/cash-only
704-757-0574 fax #   sfkg-free/p. sale-$10 + 12¢/sh
704-758-2910 InvRe   rec common
www.lowes.com

Lubrizol Corp (N-LZ) (div/yr: $ 1.04) [S&P ranking: B] mfg-specialty chemicals
29400 Lakeland Blvd   Buy fees: 2%to$2.50-div*
Wickliffe, OH 44092-2298 $25-10,000/day EFT(240)
877-573-3998 admr   DIP: $250 + $2.50 + 10¢/sh
440-943-4200 InvRe   cash-only option
www.lubrizol.com   sfkg-$7.50/p. sale-$15 + 10¢/sh
                                        common
                                        div deposit/gifting free
NOTE: *$2.50 + 10¢/sh for cash purchases

Luby's Inc (N-LUB) (div/yr: $0.00) [S&P ranking: C] food-restaurants
P O Box 33069   Buy fees: no cost
San Antonio, TX 78265-3069 $20-5,000/qtr*(12)
210-654-9000 CorpSecy   sfkg-free/p. sale-avail
800-278-4353 admr   common
www.lubys.com   div deposit
NOTE: *only recordholders may part. in cash plan/co does not pay div

Lucent Technologies Inc (N-LU) (div/yr: $0.00) [S&P ranking: C] mfg-telecommunications
equip/Bell Labs research
600 Mountain Rd 3D-548   Buy fees: $3 + 10¢/sh
Murray Hill, NJ 07974 $100-50,000/pymt*(250)
888-582-3686 admr   DIP: $1,000 + $10 fee +
908-508-2576 fax #   partial DR option
908-582-8500 InvRe   sfkg-free/p. sale-$15 + 10¢/sh
e-mail: lu-shareholders-svcs@email.bony.com   gifting $7.50
www.lucent.com
NOTE: + or $100/mo EFT + $10 fee/*cash pymt fees: 10¢/sh + $5 check/$3.50 EFT
/omitted div 9/1/01

Lyondell Chemical Co (N-LYO) (div/yr: $ 0.90) [S&P ranking: B-] energy-chemicals/petroleum refining

c/o American Stock Transfer & Trust
✂ 59 Maiden Ln, 1st Floor
New York, NY 10038
877-749-4981 admr
713-309-7799 fax #
713-652-4590 InvRe
www.lyondell.com

Buy fees: no cost
$25-10,000/qtr(4)
sfkg-free
rec common

M

M & T Bank Corp (N-MTB) (div/yr: $ 1.80) [S&P ranking: A +] banking

One M & T Plaza, 12th Flr
Buffalo, NY 14203-2399
800-368-5948 admr
716-842-4306 fax #
716-842-5986 ShrRe
e-mail: ir@mandtbank.com
www.mandtbank.com
NOTE: frmly: First Empire State

Buy fees: 5% up to $2.50 + bkg fee
$10-1,000/mo EFT(12)
sfkg-free
rec common
div deposit

MASSBANK Corp (NDQ-MASB) (div/yr: $ 1.04) [S&P ranking: B +] banking

✂ 159 Haven St
Reading, MA 01867
877-611-7981 admr
781-942-8194 fax #
781-942-8120 InvRe
www.massbank.com

Buy fees: no cost
$50-5,000/qtr(4)
part. DR/cash-only
sfkg-free/p. sale-avail
rec common

MDS Inc (N-MDZ) (div/yr: $ 0.13) [S&P ranking: B +] drug/pharmaceuticals-drug research & develop-CDN

✂ 100 International Blvd
% Toronto, ONT M9W 6J6, Canada
800-387-0825 admr
416-675-4095 fax #
416-675-7661 x2695
e-mail: smathers@mdsintl.com
www.mdsintl.com
NOTE: *US res not eligible for cash plan/frmly: MDS Health Group Ltd

Buy fees: no cost
5% disc-div
$50-3,000/s-a(2)
common

MDU Resources Group Inc (N-MDU) (div/yr: $ 0.72) [S&P ranking: A] energy/utility-elec/natural resources

P O Box 5650/918 E Divide Ave
✂ Bismarck, ND 58506-5650
877-536-3553 admr
★ 701-222-7801 fax #
800-437-8000 InvRe
e-mail: investor@mduresources.com
www.mdu.com
NOTE: *pref div purchases common/**sales limited to $25,000 or less

Buy fees: no cost
$25-10,000/mo EFT(52)
DIP: $250
part. DR/cash-only
sfkg-free/p. sale-$10 + 10¢/sh**
rec comm/preferred*/no residency restrict.
div deposit/gifting avail

✂ **MET-PRO Corp** (N-MPR) (div/yr: $ 0.31) [S&P ranking: B +] mfg-pollution control devices

P O Box 144
% Harleysville, PA 19438-0144
215-723-6751 co #
★ 215-723-6758 fax #
800-278-4353 admr
e-mail: mpr@met-pro.com
www.met-pro.com

Buy fees: no cost
3% disc-div (only on orig iss)
$100-5,000/mo EFT(12)
DIP: $1,000 +
partial DR option
sfkg-free/p. sale-$15 + bkg
comm-min 10 shs
div deposit

MGE Energy Inc (NDQ-MGEE) (div/yr: $ 1.37) [S&P ranking: B +] utility-elec/gas
P O Box 1231/133 S Blair St $25-25,000/qtr(12)
Madison, WI 53701-1231   DIP: $50   ★
  800-356-6423 Treas   part. DR/cash-only
  608-252-7098 fax #   sfkg-free/p. sale-avail
  608-252-4744 InvRe   rec common
  e-mail: investor@mge.com   div deposit/gifting avail
  www.mgeenergy.com

3M (N-MMM) (div/yr: $ 1.68) [S&P ranking: A-] mfg-diversified technology/office supplies
3M Center   Buy fees: no cost
St Paul, MN 55144-1000 $10-10,000/qtr(12)   ✄
  651-450-4064 CorpSecy   sfkg-free
  800-401-1952   rec common/no residency restrict.
  e-mail: stocktransfer@wellsfargo.com
  www.investor.3m.com
NOTE: blanket req for full-share certificates/NB: check website for details of plan

MTS Systems Corp (NDQ-MTSC) (div/yr: $ 0.32) [S&P ranking: B +] mfg-testing systems for
materials evaluation
14000 Technology Dr   Buy fees: 5%to$3-div + 5¢/sh
Eden Prairie, MN 55344-2247 $50-25,000/mo EFT*(12)
  800-468-9716 admr   sfkg-free/p. sale-$5 + 15¢/sh
  952-937-4515 fax #   rec common
  952-937-4000 InvRe
  e-mail: info@mts.com
  www.mts.com
NOTE: *cash purchase fees: 5¢/sh + $3 checks/$2 EFT

MacDermid Inc (N-MRD) (div/yr: $ 0.24) [S&P ranking: A-] mfg-specialty chemicals
P O Box 671   Buy fees: no cost   ✄
Waterbury, CT 06720-0671 $50 or more/pymt(4)
  203-575-5700 CorpSecy   partial DR option
  212-608-8440 admr   common/no residency restrict.
  www.macdermid.com

Macerich Co (The) (N-MAC) (div/yr: $ 2.60) [S&P ranking: B +] REIT-regional/community
shopping centers
401 Wilshire Blvd   Buy fees: no cost   ✄
Santa Monica, CA 90401 $50-250,000/yr EFT
  800-317-4445 admr   DIP: $250
  310-394-6000 InvRe   sfkg-avail/p. sale-$10   ★
  e-mail: macerich@macerich.com   no residency restrict.
  www.macerich.com

Mack-Cali Realty Corp (N-CLI) (div/yr: $ 2.52) [S&P ranking: B +] REIT-office properties   ✄
11 Commerce Dr   Buy fees: no cost
Cranford, NJ 07016-3599 $100-5,000/qtr EFT(12)   ★
  800-317-4445 admr   DIP: $2,000
  908-272-8000 InvRe   part. DR/cash-only
  e-mail: investorrelations@mack-cali.com   sfkg-free/p. sale-$15 + 12¢/sh
  www.mack-cali.com/drsp   div deposit/gifting free
NOTE: plan may prohibit participation for excessive trading

Manitowoc Co Inc (The) (N-MTW) (div/yr: $ 0.28) [S&P ranking: B] mfg-ice/beverage dispens-
ers/cranes/ship repair
P O Box 66   Buy fees: no cost
Manitowoc, WI 54221-0066 $10-60,000/yr(12)   ✄
  201-324-0498 admr   sfkg-free/p. sale-avail
  920-652-9778 fax #   rec common
  920-684-4410 InvRe   div deposit
  e-mail: skhail@manitowoc.com
  www.manitowoc.com

Manpower Inc (N-MAN) (div/yr: $ 0.40) [S&P ranking: B+] svcs-temporary employment
agency
P O Box 2053   Buy fees: no cost
Milwaukee, WI 53217 $25-10,000/yr(12)
414-906-6350 InvRe   part. DR/cash-only
800-851-9677 admr   sfkg-free/p. sale-avail
www.manpower.com   common

Marathon Oil Corp (N-MRO) (div/yr: $ 1.12) [S&P ranking: B+] energy-oil/gas exp/dev/distr
539 S Main St Rm 840M   Buy fees: no cost
FindleyHouston, OH 45840-4301   0-3% disc-div/cash*
% 888-843-5542 admr $50-10,000/mo+EFT(52)
419-421-4301 ShrSv   DIP: $500 + $10
★ www.marathon.com   part. DR/cash-only
                                          sfkg-free/p. sale-$10+5¢/sh
                                          rec common
                                          gifting ***
NOTE: $35,000 div amt limit/+greater cash pymt with approval/*discount at co discre-
tion, call co for current discount/***trans of 5 or more shs to another acct

Marcus Corp (N-MCS) (div/yr: $ 0.22) [S&P ranking: B] food/ent-hotels/restaurants/theaters
100 E Wisconsin Ave Ste 1900   Buy fees: no cost
Milwaukee, WI 53202-4132 $100-1,500/mo(12)
414-274-0389 InvRe   part. DR/cash-only
414-905-2669 fax #   p. sale-$5 + bkg
800-637-7549 InvRe   common
www.marcuscorp.com

Marriott International Inc (N-MAR) (div/yr: $ 0.34) [S&P ranking: B+] rec/enter-hotels/food
svc
10400 Fernwood Rd   Buy fees: 5% to $3+3¢/sh**
Bethesda, MD 20817 $25-350,000/yr EFT(52)
800-446-2617 admr   DIP: $350 + $18+ 3¢/sh*
301-380-5067 fax #   part. DR/cash-only
★ 301-380-7418 InvRe   sfkg-free/p. sale-$15+12¢/sh
www.marriott.com   rec common
                                          gifting free
NOTE: *or $25/mo for 14 months/**cash purchase fees = $5 check/$2 EFT + 3¢/sh

Marsh & McLennan Cos Inc (N-MMC) (div/yr: $ 0.68) [S&P ranking: A-] insurance/adm & con-
sultg/invst mgt svc
c/o Bank of New York $10-3,000/qtr(4)
P O Box 11258, Church St Sta   partial DR option
New York, NY 10286-1258   sfkg-free
800-457-8968 admr   common
212-345-6138 fax #
212-345-5475 InvRe
e-mail: shareowner-svcs@email.bankofny.com
www.mmc.com

Marsh Supermarkets Inc (NDQ-MARSA) (div/yr: $ 0.52) [S&P ranking: B+] food-supermarkets
9800 Crosspoint Blvd   Buy fees: no cost
Indianapolis, IN 46256-3350 $100-5,000/month(12)
317-594-2627 InvRe   part. DR/cash-only
317-594-2704 fax #   sfkg-free
216-575-2494 admr   rec comm A & B*
e-mail: investor@marsh.net
www.marsh.net
NOTE: *dividends reinvest in same class

Marshall & Ilsley Corp (N-MI) (div/yr: $ 0.96) [S&P ranking: A] banking
770 N Water St   Buy fees: no cost
Milwaukee, WI 53202 $25-20,000/yr(12)
  800-529-3163 admr   part. DR/cash-only
  414-298-2921 fax #   sfkg-free/p. sale-$10
  414-765-7801 CorpSecy   rec common
  e-mail: lisa.burmeister@micorp.com   div deposit
  www.mibank.com

Mattel Inc (N-MAT) (div/yr: $ 0.45) [S&P ranking: B +] consumer prod-toys
333 Continental Blvd   Buy fees: no cost-div
El Segundo, CA 90245-5032 $100-100,00/yr EFT(12)
  888-909-9922 admr   DIP: $500 + $10 + 8¢/sh
  310-252-2567 fax #   cash-only option
  310-252-4859 co #   p. sale-$10 + 15¢/sh
  www.mattel.com   common
NOTE: $5 check/$2.50 EFT fee for cash pymts

May Department Stores Co (N-MAY) (div/yr: $ 0.98) [S&P ranking: B +] retail-dept store chain
c/o Bank of New York $25-no max(52)
P O Box 11260 Church St Sta   sfkg-$5
New York, NY 10286   common
  800-292-2301 admr
  314-342-6413 ShrRe
  www.maycompany.com
NOTE: to be acquired by Federated Dept Stores, approximately 4th Q 05

Maytag Co (N-MYG) (div/yr: $ 0.72) [S&P ranking: B] consumer prod-home appliances
P O Box 39, 403 W 4th St N   Buy fees: no cost
Newton, IA 50208 $25-5,000/mo EFT(12)
  641-787-8344 ShSvc   cash-only option
  641-787-8102 fax #   sfkg-free/p. sale-avail
  888-237-0935 admr   rec common/no residency restrict.
  e-mail: cwalls@maytag.com   div deposit
  www.maytagcorp.com

McCormick & Co Inc (N-MKC) (div/yr: $ 0.64) [S&P ranking: A +] food-spices
P O Box 6000   Buy fees: no cost-orig is*
Sparks, MD 21152-6000 $50-50,000/yr EFT(52)
  410-771-7537 InvRe   DIP: $250 + $10 + 5¢/sh**
  410-527-8222 fax #   part. DR/cash-only
  800-468-9716 admr   sfkg-free/p. sale-$10 + 10¢/sh
  www.mccormick.com   rec comm/non-vtg*
                                        div deposit
NOTE: *market purch fees: 5¢/sh div & 10¢/sh cash purch/stock reinvests in same
class/**DIP purchases non-voting stock/telephone sales

McDonald's Corp (N-MCD) (div/yr: $ 0.55) [S&P ranking: A] food-restaurants
One Kroc Drive Dept 300   Buy fees: no cost-div*
Oak Brook, IL 60523 $50-250,000/yr EFT(240)
  800-621-7825 admr   DIP: $500 + $5 fee or $50/mo EFT
  630-623-5818 fax #   cash-only option
  630-623-7428 InvRe   sfkg-free/p. sale-$15 + 15¢/sh
  201-222-4489 TDD   rec common 10 sh min/U S residents
  www.mcdonalds.com/corporate/investor gifting free
NOTE: *cash pymt fees: $1.50 EFT, $6 single pymt

McGraw-Hill Cos Inc (N-MHP) (div/yr: $ 0.66) publishing/information svcs
1221 Ave of the Americas   Buy fees: no cost
New York, NY 10020-1001 $100-10,000/mo EFT(52)
✂ 888-201-5538 admr   DIP: $500* + $10
  212-512-2000 co #   partial DR option
★ e-mail: investor_relations@mcgraw-hill.com sfkg-free/p. sale-$15 + 12¢/sh
  www.mcgraw-hill.com   div deposit/gifting free
                                           rec comm-5 shs min
NOTE: *or $100/mo EFT for one year/**co not ranked because S&P is a subsidiary

McKesson Corp (N-MCK) (div/yr: $ 0.24) [S&P ranking: B] distr-drugs
One Post St   Buy fees: 10%to$3 + 10¢/sh +
San Francisco, CA 94104-5296 $10-10,000/mo EFT**(12)
866-216-0306 admr*   part. DR/cash-only
415-983-7026 fax #   sfkg-free/p. sale-$15 + 10¢/sh
415-983-8367 CorpSecy   rec comm
e-mail: investors@mckesson.com   gifting free
www.mckesson.com
NOTE: + cash pymt fee $5 + 10¢/sh(EFT $1 + 10¢/sh)/*hearing impaired 800-936-
4237/**monthly EFT of cash payments ($1/transaction)

✂ **MeadWestvaco Corp** (N-MWV) (div/yr: $ 0.92) [S&P ranking: B-] mfg-paper
  1 Highridge Park   Buy fees: no cost
  Stamford, CT 06903-0009   up to $5,000/qtr(12)
  800-432-9874 co #   DIP: $250 + $7.50
★ 203-461-7400 CT res 800-432-0140   partial DR option
  admr   sfkg-free/p. sale-avail
  www.westvaco.com   rec common/no residency restrict.

✂ **Meadowbrook Insurance Group Inc** (N-MIG) (div/yr: $0.00) [S&P ranking: B-] insurance
  26255 American Dr   Buy fees: no cost
★ Southfield, MI 48034 $25-50,000/yr EFT(52)
  800-246-5761 admr   DIP: $250
  248-358-1614 fax #   partial DR option
  248-358-1100 Treas   sfkg-free
  www.meadowbrook.com   common
                                          div deposit/gifting free

  NOTE: co does not pay div

✂ **Media General Inc** (N-MEG) (div/yr: $ 0.84) [S&P ranking: B] publishing/communications/TV
  P O Box 85333   Buy fees: no cost
% Richmond, VA 23293-0001   5% disc-div
  804-649-6619 AsstSecy $25-5,000/month(12)
  804-775-8105 fax #   part. DR/cash-only
  800-937-5449 admr   sfkg-free
  www.media-general.com   rec common Cl A
                                          div deposit

Medtronic Inc (N-MDT) (div/yr: $ 0.34) [S&P ranking: A-] healthcare-mfg medical devices
c/o Wells Fargo Bank Minnesota NA   Buy fees: 5% to $5-div*
PO Box 738 $25-50,000/qtr*EFT(52)
South St Paul, MN 55075-0738   DIP: $250 + $10 + 4¢/sh
★ 888-648-8154 admr   partial DR option
  763-505-2515 fax #   sfkg-free/p. sale-$10 + 10¢/sh
  763-505-3030 ShrSv   comm - 1 sh min/no residency restrict.
  e-mail: shareholder.services@medtronic.com div deposit/gifting avail
  www.medtronic.com
  NOTE: *plus 4¢/sh/cash pymt fees: $3 cash/$1 EFT

Mellon Financial Corp (N-MEL) (div/yr: $ 0.80) [S&P ranking: A-] banking
One Mellon Bank Ctr
Pittsburgh, PA 15258-0444
800-205-7699 DRP
412-236-5461 fax #
412-234-4633 ShRel
www.mellon.com or www.melloninvestor.com

Buy fees: no cost
$100-100,000/mo EFT(52)
DIP: $500 + $6 + 12¢/sh
partial DR option
sfkg-free/p. sale-$15 + 12¢/sh
rec comm
gifting free

Mercantile Bankshares Corp (NDQ-MRBK) (div/yr: $ 1.40) [S&P ranking: A] banking
P O Box 1477/2 Hopkins Plaza
Baltimore, MD 21203-1477
800-937-5449 admr
410-237-5900 co #
e-mail: investor.relations@mercantile.com
www.mercantile.net

Buy fees: no cost
5% disc-div
$25-5,000/qtr(4)
rec common/no residency restrict.

Merck & Co Inc (N-MRK) (div/yr: $ 1.52) [S&P ranking: A+] drug/pharmaceuticals
P O Box 100 (WS 3AB-40)
Whitehouse Station, NJ 08889-0100
800-613-2104 admr
908-735-1225 fax #
908-423-6627 ShSvc
www.merck.com

Buy fees: 4% to $2 + 1¢/sh
$50-50,000/yr EFT*(52)
DIP: $350 + $5 or $50/mo EFT
part. DR/cash-only
sfkg-free/p. sale-$5 + 1¢/sh
rec common/no residency restrict.
gifting free
NOTE: *$5 ($2 EFT) svc + 1 ¢/sh for cash pymts

Meredith Corp (N-MDP) (div/yr: $ 0.56) [S&P ranking: A+] publishing-magazines/TV stations
1716 Locust St
Des Moines, IA 50309-3023
800-468-9716 admr
515-284-3000 co #
www.meredith.com

no cash plan(4)
partial DR option
sfkg-free/p. sale-$15 + fees
rec common
div deposit

Meridian Bioscience Inc (NDQ-VIVO) (div/yr: $ 0.48) [S&P ranking: B] healthcare-immunodi-
agnostic test kits
3471 River Hills Dr
Cincinnati, OH 45244
888-294-8217 admr
513-271-3762 fax #
513-272-5228 CorpSecy
www.meridianbioscience.com

Buy fees: 5% to $3-div*
$50-2,000/mo EFT(12)
partial DR option
sfkg-free/p. sale-$12.50 + fee
common
NOTE: *cash pymt fees: $2.50 EFT, $5 check + bkg fee/4 pymts/yr required (total div +
cash pymts)

Merrill Lynch & Co Inc (N-MER) (div/yr: $ 0.80) [S&P ranking: A-] fin svcs-securities
101 Hudson St, 9th Flr
Jersey City, NJ 07302
888-460-7641 admr
201-557-2093 fax #
201-557-2076 DRP

Buy fees: no cost-div
no cash plan
cash-only option
p. sale-$10 + 10¢/sh
rec common/no residency restrict.

Michaels Stores Inc (N-MIK) (div/yr: $ 0.28) [S&P ranking: B] retail stores-crafts, home decor
8000 Bent Branch Dr
Irving, TX 75063
800-577-4676 admr
972-409-1555 fax #
972-409-1300 InvRe
www.michaels.com

Buy fees: no cost
0-5%-cash*
$100-2,500/mo(12)
DIP: $500
part. DR/cash-only
sfkg-free/p. sale-$10 + 12¢/sh
common
NOTE: *call co for current discount policy 888-515-MIKE

Microsoft Corp (NDQ-MSFT) (div/yr: $ 0.32) [S&P ranking: B +] svcs-software mfg
One Microsoft Way   Buy fees: div-6¢/sh *
Redmond, WA 98052-6399 $50-250,000/yr EFT*(52)
 425-882-8080 ShrRe   DIP: $1,000 + $10 + 6¢/sh
 800-285-7772 admr   part. DR/cash-only
★ e-mail: msft@microsoft.com   sfkg-free/p. sale-$15 + 12¢/sh
                                          no residency restrict.
                                          div deposit/gifting free
NOTE: *accts w/less 100 shs automatically enrolled in DRP & no cost; 100 shs-5% to
$3/cash pymt fees: 6¢/sh + $5 (check), $2.50 (auto EFT), $3 (single EFT)

Mid Penn Bancorp Inc (A-MBP) (div/yr: $ 0.79) banking
349 Union St   Buy fees: no cost
✂ Millersburg, PA 17061 $100-5,000/qtr EFT(4)
 717-692-2133 InvRe   partial DR option
 717-692-4861 fax #   common
 800-468-9716 admr

Mid-State Bancshares (Calif) (NDQ-MDST) (div/yr: $ 0.64) banks/banking
P O Box 580   Buy fees: 12¢/sh-div*
Arroyo Grande, CA 93421-0580 $50-5,000/mo EFT(52)
★ 888-540-9878 admr   DIP: $1,000 + $5 + 12¢/sh
 805-473-7752 fax #   partial DR option
 805-473-7700 ShrRe   sfkg-free/p. sale-$15 + 12¢/sh
 www.midstatebank.com   div deposit/gifting free
NOTE: *cash pymt fees: $5 + 12¢/sh

✂ **MidSouth Bancorp Inc** (A-MSL) (div/yr: $ 0.24) [S&P ranking: A +] banks/banking
PO Box 3745/102 Versailles Blvd   Buy fees: no cost
Lafayette, LA 70502 $100-10,000/mo EFT(12)
 888-216-8113 admr   DIP: $1,000/$100 mo EFT
 337-291-4980 fax #   partial DR option
 337-237-8343 InvRe   sfkg-free/p. sale-$15 + 12¢/sh
 e-mail: stock@midsouthbank.com   rec common
 www.midsouthbank.com   gifting avail
NOTE: phone sales/IRA annual fee-$48

Middlesex Water Co (NDQ-MSEX) (div/yr: $ 0.67) [S&P ranking: B +] utility-water
P O Box 1500   Buy fees: no cost
✂ Iselin, NJ 08830-0452 $25-25,000/qtr(12)
 732-634-1500 CorpSecy   part. DR/cash-only
 732-750-5981 fax #   sfkg-avail/p. sale-avail
 800-368-5948 admr   rec comm-10 sh min
 e-mail: mreynolds@middlesexwater.com
 www.middlesexwater.com

Miller (Herman) Inc (NDQ-MLHR) (div/yr: $ 0.29) [S&P ranking: B +] mfg-office furniture
✂ P O Box 302 - 855 E Main Ave   Buy fees: no cost-div*
Zeeland, MI 49464-0302 $25-60,000/yr EFT*(12)
 616-654-3000 co #   sfkg-free/p. sale-avail
 616-654-7221 fax #   common
 800-446-2617 admr
 e-mail: investor@hermanmiller.com
 www.hermanmiller.com
NOTE: *5% to $3 + bkg fee for cash pymt + $1 EFT fee

Millipore Corp (N-MIL) (div/yr: $0.00) [S&P ranking: B] mfg-biotechnology tools & svcs
80 Ashby Rd
Bedford, MA 01730-2237
 781-533-2557 InvRe
 781-533-3110 fax #
 800-730-4001 admr
www.millipore.com

Buy fees: no cost
$25-3,000/qtr(4)
cash-only option
rec common

NOTE: co does not pay div

✂

Mills Corp (The) (N-MLS) (div/yr: $ 2.51) [S&P ranking: A] REIT-regional malls
1300 Wilson Blvd, Ste 400
Arlington, VA 22209
 800-446-2617 admr
 703-526-5237 fax #
 703-526-5102 CorpSecy
www.millscorp.com

Buy fees: 5% to $3 + 3¢/sh*
$25-250,000/yr EFT(52)
DIP: $250 + $13 + 3¢/sh **
partial DR option
sfkg-free/p. sale-$15 + 12¢/sh
common/no residency restrict.
gifting free

★

NOTE: *$5 + 3¢/sh for cash purchases/$2 + 3¢/sh EFT/** or $25 EFT for 10 months

---

Modine Manufacturing Co (N-MODI) (div/yr: $ 0.65) [S&P ranking: A-] mfg-auto parts
1500 De Koven Ave
Racine, WI 53403-2552
 262-636-1200 InvRe
 262-636-1424 fax #
 800-468-9716 admr
e-mail: invest@modine.com
www.modine.com

Buy fees: no cost
$10-5,000/mo EFT(52)
DIP: $500 + $10 or $100/mo
part. DR/cash-only
sfkg-free/p. sale-$10 + 15¢/sh
rec common
gifting $10

✂
★

Monaco Coach Corp (N-MNC) (div/yr: $ 0.50) [S&P ranking: B] mfg-motor coashes/rec veh
91320 Industrial Way
Coburg, OR 97408
 800-468-9716 admr
 541-686-8011 InvRe
www.monaco-online.com

Buy fees: no cost
$40-10,000/qtr(12)
sfkg-free/p. sale-$15 + 10¢/sh (< $25,000)
rec comm-1 sh min
gifting avail

✂

Monmouth Capital Corporation (NDQ-MONM) (div/yr: $ 0.50) [S&P ranking: B] REIT
3499 Rt 9 North, Ste 3-C
Freehold, NJ 07728
 877-611-7981 admr
 732-577-9981 fax #
 732-577-9996 InvRe
www.monmouthcapital.com

Buy fees: no cost
5% disc-div/cash
$500-1,000/mo**(12)
part. DR/cash-only
common*

✂
%

NOTE: *B/O "street name" holders elig for only cash plan/**req waiver > $1,000

Monmouth Real Estate Investment Corp (NDQ-MNRTA) (div/yr: $ 0.58) [S&P rank: B +] REIT
3499 Route 9 North Ste C-3
Freehold, NJ 07728
 877-611-7981 admr
 732-577-9981 fax #
 732-577-9997 InvRe
e-mail: mreic@mreic.com
www.mreic.com

Buy fees: no cost
5% disc-div/cash
$500-1,000/mo**(12)
part. DR/cash-only
common*
gifting avail

✂
%

NOTE: *B/O elig for cash option only/**req waiver for amts > $1,000

Monsanto Co (N-MON) (div/yr: $ 0.68) mfg-agricultural chemicals/herbicides
800 N Lindbergh Blvd
St Louis, MO 63167
 888-725-9529 admr
 314-694-1057 fax #
 314-694-8148 InvRe
e-mail: info@monsanto.com
www.monsanto.com

Buy fees: 5% to $3 + 6¢/sh*
$25-250,000/yr EFT(52)
DIP: $250 + $15 + 6¢/sh
part. DR/cash-only
sfkg-free/p. sale-$15 + 12¢/sh
rec common
div deposit/gifting free

★

NOTE: *cash pymt fees: 6¢/sh + $2 EFT/$5 check

Morgan Stanley (N-MWD) (div/yr: $ 1.08) [S&P ranking: A-] fin svcs-brokerage/credit card issuance

✂   1585 Broadway   Buy fees: no cost
★   New York, NY 10036 $100-40,000/yr(24)
    800-622-2393 admr   DIP: $1,000
    212-507-3341 fax #   part. DR/cash-only
    212-762-8131 InvRe   sfkg-free/p. sale-$5 + 5¢/sh
    www.morganstanley.com   rec common or*
                                       gifting free

NOTE: *or Morgan Stanley acct shareholders

Motorola Inc (N-MOT) (div/yr: $ 0.16) [S&P ranking: B +] mfg-comm eq/semiconductors
    1303 E Algonquin Rd   Buy fees: no cost-div*
✂   Schaumburg, IL 60196-1065 $100-250,000/yr EFT(52)
    800-262-8509 InvRe   DIP: $500 + $10 + 10¢/sh
★   800-526-0801 admr   partial DR option
    e-mail: invest1@email.mot.com   sfkg-free/p. sale-$10 + 10¢/sh
    www.motorola.com/investor   common min 1 sh min
                                       gifting free

NOTE: *$5 ($2.00 EFT) + 10¢/sh for cash purch

Myers Industries Inc (N-MYE) (div/yr: $ 0.20) [S&P ranking: B +] mfg-tire svc equip/plastic/rubber products
✂   1293 S Main St   Buy fees: no cost
    Akron, OH 44301-1339 $50-2,500/qtr(4)
    800-622-6757 admr   part. DR/cash-only
    330-253-5592 co #   sfkg-free/p. sale-avail
    www.myersind.com   record common/US residents only

Mylan Laboratories Inc (N-MYL) (div/yr: $ 0.12) [S&P ranking: A-] drugs/pharmaceutical mfg
    1500 Corporate Dr Ste 400 $50-5,000/qtr EFT(4)
    Canonsburg, PA 15317   sfkg-free/p. sale-$7.50 + bkg
    800-937-5449 admr   rec comm-25 shs min
    724-514-1870 fax #
    724-514-1800 InvRe
    e-mail: investor_relations@mylan.com
    www.mylan.com/newindex.html

N

NCR Corp (N-NCR) (div/yr: $0.00) [S&P ranking: B +] mfg/svcs-business systems-ATM
    1700 S Patterson Blvd   Buy fees: $15 + 12¢/sh-cash
    Dayton, OH 45479 $25-10,000/day EFT(52)
    800-627-2303 admr   DIP: $250
★   937-445-5000 InvRe   sfkg-free/p. sale-$15 + 12¢/sh
    e-mail: investor.relations@ncr.com common
    www.ncr.com
NOTE: co does not pay dividends

NDC Health Corp (N-NDC) (div/yr: $ 0.16) svcs-information processing
    c/o SunTrust Bank   Buy fees: bkg fees
    P O Box 4625, MC 258 $25-1,000/qtr(12)
    Atlanta, GA 30302   sfkg-free
    800-568-3476 admr   rec common
    404-332-3875 fax #
    404-728-2000 GenCo
    e-mail: investorinfo@ndchealth.com
    www.ndchealth.com

NIKE Inc (N-NKE) (div/yr: $ 1) [S&P ranking: A] mfg-sports footwear
1 Bowerman Dr   Buy fees: 5% to $3-div*
Beaverton, OR 97005-6453 $50-250,000/yr EFT(52)
 503-671-6453 co #   DIP: $500 + $13
 800-756-8200 admr   sfkg-free/p. sale-$15
 www.nike.com   Cl B common/no residency restrict.   ★
 *$2 EFT/$5 ck-cash

NSTAR (N-NST) (div/yr: $ 2.32) [S&P ranking: B +] utility-electric/gas
800 Boylston St, 16th Floor   Buy fees: 4¢/sh*
Boston, MA 02199-8003 $50-250,000/yr EFT(52)
 800-338-8446 admr   DIP: $500 + $10 + 4¢/sh
 781-441-8121 InvRe   part. DR/cash-only
 e-mail: ir@nstaronline.com   sfkg-free+/p. sale-$15 + 12¢/sh ★
 www.nstaronline.com   comm/pref**
                      div deposit/gifting avail
NOTE: *cash pymt fees: $5 check/$2.50 EFT/**Boston Edison preferred div purchases
common/+skg for common shares only

Nash Finch Co (NDQ-NAFC) (div/yr: $ 0.72) [S&P ranking: B] food-wholesale/retail distributor
PO Box 355 - 7600 France Ave S Buy fees: no cost
Minneapolis, MN 55440-0355 $10-1,000/month(12*)   ✄
 800-468-9716 admr   partial DR option
 952-844-1235 fax #   rec common
 952-844-1147 AsstSecy
 www.nashfinch.com
NOTE: *monthly investment if aggregate amt buys 100-sh lots

Nashua Corp (N-NSH) (div/yr: $0.00) [S&P ranking: B-] mfg-office products
11 Trafalgar Sq, 2nd Floor   Buy fees: no cost
Nashua, NH 03063 $100-5,000/qtr(8)   ✄
 800-937-5449 admr   sfkg-free
 603-880-2323 Treas   rec common
 www.nashua.com   NOTE: co does not pay div

National City Corp (N-NCC) (div/yr: $ 1.40) [S&P ranking: A] banking
P O Box 92301 Corporate Trust Buy fees: no cost
Cleveland, OH 44193-0900 $20-25,000/mo(12)   ✄
 800-622-6757 admr   part. DR/cash-only
 216-476-8367 fax #   sfkg-avail/p. sale-$10 + fee
 216-575-2467 CpTru   common/pref
 e-mail: investor.relations@nationalcity.com
 www.national-city.com
NOTE: *or 20¢/sh up to $25,000/qtr/div amt limited to $25,000/qtr

National Financial Partners Corp (N-NFP) (div/yr: $ 0.48) fin svcs-life ins/fin planning
787 7th Ave, 11th Floor   Buy fees: no cost-div*
New York, NY 10019 $15-250,000/yr EFT*(52)   ✄
 866-637-7865 admr   DIP: $500 + $15 + 6¢/sh
 212-301-4140 fax #   part. DR/cash-only
 212-301-4040 InvRe   sfkg-free/p. sale-$15 + 12¢/sh ★
 www.nfp.com   no residency restrict.
                      div deposit/gifting free
NOTE: cash pymt fees: *6¢/sh + $2 EFT/$5 check

National Fuel Gas Co (N-NFG) (div/yr: $ 1.12) [S&P ranking: B +] utility-gas, energy
6363 Main St   Buy fees: no cost   ✄
Williamsville, NY 14221 $100-120,000/yr EFT(52)
 800-648-8166 admr   DIP: $1,000 + $15   ★
 716-857-7439 fax #   part. DR/cash-only
 716-857-7340 InvRe   p. sale-avail
 www.natfuel.com   rec common
                      div deposit

National Health Investors Inc (N-NHI) (div/yr: $ 1.80) REIT-health care facilities
100 Vine St
Murfreesboro, TN 37130
615-890-9100 co #
615-890-0123 fax #
800-568-3476 admr

Buy fees: 8¢/sh/no svc chg
$100-5,000/qtr(12)
partial DR option
rec comm/pref
div deposit

National Penn Bancshares Inc (NDQ-NPBC) (div/yr: $ 0.80) [S&P ranking: A+] banks/banking
Philadelphia & Reading Sts
✂ Boyertown, PA 19512
800-720-0181 admr
610-369-6128 InvRe
www.natpennbank.com

Buy fees: no cost-div/check pymt-$5
$100-2,000/mo EFT(12)
partial DR option
sfkg-avail/p. sale-$15 + 12¢/sh
no residency restrict.
div deposit/gifting avail

Nationwide Financial Services Inc (N-NFS) (div/yr: $ 0.76) [S&P ranking: B +] insurance
c/o Mellon Investor Services
P O Box 3316
,S Hackensack, NJ 07606
★ 866-541-9688 admr
614-249-8437 InvRe
www.nationwidefinancial.com

Buy fees: 5% to $3 + 3¢/sh
$100-120,000/yr EFT
DIP: $500 + $15 + fee
p. sale-$15 + 12¢/sh
common

Nationwide Health Properties Inc (N-NHP) (div/yr: $ 1.48) [S&P ranking: B +] REIT-health
care facilities
✂ 610 Newport Center Dr Ste 1150
Newport Beach, CA 92660
% 800-524-4458 admr
949-759-6876 fax #
★ 949-718-4400 InvRe
e-mail: investorelations@nhp-reit.com
www.nhp-reit.com

Buy fees: no cost
2%-div/cash orig iss
$100-10,000/mo EFT(12)
DIP: $750
part. DR/cash-only
sfkg-free
common
gifting free

NOTE: discount may range from 0-5%/ownership may not exceed 9.9% of voting
shares/upon approval from co may obtain waiver to purchase more than $10,000/mo

Neiman Marcus Group (The) (N-NMG) (div/yr: $ 0.60) retail/specialty-dept stores
1618 Main St
✂ Dallas, TX 75201
214-741-6911 InvRe
617-575-3170 admr
www.neimanmarcus.com
NOTE: div omitted 1/95

Buy fees: no cost
$25-2,500/qtr(12)
cash-only option
common

New Jersey Resources Corp (N-NJR) (div/yr: $ 1.36) [S&P ranking: A] utility-gas
PO Box 1468
✂ Wall, NJ 07719-1468
800-817-3955 admr
732-938-1230 ShRel
www.njresources.com

Buy fees: no cost
$25-60,000/yr(24)
part. DR/cash-only
sfkg-free
rec common/no residency restrict.

New Plan Excel Realty Trust Inc (N-NXL) (div/yr: $ 1.65) [S&P ranking: A] REIT-shopping ctrs
✂ 1120 Ave of the Americas
New York, NY 10036
800-730-6001 admr
212-869-3989 fax #
212-869-3000 admr
www.newplan.com

Buy fees: no cost
$100-20,000/qtr(12)
part. DR/cash-only
sfkg-avail/p. sale-$15 + 15¢/sh
common

New York Times Co (The) (N-NYT) (div/yr: $ 0.66) [S&P ranking: A-] publishing
c/o Mellon Investor Svcs
P O Box 3316
S Hackensack, NJ 07606
800-851-9677 admr
212-556-4634 fax #
212-556-1234 legal
www.nytimes.com

Buy fees: 5% to$3.50 + 3¢/sh
$10-3,000/qtr(4)
cash-only option
sfkg-free/p. sale-$15 + 12¢/sh
common Class A
div deposit/gifting avail

Newell Rubbermaid Inc (N-NWL) (div/yr: $ 0.84) [S&P ranking: B] consumer prod-mfg/mktr
10B Glenlake Parkway Ste 600
Atlanta, GA 30328-0943
800-432-0140 admr
770-407-3987 fax #
770-407-3829 AsstSecy
e-mail: investor.relations@newellco.com
www.newellrubbermaid.com
NOTE: *$2 EFT fee for cash pymts

Buy fees: no cost
$10-100,000/yr EFT*(12)
DIP: $250
part. DR/cash-only
sfkg-free/p. sale-avail
common
div deposit

✄
★

Newport Corp (NDQ-NEWP) (div/yr: $0.00) [S&P ranking: C] mfg-laser/electro-optical equip
1791 Deere Ave
Irvine, CA 92606
949-863-3144 co #
888-200-3169 admr
e-mail: investor@newport.com
www.newport.com

Buy fees: $1.50 + 10¢/sh div*
$25-10,000/pymtEFT(52)
DIP: $250
part. DR/cash-only
sfkg-free/p. sale-$7.50 + 10¢/sh
common
gifting free

★

NOTE: *$2.50 + 10¢/sh-cash purchase/co does not pay div

NiSource Inc (N-NI) (div/yr: $ 0.92) [S&P ranking: B] utility-electric/gas
801 East 86th Ave
Merrillville, IN 46410
219-647-6132 ShrRe
219-647-6180 fax #
888-884-7790 admr
e-mail: questions@nisource.com
www.nisource.com

Buy fees: no cost
$25-5,000/qtr(12)
sfkg-free/p. sale-$15 + bkg fee
common

✄

Nicor Inc (N-GAS) (div/yr: $ 1.86) [S&P ranking: B] energy-natural gas-trans/dist; container
shipping
P O Box 3014
Naperville, IL 60566-7014
630-305-9500 CorpSecy
630-983-7077 fax #
630-305-9500 x2749 ShSvc
www.nicor.com

Buy fees: no cost
$50-5,000/month(12)
sfkg-free
comm/pref

✄

Noranda Inc (N-NRD) (div/yr: $ 0.48) [S&P ranking: B-] metals/mining-CDN
181 Bay St #4100, PO Box 755
Toronto, ONT M5J 2T3, Canada
800-387-0825 admr
416-982-7490 fax #
416-982-7111 CorpSecy
e-mail: request@noranda.com
www.noranda.com

Buy fees: no cost
no cash plan
partial DR option
common/Canada res only

Nordson Corp (NDQ-NDSN) (div/yr: $ 0.64) [S&P ranking: B] mfg-indus application equip
28601 Clemens Rd
Westlake, OH 44145-1119
440-414-5344 ShRel
440-892-9507 fax #
800-622-6757 admr
e-mail: bprice@nordson.com
www.nordson.com

Buy fees: no cost
$10-4,000/qtr(4)
sfkg-avail
rec common

✄

Norfolk Southern Corp (N-NSC) (div/yr: $ 0.44) [S&P ranking: B] trans-railroad
c/o Bank of New York
P O Box 11258, Church St Sta
New York, NY 10286
 757-533-4810 StkRec
 757-533-4917 fax #
 866-272-9472 admr
 e-mail: ldtyree@nscorp.com
 www.nscorp.com
Buy fees: 10%to$3.00 + bkg fee*
$10-1,000/mo(12)
rec common/no residency restrict.
NOTE: *$5 + bkg fee for cash payments

North Fork Bancorp Inc (N-NFB) (div/yr: $ 0.88) [S&P ranking: A] banking
275 Broadhollow Rd
Melville, NY 11747
 800-317-4445 admr
 631-501-5521 fax #
 631-844-1004 CorpSecy
 www.northforkbank.com
Buy fees: no cost
disc at co discretio
$200-15,000/mo EFT(12)
part. DR/cash-only
sfkg-free/p. sale-$15
rec common/US res only
div deposit

Northeast Utilities System (N-NU) (div/yr: $ 0.65) [S&P ranking: B] utility-elec/gas
107 Selden St
Bolin, CT 06037
 800-999-7269 admr
 860-665-4801 ShSvc
 e-mail: nucommunications@nu.com
 www.nu.com
Buy fees: 10% to $3 + *
$100/mo-10,000/inv(52)
DIP: $250 + $12.50+10¢/sh
part. DR/cash-only
sfkg-free/p. sale-$15+10¢/sh
rec common
div deposit/gifting free
NOTE: *10¢/sh-div/cash purch: by check $7.50+10¢/sh; monthly auto $2.50 + 10¢/sh/
**EFT of cash purchase

Northrop Grumman Corp (N-NOC) (div/yr: $ 1.04) [S&P ranking: B+] mfg-aerospace, elec
c/o EquiServe
PO Box 2598
Jersey City, NJ 07303-2598
 800-756-8200 admr
 310-556-4556 fax #
 310-201-3081 CorpSecy
 e-mail: investor_relations@mail.northgrum.c
 www.northropgrumman.com
Buy fees: no cost*
$100-1,000/mo EFT*(12)
partial DR option
sfkg-free/p. sale-$15+12¢/sh
rec common/no residency restrict.
div deposit/gifting free
NOTE: *$2 EFT fee/may trans shs to brokerage acct electronically (no cert issued)

Northwest Natural Gas Co (N-NWN) (div/yr: $ 1.30) [S&P ranking: B+] utility-gas
220 NW 2nd Ave
Portland, OR 97209-3944
 503-220-2590 ShrSv
 503-721-2516 fax #
 503-226-4211 x3413
 e-mail: investorinformation@nwnatural.com
 www.nwnatural.com
Buy fees: no cost-orig iss
up to $50,000/yr*(12)
part. DR/cash-only
sfkg-free
rec common/no residency restrict.
div deposit
NOTE: *EFT of cash payments

Nucor Corp (N-NUE) (div/yr: $ 0.60) [S&P ranking: B] mfg-steel
c/o American Stock Trans & Trust Co
59 Maiden Lane 1st floor
New York, NY 10038
 704-366-7000 ShSvc
 704-362-4208 fax #
 800-937-5449 admr
 e-mail: info@nucor.com
 www.nucor.com
Buy fees: no cost
$10-1,000/month(12)
common

O

OGE Energy Corp (N-OGE) (div/yr: $ 1.33) [S&P ranking: A-] utility-gas/elec
P O Box 321
Oklahoma City, OK 73101-0321
  888-216-8114 ShrRe
  405-553-3612 fax #
  405-553-3211 ShrRe
  e-mail: stock@oge.com
  www.oge.com
Buy fees: no cost
$25-100,000/yr EFT(12)
DIP: $250 + $3 + 12¢/sh
partial DR option
sfkg-free/p. sale-$10 + 12¢/sh
common/no residency restrict.
div deposit/gifting avail
NOTE: customers of OK Gas & Elec may invest through utility bills

✂
★

OM Group Inc (N-OMG) (div/yr: $0.00) [S&P ranking: B-] mfg-specialty chemicals
50 Public Sq Ste 3500
Cleveland, OH 44113
  216-781-0083 CSecy
  800-622-6757 admr
  www.omgi.com
Buy fees: no cost
$10-5,000/month(12)
part. DR/cash-only
sfkg-free/p. sale-avail
rec common
NOTE: co does not pay div

✂

ONEOK Inc (N-OKE) (div/yr: $ 0.84) [S&P ranking: A-] energy-natural gas distr
P O Box 871
Tulsa, OK 74102-0871
  866-235-0232 admr
  918-588-7961 fax #
  918-588-7941 AsstSecy
  e-mail: jrussell@oneok.com
  www.ONEOK.com
Buy fees: no cost
$25-10,000/mo EFT(52)
DIP: $250 or $25/mo EFT
part. DR/cash-only
sfkg-free/p. sale-$15 + 10¢/sh
rec common/no residency restrict.
div deposit/gifting avail

✂
★

Occidental Petroleum Corp (N-OXY) (div/yr: $ 1.24) [S&P ranking: B +] energy-petroleum
c/o Mellon Investor Services LLC
P O Box 3336
South Hackensack, NJ 07606-1938
  800-622-9231 admr
  310-208-8800 CorpSecy
  e-mail: investorrelations_newyork@oxy.com
  www.oxy.com
Buy fees: no cost
$50-10,000/month(12)
partial DR option
sfkg-$3/p. sale-$15 + bkg
rec comm/pref-25 sh*/US res only
div deposit
NOTE: *25 shs of either

✂

Ohio Casualty Corp (NDQ-OCAS) (div/yr: $0.00) [S&P ranking: B-] insurance
9450 Seward Rd
Fairfield, OH 45014
  800-317-4445 admr
  513-682-5242 fax #
  513-603-2175 ShrRe
  www.ocas.com
Buy fees: 5% to$3 + bkg fee*
$10-60,000/yr EFT*(12)
part. DR/cash-only
sfkg-free/p. sale-$15 + 12¢/sh
rec comm 1 sh min/no residency restrict.
div deposit
NOTE: *cash pymt fees: $5 cash/$2 EFT/co does not pay div

Old National Bancorp (IN) (N-ONB) (div/yr: $ 0.76) [S&P ranking: A-] banking
P O Box 929/420 Main St
Evansville, IN 47706-0929
  800-677-1749 StkTr
  812-464-1421 fax #
  812-464-1442 InvRe
  e-mail: bancorp@oldnational.com
  www.oldnational.com
Buy fees: no cost-orig iss
$50-360,000/yr EFT(12)
DIP: $500 + $10
part. DR/cash-only
sfkg-free/p. sale-15¢/sh + bkg
common- 1 sh min
div deposit/gifting free

✂
★

Old Republic International Corp (N-ORI) (div/yr: $ 0.52) [S&P ranking: A] insurance
c/o EquiServe   Buy fees: no cost
✂ P O Box 2598 # 4675 $100-5,000/qtr(4)
Jersey City, NJ 07303-2598   part. DR/cash-only
  312-346-8100 co #   sfkg-free/p. sale-avail
  781-595-2734 admr   rec common
  www.oldrepublic.com

Olin Corp (N-OLN) (div/yr: $ 0.80) [S&P ranking: B-] mfg-chemicals
c/o Mellon Investor Services LLC $50-5,000/month(12)
P O Box 750   rec common/no residency restrict.
South Hackensack, NJ 07606-1938
  800-306-8594 admr
  314-480-1400 co #*
  www.olin.com
NOTE: *Investor Relations office in Norwalk, CT 203-750-3000

Omega Financial Corp (NDQ-OMEF) (div/yr: $ 1.24) [S&P ranking: A-] banks/banking
P O Box 298   Buy fees: no cost
✂ State College, PA 16804-0619   no cash plan
  800-368-5948 admr   partial DR option
  814-231-7680 InvRe   rec common
  www.omegafinancial.com

Omega Healthcare Investors Inc (N-OHI) (div/yr: $ 0.84) [S&P ranking: C] REIT-health care facilities
✂ 9690 Deerco Rd Ste 100   Buy fees: no cost
% Timonium, MD 21093   0-5% disc-div/cash/initial purchase
  800-317-4445 admr $50-6,250/mo*EFT(12)
★ 410-427-1740 InvRe   DIP: $250
  201/222-4955 TDD   partial DR option
  www.omegahealthcare.com   sfkg-avail/p. sale-$15 + 12¢/sh
                                          rec common
                                          div deposit/gifting avail
NOTE: *waiver may be obtained for greater amounts/div omitted 2001

Omnicare Inc (N-OCR) (div/yr: $ 0.09) [S&P ranking: A-] healthcare-mfg medical prod/devices
100 E Rivercenter Blvd Ste 1600   Buy fees: no cost-div*
✂ Covington, KY 41011-4728 $30-250,000/yr EFT(12)
  800-317-4445 admr   part. DR/cash-only
  859-392-3333 fax #   sfkg-free/p. sale-$15 + 12¢/sh
  859-392-3300 InvRe   rec common/no residency restrict.
  e-mail: investor.relations@omnicare.com gifting avail
  www.omnicare.com
NOTE: *cash pymt fees: 3¢/sh + $2.50 EFT/$5 check

Omnicom Group Inc (N-OMC) (div/yr: $ 0.90) [S&P ranking: A+] misc-advert/marketing svcs
437 Madison Ave   Buy fees: no cost
✂ New York, NY 10022-7000 $75-120,000/yr EFT(52)
  877-870-2370 admr   DIP: $750
★ 212-415-3530 fax #   partial DR option
  212-415-3600 InvRe   sfkg-free/p. sale-$15 + 12¢/sh
  e-mail: ir@omnicomgroup.com   rec common
  www.omnicomgroup.com   gifting free

Omnova Solutions Inc (N-OMN) (div/yr: $0.00) mfg-emulsion polymer prod/spec chemicals/deco surf
175 Ghent Rd
Fairlawn, OH 44333-3300
800-524-4458 admr
330-869-4272 fax #
330-869-4454 ShrSv
e-mail: inforequest@omnova.com
www.omnova.com
NOTE: co does not pay div

Buy fees: no cost
$50-120,000/yr EFT(52)
DIP: $500 + $10
sfkg-free/p. sale-$10 + 10¢/sh
rec common
gifting free
✂ ★

Oneida Ltd (OTC-ONEI) (div/yr: $ 0.08) mfg-stainless steel
163-181 Kenwood Ave
Oneida, NY 13421-2829
315-361-3362 Treas
315-361-3700 fax #
800-278-4353 admr
e-mail: investor@oneida.com
www.oneida.com

Buy fees: no cost
no cash plan
partial DR option
p. sale-$1
common/US residents
✂

Otter Tail Corp (NDQ-OTTR) (div/yr: $ 1.12) [S&P ranking: A-] utility-electric/plastics/health svcs/mfg
P O Box 496/215 S Cascade St
Fergus Falls, MN 56537-0496
800-664-1259 ShSvc
218-998-3615 fax #
218-739-8479 ShSvc
e-mail: sharesvs@ottertail.com
www.ottertail.com
NOTE: *sfkg for comm shs only/**sale of max 25 shs/mo/util cust may buy initial shares

Buy fees: no cost
$10-5,000/monthEFT(12)
partial DR option
sfkg-free*/p. sale-avail**
rec comm/pref/cust/no residency restrict.
div deposit/gifting avail
✂

Owens & Minor Inc (N-OMI) (div/yr: $ 0.52) [S&P ranking: A-] health-hospital supply, drug distr
PO Box 27626/4800 Cox Rd
Glen Allen, VA 23061-7626
804-747-9794 co #
800-524-4458 admr
www.owens-minor.com

Buy fees: no cost
$25-25,000/yr(12)
partial DR option
rec common
✂

P

PFF Bancorp Inc (N-PFB) (div/yr: $ 0.60) banks/banking
350 S Garey Ave
Pomona, CA 91766-1722
800-241-6724 admr
909-623-2323 InvRe
e-mail: investor.relations@pffb.com
www.pffbank.com

Buy fees: no cost
$100-5,000/mo EFT
p. sale-$15
✂

PG&E Corp (N-PCG) (div/yr: $ 1.20) [S&P ranking: B] utility-gas/elec
P O Box 770000 Mail Code B26B
San Francisco, CA 94177-0001
800-719-9056 admr
415-267-7267 fax #
415-267-7000 CorpSecy
e-mail: invrel@pg.corp.com
www.pgecorp.com
NOTE: *cash pymt fees: 10¢/sh + $5 check, $3.50 single EFT, $2 monthly EFT

Buy fees: no cost-div
$50-100,000/yr*(52)
DIP: $250 + $10 + 10¢/sh
sfkg-free/p. sale-$15 + 10¢/sh
rec common/no residency restrict.
gifting free
✂ ★

PNC Financial Services Group Inc (N-PNC) (div/yr: $ 2) [S&P ranking: B +] banking
249 5th Ave
Pittsburgh, PA 15222-2707
✄ 800-982-7652 admr
412-762-1553 ShRel
e-mail: corporate.communications@pncbank.co
www.pnc.com

Buy fees: no cost
$50-5,000/mo EFT(16)
partial DR option
sfkg-$3/p. sale-$15 + 10¢/sh
comm/pref
gifting free

PNM Resources Inc (N-PNM) (div/yr: $ 0.94) [S&P ranking: B +] utility-elec/gas/water
PO Box 1047 - Shareholder Records
Albuquerque, NM 87103-1047
★ 800-545-4425 InvRe
505-241-2367 fax #
505-241-2054 co #
www.pnm.com

Buy fees: bkg fee
$50-10,000/mo EFT(52)
DIP: $50
part. DR/cash-only
sfkg-free/p. sale-$15 + 6¢/sh
rec common*
div deposit/gifting free
NOTE: *owners of less than 100 shs automatically enrolled in DRP

PPG Industries Inc (N-PPG) (div/yr: $ 1.88) [S&P ranking: B] mfg-coatings, glass, chemicals, fiberglass
One PPG Place
★ Pittsburgh, PA 15272-0001
800-648-8160 admr
412-434-3318 InvRe
www.ppg.com

$100-10,000/mo EFT(52)
DIP: $500
partial DR option
sfkg-free/p. sale-avail
rec comm-10 shs min/no residency restrict.
div deposit/gifting avail

PPL Corp (N-PPL) (div/yr: $ 1.84) [S&P ranking: B] utility-electric
Two North Ninth St GENTW14
✄ Allentown, PA 18101-1179
800-345-3085 InvSv
610-774-5106 fax #
610-774-5804 InvSv
e-mail: invserv@pplweb.com
www.pplweb.com

Buy fees: no cost
up to $80,000/yr(12)
part. DR/cash-only
sfkg-free*/p. sale-10¢/sh
rec comm/pref*/no residency restrict.
gifting avail
NOTE: *common shares/pref of *PPL Electric Utilities purchases common

Pall Corp (N-PLL) (div/yr: $ 0.40) [S&P ranking: B] mfg-filters
25 Harbor Park Dr
✄ Port Washington, NY 11050-4630
800-633-4236 admr
516-484-3649 fax #
516-801-9246 admr
e-mail: dfoster@pall.com
www.pall.com

Buy fees: no cost
$100-5,000/mo EFT(12)
part. DR/cash-only
sfkg-free
rec comm 50 sh min/no residency restrict.
div deposit

Parker-Hannifin Corp (N-PH) (div/yr: $ 0.80) [S&P ranking: A-] mfg-motion control components & systems
6035 Parkland Blvd
✄ Cleveland, OH 44124-4141
800-622-6757 admr
216-896-4057 fax #
216-896-3000 CorpSecy
www.parker.com

Buy fees: no cost
$10-5,000/month(12)
sfkg-free/p. sale-avail
common

Paychex Inc (NDQ-PAYX) (div/yr: $ 0.52) [S&P ranking: A +] svcs-payroll accounting svcs
✄ 911 Panorama Trail S
Rochester, NY 14625-0397
★ 877-814-9688 admr
585-383-3406 InvRe
www.paychex.com

Buy fees: no cost
$100-10,000/qtr EFT(52)
DIP: $250
part. DR/cash-only
sfkg-free/p. sale-$15 + 10¢/sh
common

Peabody Energy Corp (N-BTU) (div/yr: $ 0.30) metals/mining-coal
701 Market St
St Louis, MO 63101-1826
  800-317-4445 admr
  314-342-3400 InvRe
  e-mail: publicrelations@peabodyenergy.com
  www.peabodyenergy.com
NOTE: *cash pymt fees: $2.50 EFT/$5 check

Buy fees: no cost-div*
$50-120,000/yr EFT
sfkg-avail/p. sale-$15
rec comm-1 sh min

✂

Penney (J C) Co Inc (N-JCP) (div/yr: $ 0.50) [S&P ranking: B-] retail-dept stores
c/o Mellon Investor Services LLC
P O Box 3338
South Hackensack, NJ 07606-1938
  800-842-9470 admr
  972-531-1859 fax #
  972-431-5500 ShRel
  e-mail: jrae1@jcpenney.com
  www.jcpenney.net
NOTE: *$1.50 + 6¢/sh for cash purchase

Buy fees: no cost-div
$25-10,000/mo EFT*(12)
DIP: $250 + $10 + 6 ¢/sh
part. DR/cash-only
sfkg-free/p. sale-$15 + 6¢/sh
rec common
div deposit/gifting free

✂
★

Pennsylvania Real Estate Investment Trust (N-PEI) (div/yr: $2.16) REIT
200 S Broad St
Philadelphia, PA 19102
  800-468-9716 admr
  215-546-7311 fax #
  215-875-0700 InvRe
  e-mail: investor@preit

Buy fees: no cost
$250-5,00/mo (12)
1% disc-div/cash

✂
✂
%

Pentair Inc (N-PNR) (div/yr: $ 0.52) [S&P ranking: A-] mfg-diversified industrial products
c/o Wells Fargo Bank NA
P O Box 64856
St Paul, MN 55164-0856
  877-536-3554 admr
  763-6565400 fax #
  763-545-1730 StkPl
  www.pentair.com

Buy fees: no cost
$10-3,000/qtr EFT(12)
sfkg-free/p. sale-avail
rec common/no residency restrict.
div deposit

✂

People's Bank (CT) (NDQ-PBCT) (div/yr: $ 1.32) [S&P ranking: B +] S&L/savings bank
850 Main St
Bridgeport, CT 06604-4913
  800-526-0801 admr
  203-338-7228 ShrRe
  www.peoples.com

Buy fees: no cost
$100-10,000/mo(52)
DIP: $250
sfkg-free/p. sale-$15
common

✂
★

Peoples Energy Corp (N-PGL) (div/yr: $ 2.18) [S&P ranking: B] utility-gas
P O Box 2000
Chicago, IL 60690-2000
  800-228-6888 admr
  312-240-4000 InvRe
  e-mail: corporatecommunications@pecorp.com
  www.PECorp.com

Buy fees: no cost
$25-100,000/yr EFT(24)
DIP: $250
part. DR/cash-only
sfkg-free/p. sale-8¢/sh + tax
rec common
div deposit/gifting avai*

★

NOTE: *gifting of 5 shs or $150 to open another acct

Pep Boys-Manny, Moe & Jack (The) (N-PBY) (div/yr: $ 0.27) [S&P ranking: B] retail-auto parts, maintenance & svc
3111 W Allegheny Ave
Philadelphia, PA 19132
  215-430-9000 co #
  215-430-4661 fax #
  718-921-8283 admr
  e-mail: investorrelations@pepboys.com
  www.pepboys.com

Buy fees: no cost
$100-10,000/qtr(4)
sfkg-free
rec common

✂

P   *Directory of Companies Offering*

Pepco Holding Inc (N-POM) (div/yr: $ 1) [S&P ranking: B] utility-electric
✂ 701 9th St, N W   Buy fees: no cost
Washington, DC 20068 $25-200,000/yr(12)
866-254-6502 admr   sfkg-free/p. sale-$5 + 4¢/sh
202-872-7982 fax #   rec common/no residency restrict.
202-872-3183 ShrSv   div deposit/gifting avail
e-mail: claire.williamson@conectiv.com
www.pepcoholdings.com

PepsiAmericas Inc (N-PAS) (div/yr: $ 0.34) [S&P ranking: B-] food/beverage-soft drinks
4000 Dain Rauscher Plza, 60 S 6th   Buy fees: 5%to$3 + 5¢/sh-div
Minneapolis, MN 55402 $50-120,000/yr**(52)
877-602-7611 admr   DIP: $250 + $10 + 5¢/sh
★ 612-661-3737 fax #   part. DR/cash-only
612-661-3718 ShSvc   sfkg-free/p. sale-$10 + 10¢/sh*
e-mail: info@pepsiamericas.com   rec common/no residency restrict.
www.pepsiamericas.com   gifting avail
NOTE: *sales by phone (min $50)/**cash pymt fee: 5¢/sh + $3 check, $1 EFT

PepsiCo Inc (N-PEP) (div/yr: $ 0.92) [S&P ranking: A+] beverages-soft drink/snacks
700 Anderson Hill Rd   Buy fees: no cost
✂ Purchase, NY 10577-1403 $25-5,000/month(24)
800-226-0083 admr   part. DR/cash-only
914-253-2711 fax #   sfkg-free/p. sale-$5 + bkg fee
914-253-3055 ShRel   rec comm 5 sh min
www.pepsico.com   div deposit

PerkinElmer Inc (N-PKI) (div/yr: $ 0.28) [S&P ranking: B] mfg-life/fluid sciences, optoelectron-
ics, instrumentation
✂ 45 William St   Buy fees: no cost
Wellesley, MA 02181-4078 $25-5,000/month(12)
781-431-4306 InvRe   cash-only option
781-431-4255 fax #   sfkg-free
800-730-4001 admr   rec common
800-952-9245 TTY   div deposit
e-mail: investor_relations@perkinelmer.com
www.perkinelmer.com

Pfizer Inc (N-PFE) (div/yr: $ 0.76) [S&P ranking: A] drug/pharm industry
235 E 42nd St   Buy fees: no cost
✂ New York, NY 10017-5755 $50-120,000/yr EFT(52)
800-733-9393 admr   DIP: $500
★ 212-573-7398 fax #   partial DR option
212-733-4749 ShrSv   sfkg-free/p. sale-$15 + bkg fee
www.pfizer.com   rec common/no residency restrict.

✂ **Piedmont Natural Gas Co Inc** (N-PNY) (div/yr: $ 0.92) [S&P ranking: A-] utility-gas
P O Box 33068   Buy fees: no cost
% Charlotte, NC 28233-6097   5% disc-div
800-438-8410 ShrSv $25-120,000/yr EFT(52)
★ 704-365-8515 fax #   DIP: $250
800-937-5449 admr   part. DR/cash-only
e-mail: marty.ruegsegger@piedmontng.com sfkg-free/p. sale-avail
www.piedmontng.com   common/no residency restrict.
                                         div deposit

Pier 1 Imports Inc (N-PIR) (div/yr: $ 0.40) [S&P ranking: A-] retail-imported goods stores

100 Pier 1 Place	Buy fees: no cost
Fort Worth, TX 76102-0020	$50-5,000/mon EFT(52)
888-884-8086 admr	DIP: $490 + $10
817-252-8174 fax #	partial DR option
817-252-8063 InvRe	sfkg-free/p. sale-$15 + 12¢/sh
e-mail: sjmartin@pier1.com	rec comm-10 shs min
www.pier1.com	gifting free

✂ ★

Pinnacle West Capital Corp (N-PNW) (div/yr: $ 1.90) [S&P ranking: A] utility-elec holding co

c/o Bank of New York	Buy fees: 10¢/sh
P O Box 11258, Church St Sta	to $150,000/yr EFT(12)
New York, NY 10286	DIP: $50 + bkg fee
800-457-2983 admr	part. DR/cash-only
602-250-5511 co #	sfkg-free/p. sale-$10 + 10¢/sh
e-mail: shareowners@bankofny.com	rec comm/no residency restrict.
www.pinnaclewest.com	div deposit/gifting avail

★

Pitney Bowes Inc (N-PBI) (div/yr: $ 1.24) [S&P ranking: A-] mfg-mail/document management

1 Elmcroft Rd MSC 6313	Buy fees: no cost
Stamford, CT 06926-0700	US$100-3,000/qtr(12)
800-648-8170 admr	part. DR/cash-only
203-351-6264 fax #	sfkg-avail/p. sale-$15 + 12¢/sh
203-351-6088 StkSv	rec common/US res only
e-mail: investorrelations@pb.com	div deposit/gifting free
www.pitneybowes.com	
NOTE: TDD 800-490-1493	

✂

Polaris Industries Inc (N-PII) (div/yr: $ 1.12) [S&P ranking: A-] consumer prod-mfg snowmo-biles/ATVs/motorcycles/PWC

2100 Highway 55	Buy fees: no svc fee
Medina, MN 55340-9770	no cash plan
800-468-9716 admr	sfkg-avail
763-542-0500 co #	common
www.polarisindustries.com	
NOTE: blanket request for full shares	

PolyOne (N-POL) (div/yr: $0.00) [S&P ranking: C] mfg-chemicals-polymer products

33587 Walker Rd	Buy fees: 5%to$3 + 3¢/sh-div
Avon Lake, OH 44012	$25-250,000/yr EFT*(24)
888-767-7166 admr	DIP: $250 + $10 + 3¢/sh*
440-930-1538 InvRe	part. DR/cash-only
www.polyone.com	sfkg-free/p. sale-$15 + 12¢/sh
	rec common
	div deposit/gifting free

★

NOTE: *or $25/mo EFT for 10 months/**cash pymt fees: 3¢/sh + $5 check/$2.50 EFT/co does not pay div

Popular Inc (NDQ-BPOP) (div/yr: $ 0.64) [S&P ranking: A+] banking

P O Box 362708	Buy fees: no cost
San Juan, PR 00936-2708	5% disc-div
877-764-1893 Trust	$25-10,000/mo*(12)
787-281-5193 fax #	DIP: $100
787-765-9800 x5525	part. DR/cash-only
e-mail: investorrelations@bppr.com	sfkg-free/p. sale-avail
www.bppr.com	common

✂ % ★

NOTE: *EFT for PR residents/non-PR US citizens may be subject to PR tax, check prospectus

Post Properties Inc (N-PPS) (div/yr: $ 1.80) [S&P ranking: B] REIT-apartments
4401 Northside Pkwy, Ste 800   Buy fees: no cost
Atlanta, GA 30327-3057 $100-10,000/mo(12)
  800-633-4236 admr   part. DR/cash-only
404-504-9388 fax #   p. sale-$15 + 12¢/sh
404-846-5012 CpAdm   rec common
e-mail: ir@postproperties.com   div deposit
www.postproperties.com

Potlatch Corp (N-PCH) (div/yr: $ 0.60) [S&P ranking: B-] mfg-forest products
601 W Riverside Ave Ste 1100   Buy fees: no cost
Spokane, WA 99201-3591 $25-1,000/mo EFT(12)
509-835-1500 co #   sfkg-avail/p. sale-avail
312-360-5390 admr   rec common
e-mail: investorinfo@potlatch.com
www.potlatchcorp.com

Praxair Inc (N-PX) (div/yr: $ 0.72) [S&P ranking: A] mfg-industrial gases/coatings
39 Old Ridgebury Rd   Buy fees: no cost
Danbury, CT 06810-5113 $50-24,000/yr EFT(12)
800-368-5948 admr   partial DR option
203-837-2545 fax #   sfkg-free/p. sale-$5 + bkg fee
203-837-2264 AsstSecy   rec common/no residency restrict.
e-mail: mark_lyon@praxair.com   gifting avail
www.praxair.com

Prentiss Properties Trust (N-PP) (div/yr: $ 2.24) [S&P ranking: B+] REIT-office properties
3890 W Northwest Highway Ste 400   Buy fees: 5%to$3/qtr
% Dallas, TX 75220-5166   ***
888-290-7286 admr $100-5,000/mo*EFT(12)
★ 214-654-5818 fax #   DIP: $500 + $10
214-654-0886 CorpSecy   part. DR/cash-only
e-mail: ir@pptinc.com   sfkg-avail/p. sale-$15 + 12¢/sh
www.prentisproperties.com   comm/pref
                                      gifting avail
NOTE: *cash pymt fees: $5 check; $2 EFT &req for wavier for cash pymts
45,000/mo/***0-5% disc on cash pymts > $5,000

Presidential Realty Corp (A-PDL.B) (div/yr: $ 0.64) [S&P ranking: B+] REIT
180 S Broadway   Buy fees: no cost
White Plains, NY 10605   5% disc-div
877-611-7981 admr $100-10,000/qtr(12)
% 914-948-1327 fax #   part. DR/cash-only
914-948-1300 CorpSecy   common Cl A & B*
                                      div deposit
NOTE: both classes reinvested in Cl B

Price (T Rowe) Group Inc (NDQ-TROW) (div/yr: $ 0.92) [S&P ranking: A] fin svcs-mutual
fund distr & advisor
100 E Pratt St   Buy fees: no cost
Baltimore, MD 21202   no cash plan
410-345-7733 CorpSecy   common
800-638-5660 fund
e-mail: info@troweprice.com
www.troweprice.com
NOTE: dividends are reinvested in TRP mutual funds

ProLogis (N-PLD) (div/yr: $ 1.48) [S&P ranking: B +] REIT-industrial distribution facilities
14100 E 35th Place
Aurora, CO 80011-1631
800-956-3378 admr
303-375-8581 fax #
303-375-9292 InvRe
e-mail: infor@prologis.com
http://ir.prologis.com

Buy fees: no cost
0-2% disc-div/cash**
$200-10,000/mo*EFT(24)
DIP: $200 + $10
part. DR/cash-only
sfkg-avail/p. sale-$15
no residency restrict.
div deposit

NOTE: *request waiver for cash pymts $10,000/IRA min-$200

Procter & Gamble Co (N-PG) (div/yr: $ 1.12) [S&P ranking: A] consumer prod-household products
P O Box 5572
Cincinnati, OH 45201-5572
800-742-6253 ShSvc
513-983-3034 ShSvc
e-mail: shareholders.im@pg.com
www.pg.com

Buy fees: $1 + 3¢/sh
$100-120,000/yr* EFT(52)
DIP: $250 + $5 fee
partial DR option
sfkg-free/p. sale-$2.5 + 2¢/sh
rec common/no residency restrict.
div deposit/gifting avail

Progress Energy Inc (N-PGN) (div/yr: $ 2.36) [S&P ranking: B +] utility-electric
PO Box 1551
Raleigh, NC 27602-1551
866-290-4388 admr
919-546-2859 fax #
800-662-7232 ShrRe
e-mail: shareholderrelatons@progress-energy
www.progress-energy.com

Buy fees: no cost-orig iss
$50-25,000/mo EFT(24)
DIP: $250
part. DR/cash-only
sfkg-free/p. sale-3.5¢/sh
comm/pref*-1 sh min/no residency restrict.
div deposit/gifting free

NOTE: 3.5¢/sh for market-purchased shs; may grant appr for $25,000/**preferred of Carolina Power & Light, Florida Power and North Carolina Natural Gas Corp

Protective Life Corp (N-PL) (div/yr: $ 0.78) [S&P ranking: A] insurance-life/accident/health
2801 Hwy 280 S
Birmingham, AL 35223-2488
800-524-4458 admr
205-268-5516 fax #
205-268-3385 legal
www.protective.com

Buy fees: no cost
$25-6,000/qtr(4)
common

Provident Bankshares Corp (NDQ-PBKS) (div/yr: $ 1.08) [S&P ranking: A] banking
114 E Lexington St
Baltimore, MD 21202
866-820-0125 admr
410-277-2889 InvRe
e-mail: paferrica@provbank.com
www.provbank.com

Buy fees: no cost-div*
$50-10,000/qtr EFT*(104)
DIP: $250 + $10 + bkg fee
partial DR option
sfkg-free/p. sale-$15 + 12¢/sh
rec common/no residency restrict.
div deposit

NOTE: *cash pymt fees: $5 check/$2.50 EFT + 3¢/sh bkg fee/*EFT from US banks only

Providian Financial Corp (N-PVN) (div/yr: $0.00) [S&P ranking: B] fin svcs-credit card/consumer loans
c/o EquiServe
P O Box 43081
Providence, RI 02940-3081
800-317-4445 admr
415-278-6028 fax #
415-278-6770 InvRe
800-952-9245 TDD
www.providian.com

Buy fees: no cost-div*
0-5% disc-cash purch
$100-10,000/mo*EFT(12)
DIP: $100 + $15 + bkg**
part. DR/cash-only
sfkg-free/p. sale-$15 + 12¢/sh
rec common/no residency restrict.
gifting free

NOTE: *may obtain wavier for cash pymts over $10,000/div not paid

Public Service Enterprise Group Inc (N-PEG) (div/yr: $ 2.24) [S&P ranking: B +] utility holdg
co-elec/gas

✂ P O Box 1171   Buy fees: no cost
Newark, NJ 07101 $50-125,000/yr EFT(24)
★ 800-242-0813 StkSv   DIP: $250 + $10 fee*
973-824-7056 fax #   part. DR/cash-only
973-430-7000 co #   sfkg-free/p. sale-$10 + bkg
e-mail: stkserv@pseg.com   rec comm/pref**/no residency restrict.
www.pseg.com   div deposit
NOTE: *or $50/mo EFT/TDD-800/732-3241/**pref of Public Service Elec & Gas / to be
acq by Exelon approx by 12/05 - 3/06

Puget Energy Inc (N-PSD) (div/yr: $ 1) [S&P ranking: B] utility-electric/natural gas
c/o Mellon Investor Services LLC   Buy fees: 10¢/sh
P O Box 476, Wash Bridge Sta $250-10,000/mo EFT(52)
South Hackensack, NJ 07606-1938   DIP: $250 + $10 + 10¢/sh
800-997-8438 admr   part. DR/cash-only
★ 425-462-3515 fax #   sfkg-free/p. sale-$15 + 10¢/sh
425-462-3898 InvSv   comm/pref/no residency restrict.
www.pse.com   div deposit

Q

Quaker Chemical Corp (N-KWR) (div/yr: $ 0.86) [S&P ranking: B +] mfg-specialty chemi-
cals/chemical mgmt svcs

✂ c/o American Stock Trans & Trust Co   Buy fees: no cost
59 Maiden Lane 1st floor $300-24,000/yr EFT(24)
New York, NY 10038   cash-only option
800-278-4353 admr   sfkg-free/p. sale-$7.50 + bkg fee
610-832-4496 fax #   common
610-832-4119 AsstSecy   gifting free
e-mail: irene_kisleiko@quakerchem.com
www.quakerchem.com

Quanex Corp (N-NX) (div/yr: $ 0.54) [S&P ranking: B] mfg-vehicular & building products

✂ 1900 West Loop South, Ste 1500   Buy fees: no cost
Houston, TX 77027 $50-10,000/qtr EFT(52)
★ 800-468-9716 InvRe   DIP: $250 + $15
713-439-1016 fax #   part. DR/cash-only
713-961-4600 InvRe   sfkg-free/p. sale-$15 + 8¢/sh
e-mail: vcalvert@quanex.com   common/no residency restrict.
www.quanex.com   div deposit/gifting free
NOTE: sales limited to $25,000 or less/cert for shares up to $50,000

Questar Corp (N-STR) (div/yr: $ 0.86) [S&P ranking: A-] energy-natural gas distr

✂ P O Box 45433/180 East 1st So   Buy fees: no cost-orig iss
Salt Lake City, UT 84145-0433 $50-100,000/yr EFT(12)
★ 801-324-5885 ShSvc   DIP: $240 + $10 fee
801-324-5483 fax #   part. DR/cash-only
800-729-6788 ShSVC   sfkg-free/p. sale-up to 99 shs
e-mail: shareholder@questar.com   common
www.questar.com   gifting avail
NOTE: 5¢/sh for open market purchases or sales

R

RGC Resources Inc (NDQ-RGCO) (div/yr: $ 1.18) [S&P ranking: B +] energy-natural gas & propane distr

P O Box 13007	Buy fees: no cost
Roanoke, VA 24030	$25-40,000/yr EFT(12)
800-829-8432 admr	partial DR option
540-777-2636 fax #	sfkg-free/p. sale-avail
540-777-4427 CorpSecy	rec comm-1 sh min
e-mail: susan_miller@rgcresources.com	
www.rgcresources.com	

RLI Corp (N-RLI) (div/yr: $ 0.56) [S&P ranking: A] insurance-property/casualty

9025 N Lindbergh Dr	Buy fees: no cost
Peoria, IL 61615	$25-2,000/mo(12)
800-331-4929 co #	sfkg-avail
309-692-4634 fax #	common
800-468-9716 admr	
www.rlicorp.com	

RPM International Inc (N-RPM) (div/yr: $ 0.60) [S&P ranking: A-] mfg-chemicals

P O Box 777	Buy fees: no cost
Medina, OH 44258-0777	$25-5,000/month(24)
800-776-4488 ShRel	cash-only option
216-476-8367 fax #	sfkg-free
800-988-5238 admr	rec common/no residency restrict.
e-mail: info@rpminc.com	div deposit
www.rpminc.com	

RadioShack Corp (N-RSH) (div/yr: $ 0.25) [S&P ranking: B +] retail-consumer electronics

300 RadioShack Cir MS CF3-227	Buy fees: no cost-div*
Fort Worth, TX 76102	$50-150,000/yr*EFT(12)
866-725-0781 admr	DIP: $250 + $10
817-415-2647 fax #	part. DR/cash-only
817-415-3022 AsstSecy	sfkg-free/p. sale-$15 + 10¢/sh
e-mail: investor.relations@radioshack.com	rec common/no residency restrict.
www.RadioShackCorporation.com	gifting free

NOTE: *cash pymt fees: $5 cash/$1.50 EFT/online sales

Raven Industries Inc (NDQ-RAVN) (div/yr: $ 0.28) [S&P ranking: B +] mfg-electronic sys/flow control/engineered film

P O Box 5107	Buy fees: no cost
Sioux Falls, SD 57117-5107	$100-15,000/qtr EFT(4)
605-336-2750 InvRe	part. DR/cash-only
605-335-0268 fax #	sfkg-free
800-468-9716 admr	common
e-mail: info@ravenind.com	
www.ravenind.com	

Rayonier Inc (N-RYN) (div/yr: $ 2.48) [S&P ranking: B +] REIT

50 N Laura St	Buy fees: no cost-div/svc fee on cash
Jacksonville, FL 32202	$50-5,000/qtr(52)
800-659-0158 admr	sfkg-free/p. sale-avail
904-357-9848 fax #	common
904-357-9177 InvRe	
www.rayonier.com	

Raytheon Co (N-RTN) (div/yr: $ 0.88) [S&P ranking: B-] mfg-electronic eq
c/o EquiServe
P O Box 366
Boston, MA 02101
  781-860-2303 ShrSv
  781-860-2172 fax #
  800-360-4519 admr
  e-mail: invest@raytheon.com
  www.raytheon.com
$25-25,000/qtr(12)
sfkg-free/p. sale-$10 + 15¢/sh
rec comm-Cl A & B*
NOTE: *div of each class reinvest in same class/shareholders may enroll or terminate by phone

Reader's Digest Assn Inc (N-RDA) (div/yr: $ 0.40) [S&P ranking: B-] publishing-magazines/books
Reader's Digest Rd
✄ Pleasantville, NY 10570-7000
  914-244-5425 InvRe
★ 914-238-4559 fax #
  800-230-2771 admr
  www.readersdigest.com
Buy fees: no cost-div
$100-10,000/mo*EFT(52)
DIP: $1,000 + $5
part. DR/cash-only
sfkg-free/p. sale-$15
rec comm Cl A/no residency restrict.
gifting avail

✄ **Redwood Trust Inc** (N-RWT) (div/yr: $ 2.80) [S&P ranking: B +] REIT
One Belvedere Place Ste 300
% Mill Valley, CA 94941
  888-472-1955 admr
  415-381-1773 fax #
★ 415-389-7373 co #
  e-mail: nicole.klock@redwoodtrust.com
  www.redwoodtrust.com
Buy fees: no cost
2% disc-div*
$10-10,000/mo(12)
DIP: $100
part. DR/cash-only
sfkg-free/p. sale-$10 + 10¢/sh
common
NOTE: *discount on cash purchases may vary from 0 to 3%

✄ **Regions Financial Corp** (N-RF) (div/yr: $ 1.36) [S&P ranking: A-] fin svcs
P O Box 10247
★ Birmingham, AL 35202-0247
  205-326-7090 InvRe
  205-326-7784 fax #
  800-524-2879 admr
  e-mail: askus@regionsbank.com
  www.regions.com
Buy fees: no cost /$1 EFT fee
$25-120,000/yr EFT*(52)
DIP: $1,000-40,000
part. DR/cash-only
sfkg-free/p. sale-$15 + 12¢/sh
common/no residency restrict.
div deposit

Regis Corp (N-RGS) (div/yr: $ 0.16) [S&P ranking: A-] svcs-hair salon chain
7201 Metro Blvd
✄ Edina, MN 55439
  952-947-7777 InvRe
  952-947-7700 fax #
  800-468-9716 admr
  www.regiscorp.com
Buy fees: no cost
no cash plan
sfkg-avail/p. sale-avail
common/no residency restrict.

Reliv' International Inc (NDQ-RELV) (div/yr: $ 0.07) [S&P ranking: B] food-nutritional, diet products
c/o American Stock Trans & Trust Co
P O Box 922 Wall St Sta
★ New York, NY 10269-0560
  888-333-0203 admr
  636-537-9753 fax #
  636-537-9715 InvRe
  e-mail: fredn@relivinc.com
  www.reliv.com
Buy fees: 2%to$2.50 + 10¢/sh*
$25-10,000/day EFT(240)
DIP: $250 + $2.50 + 10¢/sh
part. DR/cash-only
sfkg-$7.50/p. sale-$15 + 10¢/sh
rec common
div deposit/gifting free
NOTE: *$2.50 + 10¢/sh for cash purchase

Reynolds & Reynolds Co (N-REY) (div/yr: $ 0.44) [S&P ranking: A-] svc-tech software to auto retailers
P O Box 2608
Dayton, OH 45401-2608
866-411-6748 admr
937-485-2787 fax #
937-485-2791 StkAd
e-mail: juliet_shadoan@reyrey.com
www.reyrey.com
NOTE: sales limited to $25,000 or less

Buy fees: no cost
$100-5,000/mo EFT(12)
sfkg-free/p. sale-$15 + 10¢/sh
rec comm Cl A
div deposit

Reynolds American Inc (N-RAI) (div/yr: $ 3.80) consumer prod-tobacco products
P O Box 2990
Winston-Salem, NC 27102-2990
877-679-5701 admr
336-728-8888 fax #
336-741-2000 InvRe
e-mail: shareholderservices@reynoldsamerica
www.reynoldsamerican.com
NOTE: *cash pymt fees: 3¢/sh + $2 EFT/$5 check /frmly: RJ Reynolds Holdings

Buy fees: 5%to$3 + 3¢/sh-div*
$50-250,000/yr EFT*(52)
DIP: $500 + $10
partial DR option
sfkg-free/p. sale-$15 + 10¢/sh
gifting free

RioCan Real Estate Investment Trust (T-REI-UN) (div/yr: $0.00) REIT-CDN
P O Box 378 Ste 700, 130 King St W
Toronto, ONT M5X 1E2, Canada
800-387-0825 admr
416-866-3022 InvRe
e-mail: inquiries@riocan.com
www.riocan.com

Buy fees: no cost
3.1% bonus units
$250-25,000/yr EFT(12)
cash-only option
common

Roanoke Electric Steel Corp (NDQ-RESC) (div/yr: $ 0.20) mfg-steel products
P O Box 13948
Roanoke, VA 24038-3948
800-633-4239 admr
540-342-9437 fax #
540-342-1831 CorpSecy
e-mail: info@roanokesteel.com
www.roanokesteel.com

Buy fees: no svc chg
no cash plan
sfkg-avail/p. sale-avail
common

Robbins & Myers Inc (N-RBN) (div/yr: $ 0.22) [S&P ranking: B] mfg-fluids mgmt products
1400 Kettering Tower
Dayton, OH 45423
937-222-3335 InvRe
937-225-3355 fax #
800-622-6757 admr
www.robbinsmyers.com

Buy fees: no cost
$50-5,000/qtr(12)
DIP: $500
part. DR/cash-only
sfkg-free/p. sale-5% +bkg fee
rec comm
div deposit

Rockwell Automation Inc (N-ROK) (div/yr: $ 0.90) [S&P ranking: B +] svc-indus automation power/control/info solutions
c/o Mellon Investor Services LLC
P O Box 3338
South Hackensack, NJ 07606-1938
414-212-5300 ShrRe
414-212-5212 fax #
800-204-7800 admr
www.rockwellautomation.com
NOTE: $5 fee + 10¢/sh-cash pymt/EFT of cash pymts

$100-100,000/yr*(52)
DIP: $1,000 + $5
partial DR option
sfkg-free/p. sale-$15 + 12¢/sh
rec common
div deposit

Rockwell Collins Inc (N-COL) (div/yr: $ 0.48) mfg-aviation electronic/comm systems
400 Collins Rd NE   Buy fees: no cost-div*
Cedar Rapids, IA 52498 $100-100,000/yr EFT(52)
✂ 888-253-4522 admr   DIP: $1,000 + $5 + 5¢/sh
319-295-1000 InvRe   part. DR/cash-only
★ e-mail: investorrelations@rockwellcollins.c   sfkg-free/p. sale-$15 + 12¢/sh
www.rockwellcollins.com   rec common
                                     div deposit/gifting avail
NOTE: *cash pymt fees: 5¢/sh + $2.50 EFT/$5 check

Rohm and Haas Co (N-ROH) (div/yr: $ 1) [S&P ranking: A] mfg-specialty chemicals
✂ 100 Independence Mall West   Buy fees: no cost
Philadelphia, PA 19106-2399 $50-100,000/yr(12)
800-633-4236 admr   partial DR option
215-592-3227 fax #   sfkg-free/p. sale-$15 + 12¢/sh
215-592-3495 InvRe   rec common
www.rohmhaas.com

Rollins Inc (N-ROL) (div/yr: $ 0.20) [S&P ranking: B +] svcs-pest control
✂ c/o SunTrust Bank-Atlanta   Buy fees: no cost
P O Box 4625   no cash plan
Atlanta, GA 30302   common 50 sh min
404-588-7822 admr
404-888-2851 fax #
404-888-2218 ShRel
e-mail: investorrelations@rollinscorp.com
www.rollinscorp.com

Ruddick Corp (N-RDK) (div/yr: $ 0.44) [S&P ranking: A-] food-supermarkets/mfg-thread & yarn
301 S Tyron St, Ste 1800   Buy fees: no cost
✂ Charlotte, NC 28202 $20-3,000/mo(12)
800-829-8432 admr   sfkg-free/p. sale-avail
704-372-5404 CorpSecy   common
www.ruddickcorp.com   div deposit

Russell Corp (N-RML) (div/yr: $ 0.16) [S&P ranking: B-] consumer prod-apparel
✂ 3330 Cumberland Blvd, Ste 800   Buy fees: no cost
Atlanta, GA 30339 $10-2,000/month(12)
800-568-3476 admr   rec common/US residents
678-742-8514 fax #
678-742-8181 InvRe
www.russellcorp.com

Ryder System Inc (N-R) (div/yr: $ 0.64) [S&P ranking: B] trans-services/leasing
✂ 3600 NW 82nd Ave   Buy fees: no cost
Miami, FL 33166-6623 $25-60,000/yr(12)
781-575-3170 admr   part. DR/cash-only
305-500-3130 fax #   sfkg-free/p. sale-5%-$1-10
305-500-4053 InvRe   rec common
e-mail: ryderforinvestor@ryder.com
www.ryder.com

Ryerson Tull Inc (N-RT) (div/yr: $ 0.20) [S&P ranking: B-] metals-processor/distr
c/o Bank of New York   Buy fees: no cost
✂ P O Box 11258 Church St Sta $25-120,000/yr EFT(52)
New York, NY 10286   DIP: $500 + $10
★ 800-524-4458 admr   sfkg-free/p. sale-$10 + 10¢/sh
773-788-4205 fax #   div deposit/gifting avail
773-788-3720 InvRe
www.ryersontull.com

S

SBC Communications Inc (N-SBC) (div/yr: $ 1.29) [S&P ranking: B+] telecommunications
c/o EquiServe Trust Co NA
P O Box 2508
Jersey City, NJ 07303-2508
 800-351-7221 admr
 210-351-2071 fax #
 210-351-2052 ShrSv
www.sbc.com
Buy fees: 5%to$2+fee-div*
$50-120,000/yr EFT(52)
DIP: $500 + $10 + bkg fee
part. DR/cash-only
sfkg-free/p. sale-$10 + bkg
rec comm-1 sh min
★
NOTE: *cash pymt ($2.50 check/$1 EFT) + bkg fee/IRA: $500 min ($35 ann, $50 term fees)

SCANA Corp (N-SCG) (div/yr: $ 1.56) [S&P ranking: B] utility-elec/gas
1426 Main St attn: Shareholder Svs
Columbia, SC 29218-0001
 800-763-5891 ShSvc
 803-217-7389 fax #
 803-217-7817 ShSvc
e-mail: shareholder@scana.com
www.scana.com
Buy fees: no svc chg-6¢/sh
$25-100,000/yr(24)
DIP: $250
part. DR/cash-only
sfkg-free*/p. sale-bkg fee
rec comm/pref+/U S resident
div deposit/gifting free
★
NOTE: *part sale & sfkg for common shs only / + preferred of South Carolina Elec&Gas

SEMCO Energy Inc (N-SEN) (div/yr: $0.00) [S&P ranking: B] utility-holding co-natural gas opns
27469 13-Mile Rd #300
Farmington Hills, MI 48334
 800-622-6757 admr
 248-702-6303 fax #
 800-225-7647 ShrSv
e-mail: shareholder.svcs@semcoenergy.com
www.semcoenergy.com
NOTE: co does not pay div
Buy fees: no cost
$25-100,000/yr EFT(52)
DIP: $250 + $10 + 5¢/sh
part. DR/cash-only
sfkg-free/p. sale-$10+ 5¢/sh
rec common
div deposit/gifting avail
✂
★

SIFCO Industries Inc (A-SIF) (div/yr: $ 0.05) mfg/repair-aircraft parts
970 E 64th St
Cleveland, OH 44103-1694
 216-432-6263 ShRel
 216-432-6281 fax #
 216-575-2532 admr
e-mail: jfrancis@sifco.com
www.sifco.com
NOTE: co does not pay div
Buy fees: no cost
$20-3,000/qtr(12)
sfkg-free
rec common
✂

SUPERVALU INC (N-SVU) (div/yr: $ 0.61) [S&P ranking: A-] retail-food wholesaler
c/o Wells Fargo Bank NA
P O Box 738
South St Paul, MN 55075-0738
 952-828-4963 ShrSv
 952-828-4403 fax #
 877-536-3555 admr
www.supervalu.com
Buy fees: no cost
$10/mo-3,000/qtr(12)
sfkg-free
common
✂

Sanderson Farms Inc (NDQ-SAFM) (div/yr: $ 0.40) [S&P ranking: B+] food-poultry processing
P O Box 988
Laurel, MS 39441-0988
 888-810-7452 admr
 601-426-1461 fax #
 601-649-4030 InvRe
e-mail: info@sandersonfarms.com
www.sandersonfarms.com
NOTE: *cash pymt fees: 12¢/sh + $5
Buy fees: 50¢ to $10-div*
$50-10,000/mo EFT(52)
DIP: $500 +$5 + 12¢/sh
partial DR option
sfkg-free/p. sale-$15 + 12¢/sh
rec comm-10 shs min/no residency restrict.
gifting free
★

Sandy Spring Bancorp Inc (NDQ-SASR) (div/yr: $ 0.80) [S&P ranking: A] banks/banking
17801 Georgia Ave
Olney, MD 20832
  301-774-6400 CorpSecy
★ 301-774-8434 fax #
  800-278-4353 admr
  e-mail: ir@ssnb.com
  www.ssnb.com
NOTE: *$2.50 + 10¢/sh for each cash purchase
Buy fees: 2%to$2.50+10¢/sh
$25-10,000/day*(250)
DIP: $250 + $2.50+10¢/sh
part. DR/cash-only
sfkg-$7.50/p. sale-$15+10¢/sh
common
div deposit

Sara Lee Corp (N-SLE) (div/yr: $ 0.79) [S&P ranking: A-] food-processed/hosiery
3 First National Plaza
Chicago, IL 60602-4260
★ 888-422-9881 ShrSv
  312-345-5782 fax #
  800-727-2533 ShrSv
  e-mail: shareholders@saralee.com
  www.saralee.com
NOTE: *cash purchase fee-$3 for check/$1.50 EFT
Buy fees: 4¢/sh-div*
$100-120,000/yr EFT(8)
DIP: $500 + $13
sfkg-free/p. sale-4¢/sh
rec comm-min 10 shs/no residency restrict.
div deposit/gifting free

Saul Centers Inc (N-BFS) (div/yr: $ 1.56) REIT-shopping centers
✄ 7501 Wisconsin Ave, Ste 1500
Bethesda, MD 20814-6522
% 800-509-5586 admr
  301-986-6113 fax #
  301-986-6333 InvRe
  e-mail: katherine.cruz@bfsaulco.com
  www.saulcenters.com
Buy fees: no cost
3% disc-div/cash
no cash plan
partial DR option
sfkg-free/p. sale-$2.50+14¢/sh
comm/lp units

Schawk Inc (N-SGK) (div/yr: $ 0.13) [S&P ranking: B] svcs-photo printing svcs
1695 River Rd
✄ Des Plaines, IL 60018
  800-446-2617 admr
  847-827-9494 InvRe
  e-mail: info@schawk.com
  www.schawk.com/
Buy fees: no cost
$50-100,000/yr EFT(52)
sfkg-free/p. sale-$10
no residency restrict.
gifting free

Schering-Plough Corp (N-SGP) (div/yr: $ 0.22) [S&P ranking: A-] drug/pharmaceuticals
2000 Galloping Hill Rd
✄ Kenilworth, NJ 70033
  908-298-7355 ShrRe
  973-822-7303 fax #
  800-432-0140 admr
  www.sch-plough.com
Buy fees: no cost
$25-36,000/yr(24)
part. DR/cash-only
sfkg-free/p. sale-avail
rec common/no residency restrict.
div deposit

Schnitzer Steel Industries Inc (NDQ-SCHN) (div/yr: $ 0.07) [S&P ranking: B] mfg-recycle met-
✄ als & mfg finished steel products
3200 N W Yeon Ave
Portland, OR 97296-0047
  800-524-4458
★ 503-321-2648 fax #
  503-224-9900 InvRe
  www.schnitzersteel.com
Buy fees: no cost
$50-100,000/yr EFT(52)
DIP: $500
sfkg-free/p. sale-$5+10¢/sh
gifting free

Schwab (Charles) Corp (N-SCH) (div/yr: $ 0.09) [S&P ranking: B +] fin svcs-discount brokerage
101 Montgomery St   Buy fees: no cost
San Francisco, CA 94104 $10-5,000/mo EFT(12)   ✂
800-468-9716 admr   part. DR/cash-only
415-636-9820 fax #   sfkg-free/p. sale-$10 + 5¢/sh
415-636-9869 InvRe   rec common
e-mail: SCHstock@aol.com
www.schwab.com

Scientific-Atlanta Inc (N-SFA) (div/yr: $ 0.04) [S&P ranking: A-] mfg-broadband comm
equip/TV set-top boxes
5030 Sugarloaf Pkwy   Buy fees: no cost
Lawrenceville, GA 30044 $25-40,000/yr(12)   ✂
770-236-5000 InvRe   cash-only option
770-236-4775 fax #   sfkg-avail
800-524-4458 admr   common
e-mail: investor@sciatl.com
www.scientificatlanta.com

Scripps (The E W) Co (N-SSP) (div/yr: $ 0.44) [S&P ranking: A-] publishing-newspapers/broad-
cast TV/category TV
P O Box 5380   Buy fees: no cost
Cincinnati, OH 45201 $100-2,500/qtr EFT(4)   ✂
800-829-8432 admr   partial DR option
513-977-3811 fax #   p. sale-avail
513-977-3835 co #   rec comm-Cl A
e-mail: ir@scripps.com
www.scripps.com

Selective Insurance Group (NDQ-SIGI) (div/yr: $ 0.76) [S&P ranking: B +] insurance
40 Wantage Ave   Buy fees: no cost   ✂
Branchville, NJ 07890-0001 $100-1,000/qtr(4)
866-877-6851 admr   partial DR option
973-948-0282 fax #   rec common/no residency restrict.
973-948-1310 CorpSecy   div deposit
www.selective.com

Sempra Energy (N-SRE) (div/yr: $ 1.16) [S&P ranking: B] utility-gas/elec
101 Ash St   Buy fees: no cost
San Diego, CA 92101-3017 $25-150,000/yr EFT(52)
877-773-6772 admr   DIP: $500 + $15 or $50/mo*   ✂
619-696-2374 fax #   part. DR/cash-only   ★
619-696-2143 ShSvc   sfkg-free/p. sale-$10 + 3¢/sh
e-mail: ncarusa@sempra.com   rec common/no residency restrict.
www.sempra.com   div deposit/gifting free
NOTE: *EFT for 10 months/50cents for EFT transactions/line of credit-$35 + int/free cost
basis data for 2 previous yrs, $5/yr past yrs to$25

Sensient Technologies Corp (N-SXT) (div/yr: $ 0.60) [S&P ranking: A-] mfg-distr/flavors (food)
& colors (ink)
777 E Wisconsin Ave Ste 1100   Buy fees: no cost   ✂
Milwaukee, WI 53202-5304 $25-1,500/month(12)
414-271-6755 Admin   partial DR option
414-347-3785 fax #   sfkg-free/p. sale-avail
800-468-9716 admr   rec common/no residency restrict.
www.sensient-tech.com.com
NOTE: if half of plan shares sold, no cash pymt accepted for 2 months afterwards/frmly:
Universal Foods

ServiceMaster Co (N-SVM) (div/yr: $ 0.44) [S&P ranking: A] svcs-cleaning svcs/pest control/lawn care
3250 Lacey Rd Ste 600
Downers Grove, IL 60515
 800-858-0840 admr
 630-663-2001 fax #
 630-663-2000 CorpSecy
 www.svm.com

Buy fees: no cost
$25-5,000/mo EFT(12)
partial DR option
sfkg-free
rec common
div deposit

Sherwin Williams Co (The) (N-SHW) (div/yr: $ 0.82) [S&P ranking: A] mfg-paint
PO Box 6027 - Investor Rels #133
Cleveland, OH 44101-1027
 866-537-8703 admr
 216-566-3670 fax #
 216-566-2140 InvRe
 www.sherwin-williams.com

Buy fees: no cost
$10-2,000/month(12)
sfkg-free/p. sale-avail
rec comm/deben

NOTE: blanket req for whole share certificates avail

Shurgard Storage Centers Inc (N-SHU) (div/yr: $ 2.20) [S&P ranking: B] REIT-self-storage warehouses
P O box 900933
Seattle, WA 98109
 800-937-5449 adrm
 800-582-0238 InvRe
 e-mail: investorrelations@shurgard.com

Buy fees: no cost
2% disc-div
no cash plan
partial DR option
p. sale-$15 + bkg fee

Sierra Pacific Resources (N-SRP) (div/yr: $0.00) [S&P ranking: C] utility-elec/gas/water
P O Box 30150
Reno, NV 89520-3150
 800-662-7575 ShRel
 775-834-3614 fax #
 800-468-9716 admr
 www.sierrapacific.com

Buy fees: no cost-orig iss
$50-100,000/yr(12)
DIP: $250
partial DR option
sfkg-free/p. sale-6¢/sh
rec common/no residency restrict.

NOTE: co omitted div 2002

Simon Property Group (N-SPG) (div/yr: $ 2.80) [S&P ranking: B +] REIT-regional malls
P O Box 7033
Indianapolis, IN 46207
 800-454-9768 InvRe
 317-685-7270 fax #
 317-685-7330 InvRe
 www.simon.com

Buy fees: no cost
no cash plan
common
div deposit

Skillsoft plc (NDQ-SKIL) (div/yr: $0.00) svcs-elearning software-IRELAND
107 Northeastern Blvd
Nashua, NH 03062-1916
 800-345-1612 admr
 603-324-3000 US IR
 e-mail: information@skillsoft.com
 www.skillsoft.com

Buy fees: 5% to $5 + 10¢/sh
$50-250,000/yr EFT(52)
DIP: $200 + $10 + 10¢/sh
part. DR/cash-only
sfkg-$5/p. sale-$5 + 10¢/sh
ADR
gifting $5

NOTE: *$5 + 10¢/sh cash pymt

Sky Financial Group (NDQ-SKYF) (div/yr: $ 0.88) banks/banking
10 E Main St
Salinville, OH 43945
 888-683-4901 admr
 419-327-6300 InvRe
 e-mail: shareholder@skyfi.com
 www.skyfi.com

Buy fees: no cost-div*
$50-10,000/mo*EFT(52)
DIP: $500 + $7.50
part. DR/cash-only
sfkg-free/p. sale-$10 + 5¢/sh
gifting free

NOTE: *cash pymt fees: 5¢/sh+ $1 EFT/$2 check

Smith (A O) Corp (N-AOS) (div/yr: $ 0.64) [S&P ranking: B-] mfg-electric mtors & water heaters
11270 West Park Place
Milwaukee, WI 53224-3690
414-359-4400 InvRe
414-359-4198 fax #
800-637-7549 admr
e-mail: cwatson@aosmith.com
www.aosmith.com
Buy fees: no cost
to $5,000/qtr(4 +)
rec comm & Cl A*
NOTE: + if enough cash to buy 100-sh lots/*div buys comm or A respectively

Smucker (J M) Co (N-SJM) (div/yr: $ 1.08) [S&P ranking: A-] food-jam/jellies/beverage/toppings
One Strawberry Lane
Orrville, OH 44667-0280
800-456-1169 InvRe
330-684-3026 fax #
330-684-3668 InvRe
e-mail: investorrelations@jmsmucker.com
www.smuckers.com
Buy fees: no cost-div*
$25-50,000/yr EFT*(52)
DIP: $250 + $10 + 10¢/sh
part. DR/cash-only
sfkg-free/p. sale-$10 + 10¢/sh
record comm/no residency restrict.
gifting free
NOTE: *cash pymt fees: $5 + 10¢/sh-check; $1.50 + 10¢/sh EFT

Snap-on Inc (N-SNA) (div/yr: $ 1.10) [S&P ranking: B] mfg-hand tools, auto/indus maintenance
c/o EquiServe Trust Co NA
P O Box 2598
Jersey City, NJ 07303-2598
800-446-2617 admr
262-656-5717 fax #
262-656-5200 CorpSecy
www.snapon.com
Buy fees: no cost
$100-150,000/yr**(52)
DIP: $500 ($100/mo EFT*)
part. DR/cash-only
sfkg-free/p. sale-$15 + 15¢/sh
rec common
gifting avail
NOTE: *for 5 months/**$2 per EFT pymt

Sonoco Products Co (N-SON) (div/yr: $ 0.92) [S&P ranking: B +] mfg-industrial & consumer packaging
P O Box 160/One North Second St
Hartsville, SC 29551-0160
800-633-4236 admr
843-383-7066 fax #
843-383-3392 AsstTreas
e-mail: george.hartley@sonoco.com
www.sonoco.com
Buy fees: 10¢/sh + no svc ch
$10*-120,000/yr EFT(12)
DIP: $250 + $13 + 10¢/sh*
part. DR/cash-only
sfkg-free/p. sale-10¢/sh
rec common/no residency restrict.
div deposit/gifting avail
NOTE: *or $50/mo EFT for 5 months

South Financial Group Inc (The) (NDQ-TSFG) (div/yr: $ 0.64) [S&P ranking: B +] banking
PO Box 1029
Greenville, SC 29602
800-368-5948 admr
864-239-2280 fax #
864-239-6459 ShRel
e-mail: angie.bain@thesouthgroup.com
www.thesouthgroup.com
Buy fees: no cost
5% disc-div
$25-10,000/mo(12)
partial DR option
sfkg-free/p. sale-avail
common
div deposit/gifting avail

South Jersey Industries Inc (N-SJI) (div/yr: $ 1.70) [S&P ranking: B +] utility-gas
One S Jersey Plaza, Route 54
Folsom, NJ 08037
609-561-9000 co #
609-561-7130 fax #
888-SJI-3100 admr
e-mail: investorrelations@sjindustries.com
www.sjindustries.com
Buy fees: no cost
2% disc-orig/tre shs
$25-100,000/yr(12)
DIP: $100
part. DR/cash-only
rec common/no residency restrict.
NOTE: *all accts of same entity combined for maximum cash limit

S

Southern Co (N-SO) (div/yr: $ 1.49) [S&P ranking: A-] utility-electric
P O Box 54250 - Stockholder Svcs
Atlanta, GA 30308-0250
800-554-7626 admr
404-506-0945 fax #
404-506-0990 ShSvc
e-mail: stockholders@southerncompany.com
www.southernco.com

Buy fees: no cost
$25-300,000/yr EFT(24)
DIP: $250 + $10
part. DR/cash-only
sfkg-free/p. sale-avail
rec common/no residency restrict.
div deposit/gifting avail

Southern Union Co (N-SUG) (div/yr: $0.00) [S&P ranking: B] energy-natural gas distribution & transmission
One PEI Center, 2nd Floor
Wilkes Barre, PA 18711-0601
800-793-8938 admr
570-820-2401 fax #
570-829-8662 InvRe
www.southernunionco.com
NOTE: co does not pay div

$50-100,000/yr EFT(24)
DIP: $250
sfkg-free/p. sale-$10 + 15¢/sh
common
gifting avail

Southwest Gas Corp (N-SWX) (div/yr: $ 0.82) [S&P ranking: B +] utility-gas
PO Box 98511
Las Vegas, NV 89193-8511
800-331-1119 ShSvc
702-871-9942 fax #
702-876-7280 ShSvc
www.swgas.com

Buy fees: no cost
$25-100,000/yr EFT(24)
DIP: AZ, CA & NV res-$100
sfkg-free/p. sale-avail
rec common-100 shs**/no residency re-strict.

NOTE: *partial reinvestment avail for owner of 250 shs/partial sales of shs avail, must have 100 shs in plan

Southwest Georgia Financial Corp (A-SGB) (div/yr: $ 0.52) [S&P ranking: B +] banks/banking
201 1st St SE
Moultrie, GA 31768-4747
800-278-4353 admr
229-890-2211 fax #
229-985-1120 Treas
www.sgfc.com

Buy fees: no cost
$5-5,000/month(12)
partial DR option
sfkg-free
common

Southwest Water Co (NDQ-SWWC) (div/yr: $ 0.20) [S&P ranking: B +] utility-water
624 S Grand Ave Ste 2900
Los Angeles, CA 90017-3872
800-356-2017 admr
213-929-1800 Contr
e-mail: lcline@southwestwater.com
www.southwestwater.com

Buy fees: no cost
5% disc-div
$25-3,000/qtr(4)
part. DR/cash-only
sfkg-free
rec common

Southwestern Energy Co (N-SWN) (div/yr: $0.00) [S&P ranking: B] energy-natural gas
c/o EquiServe
P O Box 2506
Jersey City, NJ 07303-2506
800-446-2617 admr
479-521-1147 fax #
251-618-4700 ShSvc
www.swn.com

Buy fees: $2-5 + 3¢/sh
$25-120,000/yr EFT(52)
DIP: $250 + $10 + 3¢/sh
cash-only option
sfkg-free/p. sale-$10 + 12¢/sh
rec common/no residency restrict.
gifting free

NOTE: co does not pay div/line of credit on plan shs/Sh Svcs located at PO Box 13408, Fayetteville AR 72702

Sovereign Bancorp Inc (N-SOV) (div/yr: $ 0.16) [S&P ranking: B +] banks/banking
1130 Berkshire Blvd
Wyomissing, PA 19610
800-685-4254 admr
215-557-4630 InvRe
e-mail: investor@sovereignbank.com
www.sovereignbank.com
NOTE: *cash pymt fees: $2-3.50EFT/$5 check

Buy fees: no cost-div*
$25-10,000/mo EFT(12)
DIP: $250 + $15
part. DR/cash-only
sfkg-free/p. sale-$15 + 12¢/sh
gifting free

✂ ★

Spartech Corp (N-SEH) (div/yr: $ 0.48) [S&P ranking: A-] mfg-thermoplastics
120 S Central Ste 1700
Clayton, MO 63105-1705
314-721-4242 InvRe
314-721-1447 fax #
888-213-0965 admr
e-mail: investorrelations@spartech.com
www.spartech.com

Buy fees: no cost
$250-10,000/month(12)
sfkg-free/p. sale-avail
common

✂

Sprint Corp (N-FON) (div/yr: $ 0.50) [S&P ranking: B] telecommunications
6200 Sprint Parkway
Overland Park, KS 66251
800-259-3755 #4
913-523-9692 fax #
913-794-1421 ShRel
e-mail: shareholder.sprintcom@mail.sprint.com
www.sprint.com

Buy fees: 2% to $2.50 + 10¢/sh
$25-5,000/qtr(12)
part. DR/cash-only
sfkg-$7.50/p. sale-$10 + 10¢/sh
rec common
gifting avail

St Paul Travelers Cos Inc (N-STA) (div/yr: $ 0.88) insurance
385 Washington St
St Paul, MN 55102-1396
651-310-7911 x7788
651-310-3386 fax #
888-326-5102 admr
www.stpaul.com

Buy fees: no cost
$10-60,000/yr EFT(12)
partial DR option
sfkg-free/p. sale-avail
comm - 1 sh min

✂

Standard Commercial Corp (N-STW) (div/yr: $ 0.35) [S&P ranking: B] misc-processor/whole-
saler-tobacco & wool
P O Box 450
Wilson, NC 27894-0450
252-237-1106 admr
252-237-0018 fax #
252-291-5507 InvRe
e-mail: kmerrick@sccgroup.com
www.sccgroup.com

Buy fees: no cost
$25-3,000/mo(12)
part. DR/cash-only
sfkg-free/p. sale-avail
rec common/no residency restrict.
div deposit

✂

Standard Register Co (N-SR) (div/yr: $ 0.92) [S&P ranking: B-] mfg-business forms & data sys-
tems equip
P O Box 1167
Dayton, OH 45401-1167
800-633-4236 admr
937-221-3431 fax #
937-221-1540 CorpSecy
www.standardregister.com

Buy fees: no cost
$25-60,000/yr EFT(12)
part. DR/cash-only
sfkg-free/p. sale-avail
common
div deposit

✂

Stanley Works (The) (N-SWK) (div/yr: $ 1.12) [S&P ranking: B +] consumer prod-hand tools &
builders prod
1000 Stanley Dr
New Britain, CT 06053
860-409-1208 Treas
860-827-3895 fax #
800-543-6757 admr
e-mail: cperry@stanleyworks.com
www.StanleyWorks.com

Buy fees: $2 fee for div & EFT cash pymts,
$5 cash pymts by check + 5 ¢/sh*
$100-150,000/yr EFT(52)
DIP: $250 +$10
part. DR/cash-only
sfkg-free/p. sale-$15 + 12¢/sh
rec comm-20 sh min/no residency restrict.

★

Staples Inc (NDQ-SPLS) (div/yr: $ 0.17) [S&P ranking: B +] retail-office supplies
500 Staples Dr   Buy fees: 5%to$3 + 6¢/sh*
Framingham, MA 01702 $25-250,000/yr*EFT(52)
  888-875-9002 admr   DIP: $250 + $15 + 6¢/sh
  508-253-8989 fax #   part. DR/cash-only
★ 508-253-5000 InvRe   sfkg-free/p. sale-$15 + 12¢/sh
  e-mail: investor@staples.com   div deposit/gifting free
  www.staples.com
NOTE: *cash pymt fees: 6¢/sh + $2 EFT/$5 check

State Bancorp Inc (A-STB) (div/yr: $ 0.60) [S&P ranking: A] banks/banking
✂ 2 Jericho Plaza FL2-Winga   Buy fees: no cost
  Jericho, NY 11753   5% disc-orig issue
% 800-468-9716 admr $100-10,000/qtr(4)
  516-495-5110 fax #   partial DR option
  516-465-2251 InvRe   rec common/U S residents
  www.statebankofli.com

State Street Corp (N-STT) (div/yr: $ 0.68) [S&P ranking: A] fin svcs
P O Box 351, Finance M-7 $100-25,000/mo EFT(12)
Boston, MA 02101   sfkg-free/p. sale-$10 + bkg fe
  617-664-3477 InvRe   common-10 shs min
  617-664-8300 fax #   gifting avail
  800-426-5523 admr
  e-mail: ir@statestreet.com
  www.statestreet.com
NOTE: *record shrholders only elig for cash plan

Sterling Bancorp (N-STL) (div/yr: $ 0.76) [S&P ranking: A +] banks/banking
650 Fifth Ave, 4th Floor   Buy fees: 5% to$3-div*
New York, NY 10019-6108 $50-120,000/yr*(52)
★ 800-826-8045 admr   DIP: $500 + $15 + 6¢/sh
  212-757-8060 CorpSecy   partial DR option
  www.sterlingbancorp.com   sfkg-free/p. sale-$15 + 12¢/sh
                                      common/no residency restrict.
                                      div deposit/gifting free
NOTE: *$5 fee for cash pymts (EFT fee $3.50 single/$2 monthly)

Stride Rite Corp (N-SRR) (div/yr: $ 0.24) [S&P ranking: B +] consumer prod-shoe mfg
PO Box 9191 $10-1,000/month(8)
Lexington, MA 02420-9191   sfkg-free
  617-824-6028 Treas   rec common/no residency restrict.
  617-824-6969 fax #
  781-575-3170 admr
  e-mail: corpcomm@striderite.com
  www.strideritecorp.com

Suffolk Bancorp (NDQ-SUBK) (div/yr: $ 0.76) [S&P ranking: A +] banking
P O Box 9000 - 4 West 2nd St   Buy fees: no cost
✂ Riverhead, NY 11901-9000   3% disc-div/cash*
  631-727-5667 $300-5,000/qtr(4)
% 800-937-5449 admr   part. DR/cash-only
  e-mail: suffolkbancorp@scnb.com   sfkg-free
  www.scnb.com   common
                                      div deposit
NOTE: *discount only on orig issue shares

Sun Communities Inc (N-SUI) (div/yr: $ 2.52) [S&P ranking: B +] REIT-own&manage communities for manufactured homes

27777 Franklin Rd Ste 200	Buy fees: no cost
Southfield, MI 48034-8205	3% disc-div
800-317-4445 admr	no cash plan
248-208-2641 fax #	rec common
248-208-2500 InvRe	
e-mail: cpeterse@suncommunities.com	
www.suncommunities.com	

✄   %

SunTrust Banks Inc (N-STI) (div/yr: $ 2.20) [S&P ranking: A +] banking

P O Box 4625	Buy fees: no cost
Atlanta, GA 30302-4625	$10/mo-60,000/yr(12)
800-568-3476 admr	partial DR option
404-658-4782 fax #	sfkg-free
404-588-7815 co #	common/no residency restrict.
www.SunTrust.com	

✄

Sunoco Inc (N-SUN) (div/yr: $ 1.60) [S&P ranking: A +] energy-petroleum

1801 Market St	Buy fees: no cost-div
Philadelphia, PA 19103-1699	$50-250,000/qtr EFT(52)
215-977-6082 ShrSv	DIP: $250 + $10 + 3¢/sh
215-977-6733 fax #	partial DR option
800-888-8494 admr	sfkg-free/p. sale-$15 + 12¢/sh
e-mail: egerner@sunocoinc.com	rec common/no residency restrict.
www.Sunocolnc.com	

✄   ★

NOTE: *cash pymt fees: EFT $2 + 3¢/sh, $5 + 3¢/sh check

Superior Industries International Inc (N-SUP) (div/yr: $ 0.62) [S&P ranking: B +] mfg-custom auto accessories

7800 Woodley Ave	Buy fees: no cost
Van Nuys, CA 91406-1788	$50-5,000/qtr(4)
800-866-1340 admr	partial DR option
818-781*4973 InvRe	sfkg-free/p. sale-avail
e-mail: info@superiorindustries.com	rec common
www.superiorindustries.com	

✄

Susquehanna Bancshares Inc (NDQ-SUSQ) (div/yr: $ 0.92) [S&P ranking: A-] banking

c/o Bank of New York	Buy fees: no cost-div*
P O Box 11258 Church St Sta	$50-120,000/yr*EFT(52)
New York, NY 10286-1258	DIP: $250 + $7.50 + 10¢/sh
866-828-8176 admr	partial DR option
717-625-0331 fax #	sfkg-free/p. sale-$10 + 10¢/sh
717-625-6305 ShRel	common
e-mail: ir@susquehanna.net	gifting free
www.susquehanna.net	

✄   ★

NOTE: *$5 + 10¢/sh on cash purchases

Synovus Financial Corp (N-SNV) (div/yr: $ 0.73) [S&P ranking: A +] banking

P O Box 120	Buy fees: no cost-div
Columbus, GA 31902-0120	$50-250,000/yr EFT(52)
800-503-8903 CorpSecy	DIP: $235 + $15 fee
706-644-8065 fax #	sfkg-free/p. sale-$15 + 12¢/sh
706-649-5220 InvRe	rec comm-10 shs min
e-mail: snvir@synovus.com	div deposit/gifting avail
www.synovus.com	

✄   ★

Sysco Corp (N-SYY) (div/yr: $ 0.60) [S&P ranking: A+] food distr/marketer of food service
products
✂ 1390 Enclave Parkway   Buy fees: no cost-div
  Houston, TX 77077-2099 $100-10,000/mo*EFT(12)
  800-337-9726 InvRe   sfkg-free/p. sale-$10 + 15¢/sh
  281-584-2721 fax #   rec common-1 sh min
  800-730-4001 admr   div deposit
  www.sysco.com
  NOTE: *$5 + 5¢/sh for cash purchases

T

3M (see M section)

TCF Financial Corp (N-TCB) (div/yr: $ 1.85) [S&P ranking: A] banking
✂ 200 Lake St East   Buy fees: no cost-div
  Wayzata, MN 55391-1693 $25-25,000/qtr*(12)
  800-730-4001 admr   partial DR option
  952-745-2775 fax #   sfkg-free/p. sale-$15
  952-745-2755 CpCom   rec comm 1 sh min
  www.tcfexpress.com
  NOTE: *$1 fee for cash purchases

TECO Energy Inc (N-TE) (div/yr: $ 0.76) [S&P ranking: B-] utility-holding co/electric
  P O Box 111   Buy fees: no svc chg
  Tampa, FL 33601-0111 $25-100,000/yr(12)
  800-650-9222 admr   part. DR/cash-only
  813-228-1670 fax #   sfkg-free
  800-810-2032 ShSvc   rec common
  www.tecoenergy.com   div deposit/gifting avail

TXU Corp (N-TXU) (div/yr: $ 2.25) [S&P ranking: B] utility/holding co-electric/nat gas/tele-
comm
  P O Box 130059   Buy fees: no cost
  Dallas, TX 75313-0059 $25-250,000/yr EFT(48)
✂ 800-828-0812 admr   DIP: $500 + $10**
  214-812-7077 fax #   part. DR/cash-only
★ 214-812-8100 ShSvc   sfkg-free/p. sale-$10 + bkg fee
  e-mail: shareholder@txu.com   rec comm/no residency restrict.
  www.txucorp.com   div deposit/gifting free*
  NOTE: *trans min 10shs to start another acct/**DIP available only to US residents

Target Corp (N-TGT) (div/yr: $ 0.32) [S&P ranking: A+] retail-dept/disc/spec stores
✂ c/o Mellon Investor Services   Buy fees: no cost-99shs*
  P O Box 3338 $50-100,000/yr**(52)
★ South Hackensack, NJ 07606-1938   DIP: $500 + $10 +3¢/sh
  800-794-9871 InvRe   part. DR/cash-only
  612-370-6736 InvRe   sfkg-free/p. sale-$10 + 12¢/sh
  www.target.com   rec common/no residency restrict.
                                         div deposit/gifting free
  NOTE: *or less, 100+ shs 5% +3¢/sh/**cash pymts: 3¢/sh + $5 by check; EFT $2
  monthly, $3.50 singly/** or $50/mo for 10 mos/TDD: 201-222-4955

Taubman Centers Inc (N-TCO) (div/yr: $ 1.14) [S&P ranking: B-] REIT-regional malls
  P O Box 200   Buy fees: no svc fee-div
  Bloomfield Hills, MI 48303-0200 $25-25,000/mo EFT(52)
  248-258-7367 InvRe   DIP: $250 + $5 + 12¢/sh
★ 248-258-7596 fax #   partial DR option
  888-877-2889 admr   sfkg-free/p. sale-$15 + 12¢/sh
  www.taubman.com   common
                                         gifting free

Tektronix Inc (N-TEK) (div/yr: $ 0.24) [S&P ranking: B-] mfg-electronic products
14200 SW Karl Braun Dr
Beaverton, OR 97077
800-411-7025 admr
503-685-3408 fax #
503-627-7111 InvRe

Buy fees: 5%to$10+12¢/sh*
$100-10,000/mo(12)
DIP: $500 + $5 + 12¢/sh
partial DR option
sfkg-free/p. sale-$15+12¢/sh
comm-20 shs min
gifting free

★

NOTE: *div &$5+12¢/sh-cash pymt

Telephone & Data Systems Inc (A-TDS) (div/yr: $ 0.70) [S&P ranking: B] telecommunications
30 N LaSalle St, 40th Flr
Chicago, IL 60602-2587
877-337-1575 admr
312-630-1908 fax #
312-630-1900 InvRe
e-mail: tdsinfo@teldta.com
www.teldta.com

Buy fees: no cost
5% disc-div
$10-5,000/qtr(12)
part. DR/cash-only
sfkg-free
comm/Cl A/pref-10 sh/no residency restrict.

✄

%

NOTE: *all classes reinvest in common shs

Temple-Inland Inc (N-TIN) (div/yr: $ 0.90) [S&P ranking: B] mfg-paper/containers/bldg
prods/fin svcs
1300 S MoPac
Austin, TX 78746
201-324-1225 admr
201/222-4955 TDD
512-434-3750 fax #
512-434-2587 ShSvc
e-mail: investorrelations@templeinland.com
www.templeinland.com

Buy fees: no cost
$25-1,000/qtr(4)
sfkg-free
rec common
div deposit

✄

Tennant Co (N-TNC) (div/yr: $ 0.88) [S&P ranking: B] mfg-floor maintenance equip
P O Box 1452
Minneapolis, MN 55440-1452
800-468-9716 admr
763-513-1811 fax #
763-540-1553 InvRe
www.tennantco.com

Buy fees: no cost
$50-5,000/qtr(4)
sfkg-free/p. sale-avail
rec common

✄

Terasen Inc (T-TER) (div/yr: $ 0.90) [S&P ranking: C] energy-natural gas-CDN
1111 W Georgia St
Vancouver, BC V6E 4M4, Canada
800-987-0825 admr
604-443-6630 fax #
604-443-6527 AsstSecy
e-mail: investor.relations@terasen.com
www.terasen.com
frmly: BC Gas Inc

Buy fees: no cost
to C$20,000/yr(4)
part. DR/cash-only
common/US res not elig

✄

Texas Instruments (N-TXN) (div/yr: $ 0.10) [S&P ranking: B] mfg-semiconductors, electronic
equip
12500 TI Blvd
Dallas, TX 75243
972-995-3773 InvRe
972-995-4360 fax #
800-336-5236 admr
www.ti.com
NOTE: $3 certificate issuance fee

Buy fees: no cost
no cash plan
partial DR option
p. sale-avail
common

✄

Textron Inc (N-TXT) (div/yr: $ 1.40) [S&P ranking: B +] mfg-aircraft/fastening & indus products/finance

✂ 40 Westminster St
Providence, RI 02903-2596
800-829-8432 admr
704-590-4652 fax #
401-421-2800 CorpSecy
www.textron.com
NOTE: TDD-201/222-4955

Buy fees: no cost
$25-120,000/yr EFT(12)
part. DR/cash-only
sfkg-free/p. sale-$10
common/no residency restrict.

Thomas Industries Inc (N-TII) (div/yr: $ 0.39) [S&P ranking: A] mfg-pumps & compressors

✂ 4360 Brownsboro Rd Ste 300
Louisville, KY 40207
800-662-6757 admr
502-895-661 fax #
502-893-4600 Treas
e-mail: thomasmail@thomasind.com
wwwl.thomasind.com

Buy fees: no cost
$25-3,000/month(12)
part. DR/cash-only
common

Thomson Corp (The) (N-TOC) (div/yr: $ 0.80) [S&P ranking: B +] publishing-integrated information solutions-CDN

P O Box 24/Toronto Dominion Ctr
Toronto, ONT M5K 1A1, Canada
✂ 800-969-9974 CorpSecy
416-360-8812 fax #
416-360-8700 Secy
e-mail: investor.relations@thomson.com
www.thomson.com

Buy fees: no cost
no cash plan
common/Canada/UK/USA res

Thornburg Mortgage Inc (N-TMA) (div/yr: $ 2.72) [S&P ranking: B +] REIT

✂ 150 Washington Ave Ste 302
Santa Fe, NM 87501
% 877-777-0800 admr
505-954-5997 fax #
★ 505-954-5300 InvRe
e-mail: lgallagher@thornburgmortgage.com
www.thornburgmortgage.com

Buy fees: no cost-orig iss
0-5% disc-div/cash-orig iss
$100-10,000*/mo(12)
DIP: $500 (0-5% discount)
part. DR/cash-only
sfkg-free/p. sale-$15 + 10¢/sh
common
gifting avail

NOTE: *may req waiver to purchase more than cash limit

Tidewater Inc (N-TDW) (div/yr: $ 0.60) [S&P ranking: B] energy svcs-offshore oil

c/o EquiServe
P O Box 1681 MS 45-01-06
Boston, MA 02105-1681
504-568-1010 AsstSecy
504-566-4559 fax #
617-575-3170 admr
www.tdw.com
NOTE: + more often if enough funds for 100-sh lot

Buy fees: to $2.50 + 5¢/sh
$25-5,000/qtr(4 +)
sfkg-free
rec common

Tiffany & Co (N-TIF) (div/yr: $ 0.24) [S&P ranking: A] retail-high-end jewelry stores

727 Fifth Ave
New York, NY 10022
★ 888-778-1307 admr
212-755-8000 InvRe
www.tiffany.com

Buy fees: 5%to$3 + 6¢/sh*
$25-100,000/yr EFT(52)
DIP: $250 + $15 + 6¢/sh
part. DR/cash-only
sfkg-free/p. sale-$15 + 12¢/sh
no residency restrict.
gifting free

NOTE: *no cost to holders of < 100 shs; cash pymt fees: 6¢/sh + $2 EFT/$5 check

DIVIDEND REINVESTMENT PLANS T

Timken Co (N-TKR) (div/yr: $ 0.60) [S&P ranking: B] mfg-metal fabricating-bearings & steel
1835 Dueber Ave SW
Canton, OH 44706-0928
800-622-6757 admr
330-471-4421 fax #
330-471-3378 ShrSv
e-mail: invest@timken.com
www.timken.com
NOTE: *or $100/month EFT + $10

Buy fees: no cost
$100-250,000/yr EFT(52)
DIP: $1,000 + $10*
part. DR/cash-only
sfkg-free/p. sale-$5 + 5¢/sh
rec common/no residency restrict.

Tompkins Trustco Inc (A-TMP) (div/yr: $ 1.20) [S&P ranking: A] banks/banking
P O BOX 460
Ithaca, NY 14851
877-573-4008 admr
607-273-0063 fax #
607-273-3210 FinDp
e-mail: shareholder@tompkinstrust.com
www.tompkinstrustco.com

Buy fees: no cost
$50-100,000/yr EFT(52)
DIP: $100
part. DR/cash-only
sfkg-free/p. sale-10¢/sh
common
div deposit/gifting free

Torchmark Corp (N-TMK) (div/yr: $ 0.44) [S&P ranking: A] insurance/financial svcs
2001 3rd Ave S
Birmingham, AL 35233-2186
866-557-8699 admr
205-325-4198 fax #
205-325-4243 CorpSecy
www.torchmarkcorp.com

$100-3,000/qtr(8)
part. DR/cash-only
sfkg-free
common/no residency restrict.

Toro Co (N-TTC) (div/yr: $ 0.24) [S&P ranking: A-] consumer prod-home appliances
c/o Wells Fargo Bank Minnesota NA
P O Box 64854
South St Paul, MN 55164-0854
952-887-8526 AsstTreas
952-887-5924 fax #
800-468-9716 admr
e-mail: invest@toro.com
www.toro.com

Buy fees: no cost
$10-1,000/month(12)
common/no residency restrict.

Total System Services Inc (N-TSS) (div/yr: $ 0.24) [S&P ranking: A +] fin svcs-bank card processing
PO Box 120
Columbus, GA 31902
800-503-8903 admr
706-644-8065 fax #
706-649-2310 InvRe
e-mail: tssir@totalsystem.com
www.tsys.com
NOTE: *cash pymt fees:6¢/sh + $2.50check or $1 single EFT(auto EFT no chg)/**owners with less than 100 shs automatically enrolled in DRP

Buy fees: no cost-div*
$50-250,000/yr EFT*(52)
DIP: $235 + $15 + 6¢/sh
partial DR option
sfkg-free/p. sale-$15 + 10¢/sh
rec common**
div deposit/gifting free

TransAlta Corp (N-TAC) (div/yr: $ 1) [S&P ranking: B] utility-electric-CDN
110-12th Ave SW, Box 1900, Sta M
Calgary, ALB T2P 2M1, Canada
800-387-0825 admr
403-267-2590 fax #
403-267-2520 INvRe
e-mail: investor_relations@transalta.com
www.transalta.com

Buy fees: no cost
5% disc-treasury shs
up to $5,000/qtr(4)
rec comm/US res not elig

TransCanada Pipelines Ltd (N-TRP) (div/yr: $ 1.22) [S&P ranking: A-] energy-natural gas dis-
CDN
✂ P O Box 1000 Station M   Buy fees: no cost
  Calgary, ALB T2P 4K5, Canada   C$50-10,000/qtr(4)
  800-564-6253 admr   or US$35-7,000/qtr comm/pref/no resi-
  403-920-2460 fax #   dency restrict.
  403-920-6000 CorpSecy
  www.transcanada.com

TriCo Bancshares (Calif) (NDQ-TCBK) (div/yr: $ 0.44) [S&P ranking: A] banks/banking
  63 Constitution Dr   Buy fees: no cost
✂ Chico, CA 95973 $100-1,000/qtr EFT
  800-230-2574 admr   part. DR/cash-only
  530-898-0300 ShrRe   p. sale-$15 + 12¢/sh
  www.tcbk.com   no residency restrict.
                                        div deposit

Tribune Co (N-TRB) (div/yr: $ 0.72) [S&P ranking: B +] publishing/broadcasting/TV
  435 N Michigan Ave   US$50-120,000/yr*(52)
  Chicago, IL 60611-4041   DIP: $500 or $50/mo EFT
★ 312-222-9787 InvRe   part. DR/cash-only
  312-222-3148 fax #   sfkg-free/p. sale-$10 + 12¢/sh
  800-446-2617 admr   rec common
  www.tribune.com   div deposit/gifting avail
  NOTE: for 10 months/*EFT of cash pymts

Trizec Properties Inc (N-TRZ) (div/yr: $ 0.80) [S&P ranking: B-] REIT-office properties
  233 S Wacker Dr Ste 4600   Buy fees: 6¢/sh
★ Chicago, IL 60606 $100-10,000/mo*EFT(12)
  800-837-9045 admr   DIP: $300 + 6¢/sh
  312-798-6270 fax #   partial DR option
  312-798-6290 InvRe   sfkg-free/p. sale-$15 + 12¢/sh
  e-mail: info@tzh.com   gifting avail
  www.trz.com
  NOTE: *req waiver for cash amts/initial purchase $10,000

Twin Disc Inc (NDQ-TWIN) (div/yr: $ 0.70) [S&P ranking: B] mfg-power transmission equip
✂ 1328 Racine St   Buy fees: no cost-div*
  Racine, WI 53403-1700 $25-250,000/yr EFT(4)
  888-213-0935 admr   DIP: $250 + $15
  262-638-4480 fax #   sfkg-free/p. sale-avail
  262-638-4000 InvRe   common/no residency restrict.
  www.twindisc.com
  NOTE: *cash pymt: check $5/single EFT pymt $3.5/auto EFT $2

✂ **Tyson Foods Inc** (N-TSN) (div/yr: $ 0.16) [S&P ranking: B] food-poultry producer/distributor
  c/o EquiServe Trust Co NA   Buy fees: no cost-div*
★ P O Box 43081 $50 min EFT*(52)
  Providence, RI 02940-3081   DIP: $250 + $16 + 3¢/sh
  800-822-7096 admr   cash-only option
  479-290-4061 fax #   sfkg-free/p. sale-$15 + 12¢/sh
  479-290-4000 InvRe   common
  e-mail: tysonir@tysonfoodinc.com
  www.tyson.com
  NOTE: *cash pymt fees: 3¢/sh + $5 check/$2.50 EFT; min $25/mo for EFT pymts

U

U S Bancorp (N-USB) (div/yr: $ 1.20) [S&P ranking: B +] banking
800 Nicollet Mall Ste 2300   Buy fees: no cost-div*
Minneapolis, MN 55402 $25-250,000/yr EFT*(52)
888-778-1311 admr   DIP: $250 + $15 + 3¢/sh**
612-303-0782 fax #   part. DR/cash-only
612-303-0783 InvRe   sfkg-free/p. sale-$15 + 12¢/sh
www.usbank.com   rec common/no residency restrict.
    div deposit/gifting free
NOTE: *cash pymt fees: by check $5 + 3¢/sh, by single EFT $3 + 3¢/sh, by monthly EFT
$2 + 3¢/sh each/**or $50/mo for 5 months by EFT

UGI Corp (N-UGI) (div/yr: $ 1.35) [S&P ranking: A-] utility-gas/elec & propane marketing
P O Box 858   Buy fees: no cost
Valley Forge, PA 19482-0858 $25-3,000/qtr(12)
800-756-3353 admr   partial DR option
610-992-3259 fax #   sfkg-$7.50/p. sale-avail
610-337-1000 Treas   common/pref/no residency restrict.
www.ugicorp.com

UIL Holdings Corp (N-UIL) (div/yr: $ 2.88) [S&P ranking: B +] utility-electric
c/o American Stock Trans & Trust Co   Buy fees: $2.50 + 10¢/sh
59 Maiden Lane 1st floor $25-10,000/trans*(daily)
New York, NY 10038   DIP: $250 + $2.50 + 10¢/sh
203-499-2409 ShrSv   partial DR option
203-499-3626 fax #   p. sale-$7.50 + 10¢/sh
877-681-8024 admr   rec common/no residency restrict.
www.uil.com   div deposit
NOTE: *cash pymts may be made by EFT or online

UMB Financial Corp (NDQ-UMBF) (div/yr: $ 0.88) [S&P ranking: B +] banks/banking
1010 Grand Ave   Buy fees: no svc chg
Kansas City, MO 64106 $50-3,000/qtr*(12)
816-860-7000 Treas   partial DR option
816-860-7610 fax #   p. sale-avail
800-884-4225 admr   common
www.umb.com
NOTE: *waivers may be obtained for amounts > $3,000/free trans of shs to another acct

USEC Inc (N-USU) (div/yr: $0.00) energy-provider/distr of enriched uranium
6903 Rockledge Dr   Buy fees: to $3-div*
Bethesda, MD 20817 $50-250,000/yr EFT*
888-485-2938 admr   DIP: $250 + $5
301-564-3200 InvRe   sfkg-avail/p. sale-$10
e-mail: financial@usec.com   div deposit
www.usec.com
NOTE: *cash pymt fees: $2 EFT/$5 check

UST Inc (N-UST) (div/yr: $ 2.20) [S&P ranking: A-] consumer products-tobacco, wine
100 W Putnam Ave   Buy fees: no cost
Greenwich, CT 06830-5342 $10-10,000/month(24)
800-730-4001 admr   part. DR/cash-only
203-622-3626 fax #   sfkg-free/p. sale-avail
203-622-3656 co #   rec common
www.ustshareholder.com/

Umpqua Holdings Corp (NDQ-UMPQ) (div/yr: $ 0.24) fin svcs-banking/retail brokerage
200 S W Market St Ste 1900
Portland, OR 97201
800-922-2641 admr
503-546-2489 InvRe
★ www.umpquabank.com

Buy fees: 5%to$3 + 6¢/sh*
$25-250,000/yr EFT*(52)
DIP: $250 + $10 + 6¢/sh
part. DR/cash-only
sfkg-free/p. sale-$15 + 12¢/sh
no residency restrict.
div deposit/gifting free

NOTE: *cash pymt fees: 6¢/sh + $5 check/$2 EFT

UniSource Energy Corp (N-UNS) (div/yr: $ 0.76) [S&P ranking: B] utility-electric/solar
P O Box 711
Tucson, AZ 85702
✁ 520-884-3755 InvRe
520-884-3602 fax #
★ 866-537-8709 admr
e-mail: ir@UniSourceEnergy.com
www.UniSourceEnergy.com

Buy fees: no cost
$50 or more(24)
DIP: $250
part. DR/cash-only
sfkg-free/p. sale-$5 + 10¢/sh
common/no residency restrict.
div deposit

Union Pacific Corp (N-UNP) (div/yr: $ 1.20) [S&P ranking: B] trans-railroad
1400 Douglas St
✁ Omaha, NE 68179
800-317-2512 admr
402-501-2121 fax #
402-544-6604 CorpSecy
www.up.com

Buy fees: no cost
$10-60,000/yr(12)
part. DR/cash-only
sfkg-free/p. sale-avail
rec common

UnionBanCal Corp (N-UB) (div/yr: $ 1.64) [S&P ranking: A] banking
400 California St 1-001-13
✁ San Francisco, CA 94104
800-317-2512 admr
415-765-2950 fax #
415-765-2969 InvRe
e-mail: investor.relations@uboc.com
www.uboc.com

Buy fees: no cost
$25-3,000/qtr(4)
partial DR option
sfkg-$2.50
common
gifting avail

United Bankshares Inc (WV) (NDQ-UBSI) (div/yr: $ 1.04) [S&P ranking: B +] banking
514 Market St
✁ Parkersburg, WV 26102
304-424-8764 CorpSecy
304-424-8711 fax #
800-526-0801 admr
www.ubsi-wv.com

Buy fees: no cost
$25-10,000/qtr(4)
sfkg-free
rec common

United Dominion Realty Trust Inc (N-UDR) (div/yr: $ 1.20) [S&P ranking: B-] REIT-apartments
400 East Cary St
✁ Richmond, VA 23219
888-468-9716 admr
720-283-2454 fax #
720-283-6132 InvRe
e-mail: ir@udrt.com
www.udrt.com

Buy fees: no cost
$50-25,000/qtr(4)
part. DR/cash-only
sfkg-free/p. sale-avail
comm/pref

United Industrial Corp (N-UIC) (div/yr: $ 0.40) mfg-defense/energy systems
✁ 124 Industry Ln
Hunt Valley, MD 21030
800-278-4353 admr
410-629-3500 InvRe
e-mail: invest@unitedindustrialcorp.com
www.unitedindustrial.com

Buy fees: no cost
$100-5,000/mo(12)
partial DR option
sfkg-free/p. sale-$10 + bkg fee
rec common

United Mobile Homes Inc (A-UMH) (div/yr: $ 0.98) [S&P ranking: A] REIT-manufactured home communities
3499 Route 9 North Ste 3-C
Freehold, NJ 07728
732-577-9996 x 36
732-577-9981 fax #
732-577-9997 InvRe
e-mail: umh@umhsf.com
www.umh.com
Buy fees: no cost
5% disc-div/cash
$500-1,000/mo**(12)
part. DR/cash-only
common*
✂
%
NOTE: *B/O "street name" holders not eligible for dividend reinvestment, only cash plan/** waivers may be granted for cash pymts over $1,000

United Parcel Service Inc (N-UPS.B) (div/yr: $ 1.32) trans-air/ground pkg delivery service
55 Glenlake Parkway
Atlanta, GA 30328
800-758-4674 admr ##
404-828-6440 fax #
404-828-6000 InvRe
www.shareholder.com/ups/drip.cfm
Buy fees: 5%to $5 + 12¢/sh*
$100-120,000/yr EFT(52)
DIP: $250 + $15 + 12¢/sh
part. DR/cash-only
sfkg-free/p. sale-$15 + 12¢/sh
comm Cl B/no residency restrict.
div deposit/gifting free
★
NOTE: *cash pymt fees: 12¢/sh + $2 EFT/$5 check/##keep pressing the (#) and (0) until you reach a human rep

United States Steel Corp (N-X) (div/yr: $ 0.40) [S&P ranking: B-] mfg-steel/diversified businesses
600 Grant St, Rm 611
Pittsburgh, PA 15219-4776
866-433-4801 ShSvc
412-433-4818 fax #
e-mail: shareholderservices@uss.com
www.USSteel.com
Buy fees: 5¢/sh
0-3% disc-div/cash*
$50-10,000/mo+ EFT(48)
DIP: $500 + $10
part. DR/cash-only
sfkg-free/p. sale-10¢/sh
rec common
%
★
NOTE: approval for more than $15,000 reinvested div/+ or more with approval/*discount at co discretion, call co for current discount

United Technologies Corp (N-UTX) (div/yr: $ 1.76) [S&P ranking: A+] mfg-aerospace systems
United Technologies Bldg
Hartford, CT 06101
860-728-7575 InvRe
860-728-7835 fax #
800-519-3111 admr
e-mail: invrelations@corphq.utc.com
www.utc.com
Buy fees: no cost
$100-120,000/yr(12)
part. DR/cash-only
sfkg-free/p. sale-avail
comm-10 sh min
✂

Unitil Corp (A-UTL) (div/yr: $ 1.38) utility-elec/holding co
6 Liberty Lane West
Hampton, NH 03842-1720
603-772-0775 InvRe
603-773-6761 fax #
800-736-3001 admr
e-mail: whitney@unitil.com
www.unitil.com
Buy fees: no cost
$25-5,000/qtr(4)
part. DR/cash-only
sfkg-free
rec common
div deposit
✂

Unitrin Inc (N-UTR) (div/yr: $ 1.70) [S&P ranking: B] insurance-life/property
c/o Wachovia Bank NA
1525 West W T Harris Blvd 3C3NC1153
Charlotte, NC 28288-1153
312-661-4520 ShRe
312-661-4941 fax #
800-829-8432 admr
www.unitrin.com
Buy fees: div-5% to$5 + bkg*
$50-100,000/yr EFT*(52)
DIP: $500 + $10 + 5¢/sh*
partial DR option
sfkg-free/p. sale-$15 + 5¢/sh
common
gifting avail
★
NOTE: *$50/mo5 EFT for 10 mo(initial purch), cash pymt fees: 5¢/sh + $5 check/$2 EFT

Universal Corp (N-UVV) (div/yr: $ 1.68) [S&P ranking: A] misc-tobacco, agri-products
P O Box 25099
Richmond, VA 23260-5099
 800-468-9716 admr
 804-254-3594 fax #
 804-359-9311 CorpSecy
 www.universalcorp.com

Buy fees: no cost
$10-1,000/mo EFT(12)
partial DR option
sfkg-free/p. sale-avail
rec common
div deposit

Universal Health Realty Income Trust (N-UHT) (div/yr: $ 2.02) REIT-health care facilities
P O Box 61558
King of Prussia, PA 19406-0958
 800-730-6001 admr
 610-768-3336 fax #
 610-265-0688 InvRe
 www.uhrit

Buy fees: no cost-orig iss
$25-50,000/month(12)
part. DR/cash-only
sfkg-free/p. sale-avail
common

Unocal Corp (N-UCL) (div/yr: $ 0.80) [S&P ranking: B +] energy-petroleum/earth resources
2141 Rosecrans Ave #4000
El Segundo, CA 90245
 800-279-1249 admr
 310-726-7682 fax #
 800-252-2233 ShRel
 e-mail: stockholder_services@unocal.com
 www.unocal.com
NOTE: *5% to $3 fee/$5 certificate fee

Buy fees: 5¢/sh
$50-10,000/mo*(12)
part. DR/cash-only
sfkg-$5/p. sale-$15 + 5¢/sh
comm-25 sh min/US res only

UnumProvident Corp (N-UNM) (div/yr: $ 0.30) [S&P ranking: B-] insurance/employee benefit/disability
1 Fountain Sq
Chattanooga, TN 37402
 800-446-2617 admr
 423-294-2590 fax #
 423-294-1661 InvRe
 www.unumprovident.com
NOTE: *cash pymt fees: 3¢/sh + $5 by check; $2 EFT/automated sales by phone

Buy fees: 5%to $3-div*
$100-60,000/yr EFT(12)
part. DR/cash-only
sfkg-free/p. sale-$15 + 12¢/sh
rec common
div deposit/gifting avail

Urstadt Biddle Properties (N-UBP) (div/yr: $ 0.86) REIT-shopping centers
321 Railroad Ave
Greenwich, CT 06830
 203-863-8200 co #
 203-861-6755 fax #
 800-524-4458 admr
 e-mail: info@ubproperties.com
 www.ubproperties.com
NOTE: each class reinvests in itself

Buy fees: no cost
no cash plan
partial DR option
comm & Cl A
gifting avail

V

VF Corp (N-VFC) (div/yr: $ 1.08) [S&P ranking: a-B +] consumer prod-apparel
P O Box 21488
Greensboro, NC 27420
 201-324-1225 admr
 336-424-7696 fax #
 336-424-6000 CorpSecy
 e-mail: irrequest@vfc.com
 www.vfc.com

$10-3,000/qtr(4)
common

Valley National Bancorp (NJ) (N-VLY) (div/yr: $ 0.90) [S&P ranking: A] banking
1455 Valley Rd   Buy fees: no svc chg
Wayne, NJ 07470-2160 $50-5,000/mo EFT(12)
800-278-4353 admr   sfkg-free
973-305-8415 fax #   rec common
973-305-3380 ShrRe   div deposit
www.valleynationalbank.com

Valspar Corp (N-VAL) (div/yr: $ 0.80) [S&P ranking: A-] mfg-paints/coatings
1101 S 3rd St   Buy fees: no cost-div*
Minneapolis, MN 55415-1211 $100-10,000/mo EFT*(12)
800-205-8318 admr   DIP: $1,000+ $5 +12¢/sh
612-375-7313 fax #   partial DR option
612-332-7371 legal   sfkg-free/p. sale-$15+12¢/sh
www.valspar.com   rec comm-25 shs min
NOTE: *$5 check/$3 EFT fee + 12¢/sh

Vectren Corp (N-VVC) (div/yr: $ 1.18) [S&P ranking: B +] utility holding co-gas/elec
P O Box 209 - 20 N W 4th St   Buy fees: no cost
Evansville, IN 47708 $25-50,000/yr EFT*(12)
800-622-6757 admr   part. DR/cash-only
812-491-4145 fax #   sfkg-free/p. sale-$15+12¢/sh
812-491-4190 ShSvc   rec common/no residency restrict.
www.vectren.com
NOTE: *EFT fee $2

Verizon Communications Inc (N-VZ) (div/yr: $ 1.62) [S&P ranking: B] telecommunications
1095 Ave of the Americas   Buy fees: $1-2/div*
New York, NY 10036 $50-200,000/yr*EFT(52)
800-631-2355 admr   DIP: $500 + $5+3¢/sh**
212-921-2917 fax #   partial DR option
212-395-1525 ShRel   sfkg-free/p. sale-$10+ 7¢/sh
e-mail: James.M.McFarland@verizon.com   rec com-10 shs min/no residency restrict.
www.verizon.com/investor   div deposit/gifting free
NOTE: *3¢/sh on market shares + $2.50 for cash pymts or $1 for EFT pymts/IRA $500 min + $35 ann fee/**or $100/mo for 5 months EFT

Viacom Inc (N-VIA) (div/yr: $ 0.28) enter-broadcast(CBS)/cable (MTV)/publishing
c/o Bank of New York   Buy fees: 10%to$3 + 10¢/sh*
P O Box 11258 $50-120,000/yr EFT*(52)
New York, NY 10286-1258   DIP: $250 + $10
800-507-7799 admr   partial DR option
212-258-6000 InvRe   sfkg-free/p. sale-$15+10¢/sh
e-mail: info@viacom.com   comm Cl A
www.viacom.com   gifting free
NOTE: *for div/cash pymt fees: 10¢/sh + $3 EFT/$7.50 check

Volvo North America Corp (NDQ-VOLVY) (div/yr: $ 1.05) mfg-trucks, buses*/jet & ind en-gines-SWEDEN
570 Lexington Ave, 20th Floor   Buy fees: no cost
New York, NY 10022-0837 $25-5,000/month(12)
800-808-8010 admr   sfkg-free
212-418-7439 fax #   ADR
212-418-7432 InvRe
www.volvo.com
NOTE: "street" name accts may part in cash plan/*sold car division

W   *Directory of Companies Offering*

Vulcan Materials Co (N-VMC) (div/yr: $ 1.16) [S&P ranking: A-] mfg-construction
P O Box 385014   Buy fees: 10% to $3-div*
Birmingham, AL 35238-5014 $10-60,000/yr**EFT(12)
866-886-9902 admr   DIP: $250 + $10 + 10¢/sh
★ 205-298-2960 fax #   sfkg-free/p. sale-$15 + 10¢/sh
205-298-3204 CorpSecy   common/no residency restrict.
e-mail: ir@vmcmail.com   div deposit/gifting free
www.vulcanmaterials.com
NOTE: *plus 10¢/sh/**cash pymt fees: 10¢/sh + $5 by check, $2 by EFT

W

W P Carey & Co LLC (N-WPC) (div/yr: $ 1.78) svcs-manage assets for REITs & own comm
properties
50 Rockefeller Plaza   Buy fees: no cost
✂ New York, NY 10020   *
888-200-8690 admr $500-25,000/mo*EFT(12)
★ 212-492-8922 fax #   DIP: $500
212-492-1151 InvRe   part. DR/cash-only
e-mail: ir@wpcarey.com   sfkg-free/p. sale-$15 + 12¢/sh
www.wpcarey.com   rec comm - 1 sh min/no residency restrict.
                                        div deposit
NOTE: *may req waiver for cash pymts & 0-5% discount on cash pymts $25,000

WGL Holdings Inc (N-WGL) (div/yr: $ 1.33) [S&P ranking: B +] utility-gas
✂ 1100 H St NW   Buy fees: no cost-orig iss
Washington, DC 20080-0001 $25-20,000/qtr(12 +)
800-330-5682 admr   partial DR option
202-624-6446 fax #   sfkg-avail/p. sale-avail
703-750-4440 ShSvc   comm/pref**/no residency restrict.
www.wglholdings.com   div deposit
NOTE: *for part reinvest-100 sh comm min + all pref/**B/O must provide proof of ownership to participate

WPS Resources Corp (N-WPS) (div/yr: $ 2.22) [S&P ranking: B +] utility-elec/natural gas, en-
ergy-related svcs
P O Box 19001/700 N Adams St   Buy fees: no cost
✂ Green Bay, WI 54307-9001 $25-100,000/yr EFT(24)
800-236-1551 admr   DIP: $100
★ 920-433-1526 fax #   part. DR/cash-only
920-433-1057 InvRe   sfkg-free/p. sale-avail
e-mail: investor@wpsr.com   common
www.wpsr.com   div deposit

Wachovia Corp (N-WB) (div/yr: $ 1.84) [S&P ranking: A-] banking/financial svcs
✂ 301 S College St   Buy fees: no cost
Charlotte, NC 28288-0206 $20-15,000/mo EFT(12)
800-347-1246 admr   part. DR/cash-only
704-374-2140 fax #   sfkg-free/p. sale-avail
704-374-6782 InvRe   rec comm-50 shs min/no residency restrict.
e-mail: investor-relations@wachovia.com
www.wachovia.com

Wal-Mart Stores Inc (N-WMT) (div/yr: $ 0.60) [S&P ranking: A +] retail-discount stores
c/o EquiServe Trust Co NA
PO Box 43069
Providence, RI 02940-3069
800-438-6278 admr
479-273-4053 fax #
479-273-4000 ShRel
e-mail: walmartstock@delphi.com
www.walmartfacts

Buy fees: no cost-div
$110-150,000/yr*(250)
DIP: $250 + $20 + 10¢/sh**
partial DR option
sfkg-free/p. sale-$20 + 10¢/sh
rec common

✂

★

NOTE: **or $25/mo EFT/200 sh or less reinvests all div/*EFT $25 per mo min + $1-5 fee + 10¢/sh for cash purchases/trans of shs

Walgreen Co (N-WAG) (div/yr: $ 0.21) [S&P ranking: A +] retail-drug stores
200 Wilmot Rd
Deerfield, IL 60015-4681
847-914-2972
847-914-2678 fax #
888-368-7346 admr
e-mail: investor.relations@walgreen.com
www.walgreens.com

Buy fees: no cost-div*
$50-60,000/yr EFT*(52)
DIP: $50 + $10 fee
sfkg-free/p. sale-$10 + 10¢/sh
rec common/no residency restrict.

✂

★

NOTE: *cash pymt fees: EFT-$1.50 + 10¢/sh/by check $5 + 10¢/sh/free gift trans of shares

Walt Disney Co (N-DIS) (div/yr: $ 0.24) [S&P ranking: B] entertainment-film/amusement parks
P O Box 11447
Burbank, CA 91510-1447
818-553-7200 ShrSv
818-553-7210 fax #
e-mail: corp.shareholder.services@disney.co
www.disney.com/investors

Buy fees: no cost-orig iss
$100-250,000/yr**(52)
DIP: $1,000 + $10 + 1.5¢/sh*
sfkg-free/p. sale-$10 + 1.5¢/sh
rec common-10 shs/no residency restrict.

✂

★

NOTE: *or $100/mo EFT for 10 mos/**$1 EFT fee) or $5 check fee + 3¢/sh cash pymt option

Washington Mutual Inc (N-WM) (div/yr: $ 1.88) [S&P ranking: A] savings bank/financial svcs
1201 3rd Ave WMT 2140
Seattle, WA 98101-3015
206-461-3187 ShRe
206-490-2447 fax #
800-234-5835 admr
www.wamu.com

Buy fees: no cost
$50-$5,000/mo EFT(24)
cash-only option
sfkg-free/p. sale-$15 + 12¢/sh
rec comm 1 sh min

✂

Washington Real Estate Investment Trust (N-WRE) (div/yr: $ 1.57) [S&P ranking: A-] REIT-diversified properties
c/o EquiServe Trust Co Inc
P O Box 2598
Jersey City, NJ 07303-2598
301-984-9400 co #
301-984-9610 fax #
877-386-8123 admr
www.writ.com

Buy fees: 3¢/sh
$100-300,000/yr EFT(52)
DIP: $250
part. DR/cash-only
sfkg-free/p. sale-$15 + 12¢/sh
rec common/no residency restrict.
div deposit

★

Washington Trust Bancorp Inc (NDQ-WASH) (div/yr: $ 0.72) [S&P ranking: A] banks/banking
23 Broad St
Westerly, RI 02891
800-852-0354 admr
401-348-1200 Mrktg
e-mail: investor.relations@washtrust.com
www.washtrust.com

Buy fees: no cost
$25-10,000/qtr EFT
div deposit

✂

Waste Management Inc (N-WMI) (div/yr: $ 0.80) [S&P ranking: B] svcs-waste mgmt svcs
c/o Mellon Investor Services $50-100,000/yr EFT*(52)
★ P O Box 3337   DIP: $500 + $10 + 12¢/sh
S Hackensack, NJ 07606   cash-only option
  800-969-1190 admr   sfkg-free/p. sale-$15 + 12¢/sh
  713-209-9711 fax #   rec common
  713-512-6200 co #
  www.wm.com
NOTE: *$5 fee cash purchase + 12¢/sh (EFT fee $2.50 + 12¢/sh)

Wausau-Mosinee Paper Co (N-WPP) (div/yr: $ 0.34) [S&P ranking: B] mfg-writing/towel&tissue/specialty papers
  100 Paper Place   Buy fees: no svc chg
  Mosinee, WI 54455-0900 $25-5,000/qtr(4)
  800-509-5586 admr   partial DR option
  715-692-2082 fax #   sfkg-free
  715-693-4470 InvRe   common
  www.wausaumosinee.com

Weingarten Realty Investors (N-WRI) (div/yr: $ 1.76) [S&P ranking: A-] REIT-shopping centers
c/o Mellon Investor Services LLC   Buy fees: no cost
✂ P O Box 3338 $25-25,000/mo EFT*(52)
South Hackensack, NJ 07606-1938   DIP: $250 + $5 + 6¢/sh
★ 800-550-4689 admr   part. DR/cash-only
  713-866-6072 fax #   sfkg-free/p. sale-$15 + 12¢/sh
  713-866-6000 CpCom   rec comm 5 sh min/no residency restrict.
  e-mail: ir@weingarten.com   gifting free
  www.weingarten.com
NOTE: *cash pymt fees: $5 check/$3.50 single EFT/$2 auto monthly EFT

Weis Markets Inc (N-WMK) (div/yr: $ 1.12) food-supermarkets
✂ c/o American Stock Trans & Trust   Buy fees: no cost
  59 Maiden Lane 1st floor $10-3,000/qtr(4)
  New York, NY 10038   sfkg-free
  570-286-4571 co #   common 50 sh min
  800-937-5449 admr

Wells Fargo & Co (N-WFC) (div/yr: $ 1.92) [S&P ranking: A] banking
  6th & Marquette, Wells Fargo Ctr   Buy fees: 4%to$4 + 3¢/sh-div
  Minneapolis, MN 55479-1000 $25-10,000/mo EFT(52)
  612-667-9799 InvRe   DIP: $250* or $25/mo EFT
★ 651-450-4085 fax #   part. DR/cash-only
  877-840-0492 StkTr   sfkg-free/p. sale-$10 + 3¢/sh
  www.wellsfargo.com/shareownerservices   rec common/no residency restrict.
                                     div deposit/gifting
NOTE: *($10 enroll fee)/**$3 + 3¢/sh for cash pymts or $1 + 3¢/sh for EFT pymts/sales
up to $25,000

Wendy's International Inc (N-WEN) (div/yr: $ 0.54) [S&P ranking: A-] food-restaurants
  P O Box 256   Buy fees: 2%to$2.50 + 10¢/sh
  Dublin, OH 43017-0256 $25-20,000/yr EFT(52)
★ 877-681-8121 admr   DIP: $250 + $2.50 + 10¢/sh
  614-766-3775 fax #   part. DR/cash-only
  614-764-3019 InvRe   sfkg-$7.50/p. sale-$7.50 + 10¢/sh
  e-mail: marsha_gordon@wendys.com   rec common
  www.wendys-invest.com   div deposit/gifting free

WesBanco Inc (NDQ-WSBC) (div/yr: $ 1.04) [S&P ranking: A] banking
One Bank Plaza   Buy fees: no cost
Wheeling, WV 26003-3562 $10-5,000/mo EFT(12)   ✂
800-837-2755 admr   part. DR/cash-only
304-234-9476 fax #   p. sale-$15 + fees
304-834-9411 Trust   common
e-mail: webanco@webanco.com
www.wesbanco.com

West Coast Bancorp (OR) (NDQ-WCBO) (div/yr: $ 0.37) [S&P ranking: A-] banks/banking
5335 Meadows Rd Ste 201   Buy fees: no cost
Lake Oswego, OR 97035 $25-2,000/mo   ✂
800-468-9716 admr   common
503-684-0781 fax #
503-684-0884 co #
www.westcoast bancorp.com

Westamerica Bancorp (NDQ-WABC) (div/yr: $ 1.20) [S&P ranking: A] banking
P O Box 1200   Buy fees: no cost
Suisun City, CA 94585-1200 $100-3,000/month(12)
707-863-6809 ShRel   p. sale-bkg fee   ✂
707-863-6815 fax #   rec common/no residency restrict.
877-588-4258 admr   div deposit
e-mail: investments@westamerica.com
www.westamerica.com

Westar Energy Inc (N-WR) (div/yr: $ 0.92) [S&P ranking: B] utility-electric
818 Kansas, PO Box 750320   Buy fees: no cost-orig iss
Topeka, KS 66675-0320 $50-10,000/mo*(24)   ✂
800-527-2495 admr   DIP: $250
785-575-1796 fax #   part. DR/cash-only   ★
785-575-1565 ShrSv   sfkg-free/p. sale-$5 + 7.25¢/sh
e-mail: sharsvcs@wr.com   rec common/no residency restrict.
www.wr.com   div deposit/gifting free
NOTE: *monthly EFT of cash pymts-min $35/mo

Western Digital Corp (N-WDC) (div/yr: $0.00) [S&P ranking: B-] mfg-computer hard drives
20511 Lake Forest Dr   Buy fees: $2.50 + 10¢/sh
Lake Forest, CA 92630-7741 $25-10,000/day EFT(240)
888-200-3165 admr   DIP: $250 + $2.50 + 10¢/sh
949-672-5410 fax #   sfkg-$7.50/p. sale-$15 + 10¢/sh   ★
949-672-7986 StkAd   individuals only
www.wdc.com   gifting free
NOTE: co does not pay div

Weyerhaeuser Co (N-WY) (div/yr: $ 2) [S&P ranking: B] mfg-forest products
P O Box 9777   Buy fees: 4% to $1.50-div*
Federal Way, WA 98063-9777 $100-25,000/qtr *(12)
800-561-4405 admr   part. DR/cash-only
253-924-5204 fax #   sfkg-$3/p. sale-$15 + bkg
253-924-5273 ShrSv   rec common
e-mail: invrelations@weyerhaeuser.com   gifting avail
www.weyerhaeuser.com
NOTE: *$5 cash pymt fee + bkg fees

Whirlpool Corp (N-WHR) (div/yr: $ 1.72) [S&P ranking: B] consumer prod-home appliances
2000 N M 63 (MD 2800) $50-250,000/yr(52)
Benton Harbor, MI 49022-2692   DIP: $250
800-446-2617 admr   part. DR/cash-only   ★
269-923-3525 fax #   p. sale-avail
269-923-3189 InvRe   rec common/no residency restrict.
e-mail: info@whirlpool.com
www.whirlpoolcorp.com

Whitney Holding Corp (NDQ-WTNY) (div/yr: $ 1.40) [S&P ranking: B +] banks/banking
P O Box 61260   Buy fees: no cost
New Orleans, LA 70161 $50-5,000/qtr(4)
  504-586-3627 ShrSv   cash-only option
  504-552-4851 fax #   sfkg-free
  800-937-5449 admr   rec common
  e-mail: investor.relations@whitneybank.com

Wilmington Trust Co (N-WL) (div/yr: $ 1.20) [S&P ranking: A +] banking
1100 N Market St/Rodney Sq N   Buy fees: no cost
Wilmington, DE 19890-0001 $10-5,000/qtr(12)
  800-999-9867 admr   part. DR/cash-only
  302-651-8010 fax #   sfkg-free
  302-651-8069 InvRe   common
  www.wilmingtontrust.com

Wisconsin Energy Corp (N-WEC) (div/yr: $ 0.88) [S&P ranking: B] utility-electric/gas distr
PO Box 1331 (231 W Michigan)   Buy fees: no cost
Milwaukee, WI 53201-2949 $25-100,000/yr EFT(104)
★ 800-558-9663 admr   DIP: $250
  414-221-3888 fax #   part. DR/cash-only
  414-221-4259 StkSv   sfkg-free/p. sale-$15 + 5¢/sh
  e-mail: virginia.ebert@we-energies.com   comm/pref*/no residency restrict.
  www.wisconsinenergy.com   div deposit/gifting avail
  NOTE: *Wisc Elec Power pref

Woodward Governor Co (NDQ-WGOV) (div/yr: $ 1) [S&P ranking: B +] mfg-energy conrol-systems/engine & turbine parts
P O Box 7001, 5001 N 2nd St   Buy fees: 2% to $2.50-div*
Rockford, IL 61111-5800 $25-10,000/day EFT
  877-253-6843 admr   DIP: $250 + $2.50 + 10¢/sh
★ 815-639-6009 fax #   part. DR/cash-only
  815-877-7441 CorpSecy   sfkg-$7.50/p. sale-$15 + 10¢/sh
  e-mail: corp_stock@woodward.com   common
  www.woodward.com   gifting free
  NOTE: *$10¢/sh + $2.50 for cash pymts

Worthington Industries Inc (N-WOR) (div/yr: $ 0.68) [S&P ranking: B] mfg-steel
1205 Dearborn Dr   Buy fees: no cost
Columbus, OH 43085-4769 $50-5,000/mo(12)
  614-438-3059 ShrRe   part. DR/cash-only
  614-438-7508 fax #   sfkg-free/p. sale-avail
  800-622-6757 admr   rec common
  www.worthingtonindustries.com

Wrigley (Wm) Jr Co (N-WWY) (div/yr: $ 1.12) [S&P ranking: A +] food-chewing gum
410 N Michigan Ave   Buy fees: no cost
Chicago, IL 60611-4287 $50-5,000/month(12)
  800-874-0474 StkRe   sfkg-free
  312-644-7879 fax #   rec common & Cl B reinvests in comm
  312-644-2121 co #
  www.wrigley.com

Wyeth (N-WYE) (div/yr: $ 0.92) [S&P ranking: B] drug/pharm-pharmaceuticals/vac-cines/biotechnology
c/o Bank of New York   Buy fees: 5% to $3 + 5¢/sh-div*
★ P O Box 11258 Church St Sta $50-120,000/yr EFT*(52)
New York, NY 10286   DIP: $500 + $10 + 5¢/sh
  800-565-2067 admr   part. DR/cash-only
  973-660-7455 fax #   sfkg-free/p. sale-$15 + 12¢/sh
  973-660-5798 admr   rec common
  www.wyeth.com
  NOTE: *cash pymt fee: 5¢/sh + $5 by check/$2 EFT

XYZ

XM Satellite Radio Holdings Inc (NDQ-XMSR) (div/yr: $0.00) entertainment-subscription
digital satellite radio
1500 Eckington Place NE
Washington, DC 20002
 781-575-3400 admr
 202-380-4500 fax #
 866-962-2557 InvRe
 e-mail: ir@xmradio.com
 www.xmradio.com

Buy fees: 3¢/sh-markt shs*
***
$100-10,000/mo EFT*(12)
partial DR option
p. sale-$15 + 12¢/sh
comm-Cl A/no residency restrict.

NOTE: co does not pay divs/*$5 check/$2.50 EFT/ **may obtain waivers for cash pymts
$10,000 to $150 million; /***0-5% disc for cash pymts $10,000/mo

XTO Energy Inc (N-XTO) (div/yr: $ 0.20) [S&P ranking: B +] energy-oil/gas development/prod
810 Houston St Ste 2000
Fort Worth, TX 76102-6298
 800-877-2892 admr
 817-870-1671 fax #
 817-885-2260 finan
 e-mail: investor_relations@xtoenergy.com
 www.xtoenergy.com

Buy fees: 12¢/sh
$50-10,000/mo EFT(52)
DIP: $500 + 12¢/sh
partial DR option
sfkg-free/p. sale-$15 + 12¢/sh
common/no residency restrict.
div deposit/gifting free

★

Xcel Energy (N-XEL) (div/yr: $ 0.83) [S&P ranking: B] utility-electric
800 Nicollet Mall
Minneapolis, MN 55402-2023
 612-215-4534 InvRe
 612-330-5878 fax #
 877-778-6786 InvRe
 www.xcelenergy.com/ir/htm

Buy fees: 3% to $1.50*
$50-100,000/yr EFT(52)
DIP: $1,000 + $10 + 5¢/sh
part. DR/cash-only
sfkg-free/p. sale-$10 + 10¢/sh
common/no residency restrict.

★

NOTE: *plus bkg fee on market shares

Xerox Corp (N-XRX) (div/yr: $0.00) [S&P ranking: B] mfg-office equip
800 Long Ridge Rd M/S 2-4-C
Stamford, CT 06904
 800-828-6396 admr
 203-968-3917 fax #
 203-968-3883 InvRe
 www.xerox.com

Buy fees: no cost
$10-5,000/month(12)
part. DR/cash-only
sfkg-free
comm

✄

NOTE: omitted dividend 7/01

Yahoo! Inc (NDQ-YHOO) (div/yr: $0.00) [S&P ranking: B-] misc-internet communications
701 First Ave
Sunnyvale, CA 94089-1019
 877-946-6487 admr
 408-731-3300 co #
 www.yahoo.com

Buy fees: $5 + 5¢/sh*
$50-150,00/yr EFT*(104)
DIP: $250 + $5
cash-only option
sfkg-avail/p. sale-$10 + 12¢/sh
common

★

NOTE: *on cash purchases (co pays no dividends)/$2 + 5¢/sh for EFT purchases

York International Corp (N-YRK) (div/yr: $ 0.80) [S&P ranking: B] mfg-climate control devices
c/o Bank of New York
P O Box 11258
New York, NY 10286-1258
 888-663-8325 admr
 717-771-7381 fax #
 717-771-7409 admr
 www.york.com

$100-10,000/mo EFT(52)
DIP: $1,000
sfkg-free/p. sale-$15 + 12¢/sh
common
div deposit/gifting free

★

Yum! Brands Inc (N-YUM) (div/yr: $0.00) food-restaurant chains-KFC, Pizza Hut, Taco Bell
1441 Gardiner Ln $25-250,000/yr EFT(240)
Louisville, KY 40213   DIP: $250
★ 800-937-5449 admr   sfkg-avail/p. sale-$15 + 10¢/sh
502-874-8300 fax #
800-298-6986 InvRe
e-mail: yum.investor@yum.com
www.yum.com

✂ **Zions Bancorp** (NDQ-ZION) (div/yr: $ 1.44) [S&P ranking: A] banking
10 East S Temple, 3rd Floor   Buy fees: no cost
Salt Lake City, UT 84111 $10-5,000/qtr(4)
801-524-4696 StkTr   partial DR option
801-524-4838 fax #   rec comm/pref/US res only
800-736-3001 co #
www.zionsbank.com

BIBLIOGRAPHY

Books and Reports

American Reference Books Annual 1999, V. 30, Libraries Unlimited Inc.

Carlson, Charles B, *Buying Stocks Without a Broker*, McGraw-Hill, New York, 1992

Currier, Chet, and David Smyth, *No Cost/Low Cost Investing*, Franklin Watts, New York, 1987

Dammon, Robert M, and Chester S Spatt, "An Option-Theoretic Approach to the Valuation of Dividend Reinvestment and Voluntary Purchase Plans," *J of Finance*, Vol XLVII, No 1, March 1992

General Accounting Office, *SECURITIES INDUSTRY-SEC Leadership Needed to Further Automate Securities Transfers*, GAO/IMTEC-92-4, December 1991

Internal Revenue Service, *Investment Income and Expenses*, Publication 550, 2004

—, *Your Federal Income Tax for Individuals*, For use in preparing 2004 Returns, Publication 17

Levitt, Arthur, with Paula Dwyer, *Take on the Street*, Pantheon Books, New York, 2002

Quinn, Jane Bryant, *Making the Most of Your Money*, Simon & Schuster, New York, 1991

Scholes, Myron S, and Mark A Wolfson, "Decentralized Investment Banking, "The Case of Discount Dividend-Reinvestment and Stock-Purchase Plans," *J of Financial Economics* 23, 1989

Securities and Exchange Commission, Release Nos 33-7114 & 34-3504, Exemption From Rule 10b-6 for Certain Dividend Reinvestment and Stock Purchase Plans, Dec 1, 1994

Standard & Poor's Corp, *Directory of Dividend Reinvestment Plans*, New York, 1992

—, S&P Net Advantage(r), Stock Reports, New York, April 2005, proprietary internet site

—, *Security Owner's Stock Guide*, 2000

State of New York, Office of the Attorney General, "Business Ethics, Regulations and the 'Ownership Society' " speech by Eliot Spitzer, January 31, 2005

U S Congress, Jobs and Growth Tax Relief Reconciliation Act of 2003, Public Law 108-27, May 28, 2003, U S Government Printing Office, Washington, D C,

—, Sarbanes-Oxley Act of 2002, To protect investors by improving the accuracy and reliability of corporate disclosures made pursuant to the securities laws, and for other purposes, Public Law 107-204, July 30, 2002, U S Government Printing Office, Washington, D C

—, Taxpayer Relief Act of 1997, Public Law 105-34, August 5, 1997, U S Government Printing Office, Washington, D C

—, National Securities Markets Improvement Act of 1996, Public Law 104-290, October 11, 1996, U S Government Printing Office, Washington, D C

Wallace, Beatson, *Learning to Invest*, 2nd edition, Globe Pequot Press, Old Saybrook, CT, 1995

Electronic sources

American Association of Individual Investors, www.aaii.org
American Institute of Certified Public Accountants, www.aicpa.org

American Stock Transfer & Trust Co, www.investpower.com or www.am-
stock.com
Bank of New York, www.stockbny.com/adr or www.globalbuydirect.com
Bloomberg LP, Bloomberg terminals
Business Week Investor Education, proprietary online service
Citibank, www.citibank.com/adr
EquiServe Trust Co NA, www.equiserve.com
U S Government Printing Office, www.gpo.gov
J P Morgan Chase Bank, www.adr.com/shareholder
Mellon Investor Services LLC, www.melloninvestor.com
National Association of Investors Corp, www.better-investing.org
Netstock Direct or ShareBuilder, www.netstockdirect.com
Registrar & Transfer Co, www.rtco.com
Standard & Poor's *S&P NetAdvantage*, a proprietary database
U S Securities & Exchange Commission, www.sec.gov
Wells Fargo Bank, www.wellsfargo.com/com/shareowner_services

Articles

Associated Press, "For many stock owners, direct approach pays off," by John
Cunniff, January 1996
Baltimore Sun, "Investing, DRIP by DRIP," by Michael Pollick, Nov 5, 1991
Bank Securities Journal, "DRPs — Another Step to Integration and a Way to Build
Customer Loyalty?" July/Aug 1994
Barron's, "Speaking of Dividends, Now Available: DIPS and DRIPs on ADRs",
by Shirley A Lazo, Sept 8, 1997
—, "A Lot for (Almost) Nothing, The Lure of Dividend Reinvestment Plans," by
Charles Carlson, Feb 17, 1992
Better Investing,"DRPs and Direct Purchase Plans Offer Opportunity, Flexibil-
ity," by Amy T Rauch-Bank, November 1997
—, "Using Dividends and DRPs," by Marsha Bertrand, July 1996.
—, "Building Your Wealth Through Dividend Reinvestment," November 1993
—, "Additional Resources for Finding and Using DRIPs," by Amy T Rauch-Bank,
November 1993
Bloomberg Personal, "Do You Have a Date With a DRIP?" by Ed Leefeldt, May
1995
Boston Globe, "Q&A: I am interested in buying shares of stock directly...," by
Kenneth Hooker, May 13, 1996
—, "Broker can be necessary to get diversity," by Kenneth Hooker, April 16,
1992
The Buffalo News, "It's Getting easier to buy stock from firms,", by David
Robinson, June 6, 1995
—, "Sometimes you can buy stock without a broker," by David Robinson,
March 13, 1992
Business Week, "Replanting Dividends: It's Easy and Cheap," by Suzanne
Woolley, Feb 24, 1992
—, "The Thriftiest Way to Buy Stocks," by Suzanne Woolley, June 4, 1990
—, "Buying Stocks—Without a Stockbroker," Nov 7, 1988
—, "Turning Dividends into a Quick Capital Gain," by Gary Weiss, Nov 2, 1987
—, "It Can Pay to Buy Stock a Bit at a Time," by Gary Weiss, May 18, 1987
The Christian Science Monitor, "Those Buying Shares With DRIPs, Aren't
Drips,", by Guy Halverson, May 30, 1995

Consumer Reports, Money Advisor, "DRIP-toe your way into the stock market, Dividend reinvestment plans allow you to buy shares cheap," November 2004

Cosmopolitan, "So Long, Stockbroker: Investors Can Do It Themselves," by Debra Wise, January 1996

Ernst & Young's Financial Planning Reporter, "Commission-Free DRIPs Can Be More Than Convenient,", July/August 1995

—, "Dividend Reinvestment Plans," by William G Brennan, July/Aug 1991

Forbes, "Stop me before I spend," by Graham Button, June 22, 1992

—, "Drip, Drip...," by Richard Greene, July 29, 1985

—, "You can get it wholesale," by Janet Bamford, July 2, 1984

—, "Tax-free and 5% off," Feb 1, 1982

—, "Beating the broker," Sept 15, 1980

Independent Business, "An Evergreen Enterprise," Nov-Dec 1992

Kiplinger's Personal Finance Magazine, "Who Shot DRIPs?" by Ken Sheets, October 1998

—, "Computing Taxes on Stock Transactions", January 1998

—, "But cashing out can be hard to do," by Ken Sheets, April 1997

—, "Good DRIPs, Bad DRIPs," by William Giese, Jan 1994

—, "Best places to reinvest your dividends," by Ed Henry, May 1922

—, "Getting Started in Stocks," July 1991

Kiplinger's Retirement Report, "A Gift That Keeps Giving", November 1995

—, "Some DRIPs Cater to Retirees,", July 1995

Knight-Ridder News Service, "Reinvestment plan revisions may be near," by Sandra Block, June 1995

Lexington [KY] Herald-Leader, "Buying solo, Bypass your broker to boost your stocks," by Annette Kondo, Aug 7, 1995

Los Angeles Times, "How You Can Buy Stock,", by Carla Lazzareschi, May 7, 1995

—, "Money Talk," by Carla Lazzareschi, Sept 19, 1993

—, "Research a company in depth before you buy its stock," by Carla Lazzareschi, March 1989

Military Lifestyle, "Your Money—Investing DRIP by DRIP," by Mary Pawlak, January 1995

Milwaukee Journal Sentinel, "Starting Early on Stocks, DRIPs a way to buy shares for kids", by Kathleen Gallagher, November 28, 1997

—, "Despite T + 3, don't lose touch with investments," by Kathleen Gallagher, June 26, 1995

Money, "The top 10 places to put this year's tax refund, #3 Buy into a dividend-reinvestment plan," by Karen Cheney, April 1996.

—, "Investing Basics, DRIPs can help your dividends multiply," May 1990

—, "Stocks That Reinvest Your Dividends," by J Howard Green, Sept 1987

—, "Investing by the Month," by Allan Sloan, June 1982

New Choices magazine, "Stock Market Profits, DRIP by DRIP," July/August 1998

—, "Easy Reinvestment in Foreign Stocks", September 1997

—, "Buying Stocks Without a Broker," Sept 1995

—, "Stocks-Dividend Reinvesting", Nov 1994

New York Times, "New York Banks Replenish Capital," Michael Quint, Nov 13, 1989

—, "Ways to Save When Investing," by Lawrence J DeMaria, Jan 28, 1989

—, "The Allure of Reinvesting Dividends," by Richard J Maturi, Aug 8, 1988

Outlook, "Riding the Offshore Waves with ADRs," Standard & Poor's, Feb 21, 1990

—, "A + Stocks Pass Test of Time," March 19, 2003

Personal Finance, "DRIPs Made Easier", March 22, 1995

—, "DRIPS on Disk," June 8, 1994

—, "Wealth From Scratch," by Thomas Scarlett, May 27, 1992

—, "Buy Direct and Save," by Nikolas Lanyi, Jan 30, 1991

—, "Never Pay Another Commission!," by Richard E Band, May 10, 1989

—, "The Magic of Dollar-Cost Averaging," by Stanley J Cohen, KCI Communications, Arlington, VA, Oct 15, 1986

Profitable Investing newsletter, "Good Info Source on DRIPs?" Richard Band, July 1994

Retired Officer Magazine (The), "Drip by Drip Investing,"by Marsha Bertrand, February 1995

Schenectady [NY] Gazette, "No-load stocks give investors another option," by Sylvia Wood, Aug 6, 1995

SmartMoney, "Getting a Grip on DRIPs," Robert J. Toth, Aug 1994

—, "Should You Buy Direct?", by Caleb Solomon, Oct 1992

USA Today, "Cut-rate investing: reinvesting dividends," by Sandra Block, Aug 27, 1996

—, "Exxon courts small investor," by John Waggoner, March 11, 1992

Wall Street Journal, "Getting Going: A Low-Budget Way to Invest in Stocks: Dividend-Reinvestment Plans Plus ETFs," by Jonathan Clements, March 24, 2004

—, "Exxon, Hoping to Lure Small Investors, Begins Program to Sell Shares Directly," by Caleb Solomon, March 11, 1992

—, "Dividend Plays Revived with New Twists," by Michael R Sesit, Nov 21, 1990

—, "ADRs: Foreign Issues with U S Accents," by Tom Herman and Michael R Sesit, Feb 8, 1990

—, "Certain Stocks Offer Trading at Little Cost," by John R Dorfman, Jan 13, 1988

—, "Turning Cash Dividends Into Stock Pays Off for Long-Term Investors," by Robert L Rose, April 22, 1986

—, "A Tax Benefit of Utility Stock is About to End," by Karen Slater, Dec 6, 1985

—,"Tax Bill Revises the Rules for Utility Dividends, Ending Sheltered Status for Many Shareholders," July 10, 1984

—, "New Tax Break on Electric-Utility Dividends May Give the Stocks More Allure for Investors," Jan 18, 1982

The Washington Post, "In Perilous Times, Think Dividends," by James K Glassman, May 12, 1996

—, "For Shareholders, a 'Drip' Can Generate Quite a Pool," by Albert B Crenshaw, Jan 28, 1996

—, "How the Little Things Boost Long-Term Profit", by James K Glassman, June 11, 1995

—, "Trading in Stocks Without a Broker," by Michael Trimarchi, Oct 10, 1993

Working Mother , "Investing is for Kids," by Janet Bodnar, July/Aug 1996

Worth, "Toolbox: The lowdown on Drips," by Doug Garr, February 1996

—, "Don't Forget the DRIP," April 1995

Appendix A

Direct Initial Purchase (DIP) of Stock from Company

The following U S and Candian plans provide for initial purchase of stock directly from the company or transfer agent, without first using a broker. The listing gives the minimum initial payment required to join the plan. Service and/or brokerage fees may be added (see main directory listing for details).

For American Depositary Receipts (ADRs) with initial purchase plans, see ADR section on page 9.

Company	Minimum Payment	Company	Minimum Payment
ADC Telecomm	$500 + $10 ($50/mo)	Becton, Dickinson	$250 + bkg fee
AFLAC	$1,000	Bedford Prop Invest	$1,000
AGL Resources	$250	BellSouth Corp	$490 + $10
AMB Prop Corp	$500	Best Buy Co	$500 + 13 + 3¢/sh**
AMETEK	$250 + $2.50 + 10¢/sh	Blair Corp	$100 + $100 fee
Acadia Realty Tr	$250 + $2.50 + 10¢/sh	Blyth	$240 + $10 + 10¢/sh*
Acuity Brands	$500 + $15	Bob Evans Farms	$100
Advanta Corp	$1,500	Borders Group	$500 + $13 + 3¢/sh
Aetna	$500 + $10 + 10¢/sh**	Borg-Warner	$500
Air Prod & Chem	$500 + $2.50 + 10¢/sh	Boston Beer Co	$500 + $10 + 12¢/sh**
Alaska Comm Sys	$500 + 6¢/sh	Boston Properties	$100
Albertson's	$250	Bowne & Co	$500
Allegheny Tech	$1,000 + $5 + 12¢/sh		
Allete	$250	CH Energy Group	$100
Alliant Energy	$250 or $25/mo EFT	CMS Energy Corp	$250 or $50 EFT/mo**
Allstate Corp (The)	$500* + $10 + 3¢/sh	CSX Corp	$500 + $10
Altria Group	$500 + $5 + 3¢/sh	CTS Corp	$1,000 + $10
Amegy Bank of Tex	$250	CVS CORP	$100 + $7.50 + 10¢/sh
AmerUs Group	$1,000 + $10 + 12¢/sh	Calgon Carbon	$250 or $50/mo EFT
Ameren Corp	$250 + 4¢/sh**	Calif Water SvcGp	$500
Amer Elec Power	$250 or $25/mo + $10	Campbell Soup Co	$500** + $18 + 3¢/sh
American Express	$1,000 + $6 + 6¢/sh	Caraustar Ind	$250 + 10¢/sh
Amer States Water	$500	Carpenter Tech	$250 + $2.50 + 10¢/sh
American Tower	$1,000 + $10	Cascade Financial	$250 + $15 + 6¢/sh
Anadarko Petroleum	$1,000	Cash America Int'l	$250 or 5 $50/mo EFT
Aqua America	$500	Caterpillar	$250 + $15 + 3¢/sh
Arbitron	$500 ($200 for*	Cendant Corp	$250 + $15 + 6¢/sh**
Arch Chemicals	$500 + $10 + 10¢/sh	Centerpoint Energy	$250
Archstone-Smith Tr	$200 + 6¢/sh	Central Vt Pub Svc	$250
Arrow Financial	$300	Ceridian Corp	$500
ArvinMeritor	$500 + $10	Chase Corp	$250 + 10¢/sh
Ashland	$500	Chemical Financial	$50
Assoc Estates Realty	$100 + $50	Chevron	$250 + $10 fee + 5¢/sh
Atmos Energy Corp	$1,250	Cinergy Corp	$245
Avery Dennison	$500* + $10 + 3¢/sh	Citizens Banking	$100
Baldor Electric Co	$50	Comm Bank Sys	$250 + $2.50 + 10¢/sh
Bank of America	$990 + $10	ConocoPhillips	$500 + $10
Bank of New York	$1,000 + $7.50	Costco Wholesale	$250 + $15 + 3¢/sh**
Bard (C R)	$250 + $15 + bkg fee	Curtiss-Wright Corp	$2,000 + $5 + 12¢/sh

DTE Energy	$250	Granite Construction	$3,000 + $5 + 12¢/sh
Darden Restaurants	$1,000 + $10 + 10¢/sh	Gray Television	$250 + $5 + 12¢/sh
Deere & Co	$500 + $7.50 + 5¢/sh	Great Plains Energy	$500 + $5 + 5¢/sh
Del Monte Foods	$200 + $10	Green Mountain Power	Vt res $50
Delphi Corp	$500 + $10	Guidant Corp	$250 + $5 + 3¢/sh**
Delta Air Lines	$250 + $10 + 3¢/sh**	Harland (John H) Co	$500 + $10 + 10¢/sh
Diebold	$500 + $7.50 + 10¢/sh	Harley-Davidson	$500 + $10
Dollar General	$50 + $5	Harrah's Entertain	$200 + $10
Dominion Res	$350 or $40/mo-EFT*	Hawaiian Electric Ind	$250
Dow Jones & Co	$1,000 + $5	Health Care Prop	$750
Duke Energy Corp	$250	Heinz (H J) Co	$250
Duke Realty Corp	$250	Hershey Foods Corp	$250 + $15 + 6¢/sh
Duquesne Light	$100 + $5 fee	Hillenbrand Ind	$250
		Home Depot (The)	$250
Eastern Co	$250 + $5*	Home Properties	$1,000
Eastman Chemical	$250	Huffy Corp	$500 + $10 + 10¢/sh
Eastman Kodak Co	$150		
Electronic Data Sys	$250 + $2.50 + 10¢/sh	IDACorp	$200 + $10
Emerson Electric	$250 + $15	IStar Financial	$100
Energen Corp	$250 or $25/mo EFT*	ITT Industries	$500 + $7.50
Energy East Corp	CT/MA/ME/NY res*	IndyMac Bancorp	$250 or 5 $50 EFT
Entergy Corp	$1,000	Interchange Fin Svc	$100
Entertaint Prop Tr	$200	IBM	$500 + $15 fee *
Equifax	$500 + $5 + 7¢/sh	Int'l Paper Co	$500 + $5
Equity Off Prop Tr	$250	Investors Fin Svcs	$250
Estee Lauder Cos	$250 + $10 + 12¢/sh	Johnson Controls	$250 + $10
ExxonMobil Corp	$250	Kaman Corp	$250 + $5/$3(EFT)
FBL Financial Group	$250 + $10	Keithley Instruments	$250
FNB Corp (PA)	$1,000	Kellwood Co	$100
Fannie Mae	$250* + $15 + 3¢/sh	Kelly Services	$250 + $5
FedEx Corp	$1,000+ + $15 + 3¢/sh	Kerr-McGee Corp	$750
Federal Realty Tr	$250	KeySpan Corp	$250
Federal Signal Corp	$100	Kilroy Realty Corp	$750
First American Corp	$250 + $10	Kimco Realty Corp	$100 + $10 + 5¢/sh
First Commonwealth		Knape & Vogt Mfg	$100
Financial Corp	$500 + $7.50	Kraft Foods	$500 + $13 + bkg fee
First Financial Hdgs	$250		
FirstEnergy Corp	$250	LSB Bancshares	$250 + $10
Ford Motor Co	$1,000 + $13 + 3¢/sh^	Lear Corp	$250 + $2 fee
Freddie Mac	$250 + $15 + 3¢/sh	Lehman BroHolding	$500 + $7.50
Freescale Semiconductor	$500 + $15 + 6¢/sh	Libbey	$100 + $7.50 + 7¢/sh
		Lilly (Eli) & Co	$1,000 + $15
GenCorp	$500 + $7.50	Lockheed Martin	$250
General Electric Co	$250 + $7.50	Longs Drug Stores	$500 + $10 + 5¢/sh
General Growth Prop	$200 (or $50/mo) + $15	Lowe's Cos	$250
German Amer Bancorp	$100	Lubrizol Corp	$250 + $2.50 + 10¢/sh
Gillette Co	$1,000 + $10 + 8¢/sh	Lucent Tech	$1,000 + $10 fee +
Glacier Bancorp	$250 + $2.50 + 10¢/sh	MDU Resources	$250
Glenborough Realty	$250	MET-PRO Corp	$1,000 +
Glimcher Realty Tr	$100 + $10	MGE Energy	$50
Goodyear Tire & Rubber	$250 + $10 + 3¢/sh	Macerich Co (The)	$250
Gorman-Rupp Co	$500 + $100 fee	Mack-Cali Realty	$2,000

Marathon Oil Corp	$500 + $10
Marriott Int'l	$350 + $18+ 3¢/sh*
Mattel	$500 + $10 + 8¢/sh
McCormick & Co	$250+$10+5¢/sh**
McDonald's Corp	$500 + $5 fee**
McGraw-Hill Cos	$500* + $10
MeadWestvaco Corp	$250 + $7.50
Meadowbrook Ins	$250
Medtronic	$250 + $10 + 4¢/sh
Mellon Financial	$500 + $6 + 12¢/sh
Merck & Co	$350+$5 or $50/moEFT
Michaels Stores	$500
Microsoft Corp	$1,000 + $10 + 6¢/sh
Mid-State Bancsh	$1,000 + $5 + 12¢/sh
MidSouth Bancorp	$1,000/$100 mo EFT
Mills Corp (The)	$250+$13 + 3¢/sh **
Modine Mfg Co	$500+$10 or $100/mo
Monsanto Co	$250 + $15 + 6¢/sh
Morgan Stanley	$1,000
Motorola	$500 + $10 + 10¢/sh
NCR Corp	$250
NIKE	$500 + $13
NSTAR	$500 + $10 + 4¢/sh
National Fin Partners	$500 + $15 + 6¢/sh
National Fuel Gas	$1,000 + $15
Nationwide Fin Svcs	$500 + $15 + fee
Nationwide Health Properties	$750
Newell Rubbermaid	$250
Newport Corp	$250
Northeast Utilities Sys	$250 + $12.50+10¢/sh
OGE Energy Corp	$250 + $3 + 12¢/sh
ONEOK	$250 or $25/mo EFT
Old Nat'l Bancorp	$500 + $10
Omega Healthcare Investors	$250
Omnicom Group	$750
Omnova Solutions	$500 + $10
PG&E Corp	$250 + $10 +10¢/sh
PNM Resources	$50
PPG Industries	$500
Paychex	$250
Penney (J C) Co	$250 + $10 + 6 ¢/sh
People's Bank (CT)	$250
Peoples Energy Corp	$250
PepsiAmericas	$250 + $10 + 5¢/sh
Pfizer	$500
Piedmont Nat Gas	$250
Pier 1 Imports	$490 + $10
Pinnacle West Cap	$50 + bkg fee
PolyOne	$250 +$10 +3¢/sh*
Popular	$100

Prentiss Properties Tr	$500 + $10
ProLogis	$200 + $10
Procter & Gamble	$250 + $5 fee
Progress Energy	$250
Provident Bankshares	$250 + $10 + bkg fee
Providian Financial	$100 + $15 + bkg**
Public Svc Enterprise	$250 +$10 fee*
Puget Energy	$250 + $10 +10¢/sh
Quanex Corp	$250 + $15
Questar Corp	$240 + $10 fee
RadioShack Corp	$250 + $10
Reader's Digest Assn	$1,000+$5
Redwood Tr	$100
Regions Financial	$1,000-40,000
Reliv' Int'l	$250 + $2.50 +10¢/sh
Reynolds American	$500 + $10
Robbins & Myers	$500
Rockwell Automation	$1,000 + $5
Rockwell Collins	$1,000 +$5 + 5¢/sh
Ryerson Tull	$500 + $10
SBC Comm	$500 + $10 + bkg fee
SCANA Corp	$250
SEMCO Energy	$250 + $10 +5¢/sh
Sanderson Farms	$500 +$5 +12¢/sh
Sandy Spring Bancorp	$250 + $2.50+10¢/sh
Sara Lee Corp	$500 + $13
Schnitzer Steel Ind	$500
Sempra Energy	$500 +$15 or $50/mo*
Sierra Pacific Res	$250
Sky Financial Group	$500 + $7.50
Smucker (J M) Co	$250 + $10 +10¢/sh
Snap-on	$500 ($100/mo EFT*)
Sonoco Products Co	$250 + $13 + 10¢/sh*
South Jersey Ind	$100
Southern Co	$250 + $10
Southern Union Co	$250
Southwest Gas Corp	AZ, CA & NV res-$100
Southwestern Energy	$250 +$10 + 3¢/sh
Sovereign Bancorp	$250 + $15
Stanley Works (The)	$250 +$10
Staples	$250 + $15+ 6¢/sh
Sterling Bancorp	$500+ $15 + 6¢/sh
Sunoco	$250+$10+3¢/sh
Susquehanna Bancsh	$250 + $7.50 +10¢/sh
Synovus Financial	$235 + $15 fee
TXU Corp	$500 + $10**
Target Corp	$500 + $10 +3¢/sh
Taubman Ctrs	$250 + $5 + 12¢/sh
Tektronix	$500 + $5 + 12¢/sh

Thornburg Mortgage	$500 (0-5% discount)	W P Carey & Co	$500
Tiffany & Co	$250 + $15 + 6¢/sh	WPS Resources	$100
Timken Co	$1,000 + $10*	Wal-Mart Stores	$250 + $20 + 10¢/sh**
Tompkins Trustco	$100	Walgreen Co	$50 + $10 fee
Total Sys Svcs	$235 + $15 + 6¢/sh	Walt Disney Co	$1,000 + $10 + 1.5¢/sh*
Tribune Co	$500 or $50/mo EFT	Washington REIT	$250
Trizec Prop	$300 + 6¢/sh	Waste Management	$500 + $10 + 12¢/sh
Twin Disc	$250 + $15	Weingarten Realty	$250 + $5 + 6¢/sh
Tyson Foods	$250 + $16 + 3¢/sh	Wells Fargo & Co	$250* or $25/mo EFT
U S Bancorp	$250 + $15 + 3¢/sh**	Wendy's Int'l	$250 + $2.50 + 10¢/sh
UIL Holdings	$250 + $2.50 + 10¢/sh	Westar Energy	$250
USEC	$250 + $5	Western Digital Corp	$250 + $2.50 + 10¢/sh
Umpqua Hldngs	$250 + $10 + 6¢/sh	Whirlpool Corp	$250
UniSource Energy	$250	Wisconsin Energy	$250
United Parcel Svc	$250 + $15 + 12¢/sh	Woodward Governor	$250 + $2.50 + 10¢/sh
United States Steel	$500 + $10	Wyeth	$500 + $10 + 5¢/sh
Unitrin	$500 + $10 + 5¢/sh*		
		XTO Energy	$500 + 12¢/sh
Valspar Corp	$1,000 + $5 + 12¢/sh	Xcel Energy	$1,000 + $10 + 5¢/sh
Verizon Comm	$500 + $5 + 3¢/sh**	Yahoo!	$250 + $5
Viacom	$250 + $10	York Int'l Corp	$1,000
Vulcan Materials Co	$250 + $10 + 10¢/sh	Yum! Brands	$250

Individual Retirement Arrangement Plans

Altria Group   Hershey Foods Corp
American Electric Power   McDonald's Corp
Aqua America   MidSouth Bancorp
Campbell Soup Co   ONEOK
Connecticut Water Service   ProLogis
ExxonMobil Corp   SBC Communications
Fannie Mae   Verizon Communications
Ford Motor Co

Discount Plans

The following is a list of plans that grant discounts when purchasing stocks with reinvested dividends and, in some cases, cash payments. Some plans provide for periodic evaluation of the discount policy, thus resulting in changes in the discount amounts granted.

Evergreen Enterprises make an effort to track these changes. However, plans with discounts change rapidly, and we caution investors to check with plan administrators before investing. See main section for notes indicated by asterisk.

Company	Discount	Company	Discount
Advanta Corp	0-5% disc-div/cash+	Archstone-Smith Trust	0-5% disc-div/cash**
AmeriVest Properties	3% disc-div	Ball Corp	5% disc-div
American Tower	***	Bedford Prop Invest	0-3% disc-cash*
Anadarko Petroleum	5% disc*-div	Boston Properties	3% disc-div
Aqua America	5% disc-div	Brandywine Realty Trust	0-5% disc-div/cash**

Canadian Oil Sands Trust	5% disc-distribution	Monmouth Capital Corp	5% disc-div/cash
Colonial Properties Trust	5% disc-div/cash	Monmouth REI Corp	5% disc-div/cash
Commerce Bancorp (NJ)	3% disc-div/cash		
Community Banks (PA)	5% disc-div/cash	Nationwide Health Prop	2%-div/cash orig iss
Countrywide Financial	0-5% disc-orig issue	North Fork Bancorp	disc at co discretion
		Omega Healthcare Investors	0-5% disc-div/cash
Empire District Elec	3% disc-div(orig is)	Piedmont Natural Gas Co	5% disc-div
Entergy Corp	0-3% on cash*	Popular	5% disc-div
Equity One	5% disc-div/cash	Prentiss Properties Trust	***
Equity Residential	0-5% disc-cash**	Presidential Realty Corp	5% disc-div
First Commonwealth Financial	10% disc-div	ProLogis	0-2% disc-div/cash***
Fuller (H B) Co	3% disc-div	Providian Financial	0-5% disc-cash purch
Glimcher Realty Trust	0-5% disc-div/cash*		
Health Care Prop Invest	0-1% disc-orig issue	Redwood Trust	2% disc-div*
Health Care REIT	4% disc-div/cash	RioCan REIT	3.1% bonus units
Healthcare Realty Trust	5% disc-div	Saul Ctrs	3% disc-div/cash
Hibernia Corp	5% disc-div	Shurgard Storage Ctrs	2% disc-div
Highwoods Properties	0-5% disc-div	South Financial Group (The)	5% disc-div
IStar Financial	0-3% disc-div/cash	South Jersey Industries	2% disc-orig/tre shs
		Southwest Water Co	5% disc-div
Kennametal	5% disc-div	State Bancorp	5% disc-orig issue
Kilroy Realty Corp	***	Suffolk Bancorp	3% disc-div/cash*
Lafarge North America	5% disc-div*	Sun Communities	3% disc-div
MDS	5% disc-div	Telephone & Data Sys	5% disc-div
MET-PRO Corp	3% disc-div	Thornburg Mortgage	0-5% disc-div/cash*
Marathon Oil Corp	0-3% disc-div/cash*	TransAlta Corp	5% disc-treasury shs
Media General	5% disc-div	United Mobile Homes	5% disc-div/cash
Mercantile Bankshares Corp	5% disc-div	United States Steel	0-3% disc-div/cash*
Michaels Stores	0-5%-cash*	W P Carey & Co LLC	***
		XM Satellite Radio Holdings	***

*** plans grant discounts for approved amounts greater than upper limit of cash purchases.

Appendix A

NOTES

Appendix B

State of New York
Office of the Attorney General
120 Broadway
New York, NY 10271

Business Ethics, Regulation and The "Ownership Society"

Remarks by
New York State Attorney General
Eliot Spitzer

National Press Club, Washington, D C
January 31, 2005

Thank you very much for that kind introduction. I noted with interest that Hank McKinnel will be your speaker next week. Hank, the CEO of Pfizer, once introduced me to an audience of CEOs. Hank, who is a wonderful guy and great CEO, came up to the podium and said very seriously: "Eliot, we want you to know that 99 percent of the folks here are good, ethical, hardworking people."

So I went up to the podium and I said: "Hank, thank you very much for that reminder. I know that's true, but I'm not worried about the 99 percent--I'm worried about the 1 percent, who are they?"

I'm not sure my joke had the desired effect on that particular audience. I thought it would be a funny way to begin, but there were more than a few groans. So, to dig my way out of that hole, I explained I am the 63rd Attorney General of the State of New York, which is something I became aware of only when I was sworn in a few years ago. I felt I should know who my predecessors were, so I looked it up and, lo and behold, Aaron Burr was once the Attorney General of New York. So I said to Hank and to the assembled group of CEOs: "Hey, if you think I am hard to deal with, imagine how hard it could have been."

I have never challenged anyone to duel. Not yet, anyway.

What I want to do today is throw out a few facts to frame a political debate. It is an enormously important debate, and it relates to a critical issue--[what] is government's role in regulating and defining the parameters of appropriate business behavior. The facts that I want to begin with are, I think, beyond dispute: certain elements of the business community are pushing back hard against the effort to impose disclosure obligations, transparency and ethical behavior.

First, they are objecting to the Sarbanes-Oxley Act [PL 108-27, enacted May 28, 2003], and objecting to the S.E.C.'s [U S Securities and Exchange Commission] effort to mandate disclosure and certain behavior patterns. The business leadership is saying: "Enough, we got the lesson, now back off."

Second, the U. S. Chamber of Commerce, which views itself as the preeminent business lobbying group, is going to court to challenge the S.E.C.'s capacity to issue regulations relating to mutual funds, board behavior, accounting rules and other rules that the S.E.C. believes are essential to ensure integrity in the capital markets.

Third, the president of the Chamber of Commerce [Thomas J Donohue], in a rather direct attack on the cases that my office has brought, has said recently that he thinks we are targeting individuals for what he calls "honest mistakes." He said this in the context of my office's investigation of the insurance industry. You should know that my office today settled with the nation's largest insurance broker, Marsh [& McLennan Cos Inc], and that as part of the settlement the company made certain comments regarding its own actions. I'll come back to that in a moment.

Fourth, there has been an enormous effort sponsored by some in the business community to preempt the states and my office in particular. The goal of this effort is to prevent us from bringing the types of cases that we have been bringing for the past number of years.

Now, what's this all about? Well, it's a debate about the role of government in defining the boundaries of appropriate business ethics, defining what it means to participate in our economy and what the expectations are for our business leadership and also who is supposed to enforce those boundary lines. One of the interesting things about this debate is that everybody invokes the same heroes. In this regard, everybody harkens back to Alexander Hamilton and Teddy Roosevelt [President Theodore Roosevelt]. These are the two icons, the two individuals whom we all embrace and say they really understood what government should do. They understood how the economy should function. They understood how to help the private sector generate the wealth that we so desperately want.

Now the interesting aspect of this is that when Teddy Roosevelt was running for office in 1904, 100 years ago, he wasn't a favorite of the business community. In fact, when Roosevelt attacked the cartels and when he attacked what he regarded as improper behavior, he met with staunch opposition from the business community. He was reviled by the business community.

So the irony is that those who now invoke him, if they actually looked back on what he said and did, and looked back on what their predecessors in the business community said about him, if they did that, perhaps they would rethink their holding him out as an icon.

I listened recently to Roosevelt's recorded speeches, the few that are available on tape. I was stunned by remarkable things that he was saying and you would be, too. He was incredibly forceful in describing the failure of ethics in the business leadership and perverse effect on our economy of the cartels that he was pursuing. Now today, 100 years later, nobody disputes that what he did was not only beneficial to the economy, but was absolutely necessary. In fact, if he had failed to attack the cartels, failed to attack the illegal behavior, failed to open up the economy to permit true competition, then we would not have experienced the enormous growth in our economy that came in the years that followed.

I would suggest to you that we are in the midst of a similar debate today. No, I'm not comparing myself to him, as they say: hubris is terminal. What I am saying is that the debate today is akin to what it was 100 years ago. On one side, there is an element of the business leadership that is cloaking itself in the language of the free market, but which really wants to preserve an ossified system. On the other side, there are those who--I would suggest-- really understand the markets and what it takes to generate wealth. They understand that government must step in every now and again to define the boundary lines and ensure that there is indeed integrity, transparency and fair play.

Now what I want to do is run through a few of the cases that we have made in my office. I want to lay out the facts and then ask what was the response of the other side? How did those who pretend to be the voice of the free market, who pretend to be advocates of competition and capitalism, how did they react when there was evidence, overwhelming evidence of illegality and impropriety?

The first case was the analyst case. Analysts on Wall Street were distorting and misrepre- senting their true opinion of stocks in order to encourage folks to buy stocks. There was an inherent conflict of interest in the business structure of the major investment houses. By hawking the stocks and giving "strong buy" ratings, they could persuade issuing companies to bring underwriting business to their employers, the investment banks. This was ultimately a much more lucrative stream of income than what was generated from small investors. So they subverted their obligation to give honest advice to the investing public to their desire to get the underwriting business.

As a result we saw overwhelmingly positive reports on all sorts of companies that never should have been taken out into the marketplace in the first instance, and we had a bubble.

My office began to reveal the evidence of this problem and it was rather vivid evidence in the form of e-mails. And one e-mail was from a star analyst named Jack Grubman, who made an observation that really captured the problem. He said this of his profession: "What used to be viewed as a conflict of interest is now viewed as synergy."

Think about that. They had so rationalized their world view that the duty to deliver an honest opinion was all but forgotten. They said: "Hey, we can make money on both sides of this transaction!" And that is exactly what they did.

We exposed it with the help of those e-mails, and we were negotiating with one of the major companies, trying to resolve the case in a way that would produce some meaningful reforms. And the lawyer for the other side said something to me that was very revealing and true. He said: "Eliot, be careful, we have powerful friends."

He was correct. The existing system has many powerful friends because the status quo always has powerful friends. Those who benefit from the status quo never want change.

But knowing this, what was I to do? Of course, I had no choice but to file the lawsuit. I mean what was I going to do at that point? Should I back down and say: "Oh, I didn't know you had powerful friends. Now you tell me, if you had only told me that last week we wouldn't be here."

So we filed the case and then the lawyers for the company come into my office and what do they say? Now all of you in this room know high-priced lawyers. You know what they're supposed to say. They said: "You don't understand the sector. You're taking the evidence out of context. You don't really mean it. We're really nice guys." That's what high-priced defense lawyers always say.

But, interestingly, they didn't say any of that. No, they came to my office and said: "Eliot, you're right. But we want you to know that we're not as bad as our competitors."

Now how is that for a defense? Even in an era of moral relativism, it just doesn't work. But here's the interesting thing: They were telling the truth. They clearly weren't as bad as their competitors. We found that out and that's what led to the global deal in which every major investment bank signed on.

They were right in a more subtle way. Everyone of the investment banks knew what the other bank [was] doing. But what always struck me was the fact that rather than getting together and saying: "You know what? There's a problem here. This is behavior that we really aren't proud of." Instead of doing that and elevating their standards through self-regulation or a discussion about what proper standards should be in the industry, every one of the banks sank to the lowest common denominator.

And the fact that they were saying: "We've got to be as devious as our competitors in how we take advantage of it," just reinforced in my mind the notion that we had to step in and do something. So we did. But what happened next was even more fascinating.

I called some of the other regulators in and proposed some ideas to remedy the problem. But the other regulators said to me: "no we can't do that."

Even though they were simple ideas, things that were ultimately made part of the global deal, they said it couldn't be done. I asked why and they said: "Because the industry won't like it." I looked at them quizzically. "Who cares whether they like it or not? It needs to be done."

But this was the mind set of the regulatory community. Specifically, it was the view of Harvey Pitt, who was the head of the S.E.C. at the time. Harvey was a fine lawyer, but I don't think he understood his job. He was aware of this problem. He actually convened a meeting of the CEOs of the major investment houses, along with the chairman of the New York Stock Exchange [Richard Grasso]. He called them together for the express purpose of addressing the problem of structurally-flawed analytical work that was being distributed to tens of millions of Americans. But what did he say to them? He said it wasn't his problem and he left it to the industry to address.

Here was something that went to the core integrity of the marketplace. Tens of millions of investors were investing based on knowingly-wrong analytical work. And he said: "It's not my problem."

That was terrible. That shouldn't have happened. But what is worse is that when the self-regulatory bodies that were supposed to do something about it did absolutely nothing. And then the S.E.C. under Harvey Pitt went up to Capitol Hill to support a pre-emption bill that would have prevented my office and other state regulators from looking into the problem in the first place.

Harvey Pitt wouldn't do anything about the problem, but he would support a bill to place handcuffs on those who wanted to investigate.

Now the obvious harm from this scandal is that millions of Americans were investing based on bad advice. The other problem that is less often thought about is the mis-allocation of capital that resulted. If you were to go to AT&T and say: "Do you remember that year when WorldCom was getting all of those wonderful analytical reports and everybody was saying that WorldCom was the future?"

They remember it all too well. AT&T and other companies couldn't compete with their numbers, and now we know why: Those numbers were a fraud. So, it's not just that investors were hurt, companies that were trying to compete for capital, that were reporting honest numbers, that weren't playing the game in the same devious way, those companies were at a competitive disadvantage and consequently had trouble getting access to capital that they needed.

And yet what did the government, those who pretend to speak for the free market, do? They did nothing except try to put handcuffs on us.

The mutual fund scandals are the second set of cases that I want to mention. It was a similar story. We revealed a significant problem, actually, a trio of problems: timing, late-trading and fees that were driven higher by the failure of boards simply to pay attention and do what they were supposed to do.

What was the response? Once again, the S.E.C. ran to the Hill and supported a preemption bill. When we tried to say to the mutual fund companies that the failure of board members to live up to their fiduciary duty had generated higher fees to the tune of hundreds of millions of dollars a year from one company alone, the S.E.C. disagreed with us and said that we couldn't get into the issue. They said it was price fixing.

Well, it had nothing to do with price fixing. It was saying to boards of directors: "Live up to your fiduciary duty, understand whom you represent and what you have to do to provide integrity in the marketplace."

But, again, where had the S.E.C. been as this enormous scandal in the mutual fund industry unraveled? The answer is nowhere. This was another one of the scandals that was out there and nobody was doing anything about it.

The Wall Street Journal editorial page attacked us for actually daring to get into this sector, and trying to unravel the massive conflicts of interest that existed. Keep in mind that seventy billion dollars a year is what the mutual fund companies derived from fees. Seventy billion a year! And if fees are ten to twenty percent higher than they should be, which is a conservative estimate, think how much it is costing investors every year. These are enormous numbers.

Next is insurance, and some of you may know, we settled with Marsh this morning. It's a settlement that is wonderful in many respects: It's $850 million dollars and all of it, all of it, is going back to customers. In addition, there is new leadership at the company and there is an entirely new business model predicated on disclosure and transparency so that those who buy insurance in this nation will no longer be victimized by contingent payments that drove premiums up by a significant margin.

This is a significant step forward, but, again, what was the response of the Chamber of Commerce? The Head of the Chamber said that the leadership of Marsh had made "honest mistakes."

I would note that these "honest mistakes" have already produced six guilty pleas, with more to come very shortly, and many more down the road. These "honest mistakes" involved bid rigging and outright deceit and fraud.

But Marsh, to its credit, is now a new company and I think this is really a turn for the better. They issued a statement today as part of the settlement, apologizing, acknowledging that the actions of the individuals, their employees and others at other companies were "unlawful and shameful". Those were their words, not mine. There was a wonderful column in the

Wall Street Journal a couple of weeks ago written by some industry apologist, he said the mistake of these CEOs was not to realize that in the post-Enron era, bid rigging is unacceptable.

You don't need to be an antitrust scholar to know that bid-rigging was unacceptable even before Enron. But there it is again, so-called voices of the free market defending frauds as honest mistakes and making excuses for criminal actions like bid-rigging. But they aren't the voices of the free market; they are the voices of ossification and stagnation.

Now let me make one footnote to the insurance cases: The President of the United States [George W Bush], whom we all respect, is out there attacking problems that drive insurance premiums higher. And, yes, there are a multitude of problems. But I have not heard a single word from the White House saying: " Maybe, just maybe, premiums are higher because the insurance companies formed an illegal cartel."

Remember that six insurance executives at three companies have pled guilty so far, and we are just beginning. The evidence is clear, the record of misconduct is clear. But not a word, not a single word about it from the administration. Everybody else and everything else is a causative factor. But not the corruption that is rife in the industry. It's corruption that touches every line of insurance, every line, and we will keep going until we expose all of it.

Another case that we made was the Paxil case. Not to bore you with details, but Paxil was a drug that was being prescribed off-label for adolescents who suffered with depression. GlaxoSmithKline, the company that makes it, was saying to the world that it was safe, and efficacious. But the problem was that they had done five studies, and one of the studies found that Paxil was marginally better than a placebo. The other four studies found that it was either no better than a placebo, or that it generated suicidal tendencies in adolescents.

But did Glaxo tell people that? Did they reveal this danger associated with the drug? No, they didn't. And if you or I were a parent of an adolescent who had been prescribed this drug or we were doctors considering whether or not to prescribe it, we'd want that information.

So we sued Glaxo. We sued them not to say: "Take this drug off the market." We sued them on the theory that the information, the clinical testing data should be revealed to the public. We said simply: "Create a website, post the relevant data so that people will have a full array of information and they can make informed judgments."

After some push back in which they again said: "You don't understand the market," Glaxo gave in. They agreed to full disclosure and established a website to reveal clinical trial data. Forest Labs has agreed to do the same thing and other pharmaceutical companies may follow suit because it makes sense.

But where has the F.D.A. [Federal Drug Administration] been on this issue? The answer is nowhere. There has been only silence. To us and to the medical journals and to doctors and parents, it was simply a matter of decency, disclosure and integrity. Yet this F.D.A. has not said a word about revealing this critically important data so that doctors can make informed judgments.

Now back to my favorite editorial page. The Wall Street Journal wrote an editorial saying that I should back off because, and I quote, "The system is working exactly as it should."

But a system that denies doctors and patients critically important information about the known side-effects of a drug cannot be working as it should. No way. And yet the Journal, as the paragon of honesty and integrity in the free marketplace, said the old system was working exactly as it should. Ridiculous. Flat out ridiculous.

The last case I want to mention relates to predatory lending. Let me tell a short story. There was a fellow from Rensselaer County—and for those of you who are unfamiliar with New York, it is a wonderful place just east of Albany. Thirty years ago, this poor fellow took out a 25-year mortgage. There were automatic deductions from his checking account for years and years. He really hadn't paid attention. He'd been divorced and the mortgage had been bought and sold by a couple of companies--securitized as we all know these things are. Time passed, but one day he woke up and he said: "Wait a minute, why am I still paying on that? Why are they still deducting money from my checking account!"

It was a fair question. So he called the bank, but the bank, based in Texas, gave him the brush off. Worse than that, they told him he would have to pay or they'd foreclose on his house. Then he got a lawyer and the lawyer called the bank and the bank gave the lawyer the brush off, too. So then the lawyer called my office, and we called the bank and said: "Look, it was a 25-year mortgage and he has made 30 years of payments. How is that possible?"

What did we hear back from the bank? Well, they left a voice mail message on an assistant attorney general's phone. The message was: "We don't need to answer your questions anymore. The O.C.C. has told us we can ignore state attorneys general."

The O.C.C. is the Office of the Comptroller of the Currency, a division of the [U.S.] Treasury Department that regulates banks. The O.C.C. was indeed telling nationally-chartered banks that they didn't have to respond to state regulators. Why? Because the O.C.C., in an effort to get banks to move their charters from state-chartered status to federally-chartered status, had offered the banks preemption from basic state laws, including those governing predatory lending. Yes, as bizarre as it sounds, that's what the O.C.C. is doing.

Now giving the O.C.C. the benefit of the doubt, perhaps you'd say: "Well, maybe the O.C.C. will aggressively pursue cases of predatory lending and otherwise step in to protect consumers."

Well, the O.C.C. says that it's doing that, but it's not. In fact, it can't because the agency doesn't have the manpower. We have more enforcement personnel in New York State alone than the O.C.C. does nationwide. And rarely have they made consumer protection cases [a priority]. Think about it: Does anyone with a consumer problem call the O.C.C.? Do people really say: "Let's call the Comptroller of the Currency because he's on our side! He'll get it done." I don't think so.

But State Attorneys General have been doing these cases for decades. It's what the A.G.s traditionally do. But the O.C.C. want to preempt them. And why? Why is the O.C.C. doing this? Well, their preemption move is all about freeing the banks of state regulatory oversight, which is terrific for the banks. But not very good for customers like the fellow from Rensselaer County.

A postscript: As a result of a lawsuit brought by our office against the Texas bank and against the O.C.C. the fellow kept his home and eventually received a refund of more than $9,000.

Now, as I noted, my office has been attacked for not understanding the markets, for over-reaching, for being unfair to CEOs, and I make two points in response.

First, not once has the other side been able to say that we were wrong on the facts. Not once. And that's the reason companies settle so quickly with our office and acknowledge improprieties. That's what Marsh did today. That's what Merrill Lynch [& Co Inc] did. And Goldman Sachs and CSFB [Credit Suisse-First Boston] and others. And yet those who supposedly speak for the free market refuse to acknowledge that we've been right in these cases. Instead, they recede into a shell of ossification—pretending that these issues should not have been addressed in the first place.

And this raises the second point: Does anyone out there really believe that the market was better off with those problems before we revealed them? Does anybody want to go back to an era of conflicted research? Of late-trading and market timing of mutual funds? Of contingent commissions and bid-rigging in the insurance business? Of secret clinical trials of drugs? Of unaccountable mortgage institutions? Does anybody want to do that? No, of course not, even those who kicked back the most can't say they want to go back to those practices and those days.

The reality is that the market survives only because problems are revealed and confronted aggressively, and this has led me to the rule that Teddy Roosevelt advanced and which I have come to live by, which is that only government, at the end of the day, can enforce rules of integrity and transparency in the marketplace.

Remember that comment—"We're not as bad as our competitors." It was correct. Business, in many cases, will descend to a lowest common denominator. And if we believe that the market depends upon integrity and fair dealing, then government must step in to make sure that the rules are honored.

Now there are two corollaries to this: The first is that self-regulation failed utterly. I say that with real disappointment. We've gone through, in many respects, a legitimate era of deregulation where an overreaching government bureaucracy has been pulled back. And we were told: "Don't regulate us, we will regulate ourselves."

But in not one of the instances where my office has uncovered rampant fraud has a self-regulatory entity stood up to say: "Hey, we have a problem here. Let's do something about it."

And by that I mean not only the New York Stock Exchange or the other securities self regulators, but also the leading industry bodies, such as the Investment Company Institute. Did the I.C.I. say: "We have a problem here?" No, the I.C.I. was professing the purity of the mutual fund industry even after these problems were revealed.

I'll get to the second corollary by means of a quick story, not a terribly flattering story about me. My family was sitting at the dining room table a couple of weeks ago and I turned to my 15-year-old, and those of you who have teenage daughters know that every now and then you try to start up a conversation with them and you meet with utter, abject failure. So this was one of those moments, and I turned to her and I said: "Elyssa, honey, tell me your favorite word. Think about it, what would it be if you had to choose?"

Yes, I know this was a lousy effort on my part at communication. I admit it, well, she looked at me and she rolled her eyes and said: "Oh Dad, cut it out. I don't have a favorite word, but you do and I know what it is."

I was taken aback and I said: "Really, what do you think my favorite word is?

"It's two words, Dad: fiduciary duty."

Pathetic, right? But here's the point: There has been a dramatic failure to adhere to notions of honest dealing and fiduciary duty in every sector we've looked at. That was true with investment banks, mutual funds, insurance agents and pharmaceutical companies. The failure to adhere to these concepts of integrity is the thread that runs through everything that we have seen.

So let me now ask a few questions of those who pretend to be the voices of the free market:

First, how much capital has been mis-allocated by virtue of what has been done? How much capital would have gone into IRAs and 401(k)s, had there not been the bubble that was created in part by the analysts' hype and which resulted in enormous losses? How much shareholder equity has been diluted because CEOs have given themselves not only enormous options which are to a great extent unjustified in my view, but also change of control provisions? What possible justification can there be when the ratio of CEO compensation to ordinary employee compensation has gone from 41 to 1, twenty years ago, to 530 to 1, today?

Now there are other rules that we have discerned over time that relate to why and when the government should step in. These involve externalities and core values. Because I want to move to the question and answer period, I will not go into this other than to make one very quick observation.

Why does government have to pass laws relating to discrimination and the minimum wage? The answer is because the marketplace alone simply won't get us there. If you ask yourself this question: Before the Civil Rights statutes of the mid-1960s, had the market alone begun to eliminate discrimination based on race or gender? No, it hadn't. Giving government the right to enforce a core value, which is that there should not be discrimination, is what changed the system. Do we believe that someone who works a forty-hour week should be able to live at the poverty line or higher? We do, but if we didn't have a minimum wage would that be the case? No, it wouldn't be and that is why there is this consensus that these laws are appropriate and important.

I am not going to go on at length about these issues. Let me just conclude with one observation: These issues are more than an abstraction. They affect real people. Whether it is the people whose money was lost, the people who are given an improper prescription drug, or the businesses that couldn't afford to get insurance because impropriety drove up premiums, real people are affected.

We are going through a debate now relating to the privatization of Social Security. I would ask people this final question: Do you trust an administration that failed to protect investors?

If this administration had addressed the flaws in some way, I might be more sympathetic to their approach. But they are still saying that the system does not need to be fixed. And they're still fighting reform.

So now they say: "Go ahead. Take your savings, your safety net, and put it into the system."

Well, where would we be if those who are retiring had their money in Enron and WorldCom? Where would we be? Remember that question as I now conclude my remarks with one final thought: As a lawyer, I can tell you that the only thing worse than not making your best argument, is having the other side steal it from you. In this regard, President Bush has embraced what he calls the "ownership society." He claims that his administration is making it possible for the middle class to save and invest and succeed. Well, when I hear that, I say to myself: "No, that is not right at all."

It was the Democratic Party historically that did so much to create the middle class. And it has been the Democrats who have acted to protect middle class investments through the years. We are the ones who understand that government has to enforce the rules of integrity to protect small investors and honest corporations alike. We're looking out for them, not the other side. As I said, the Republicans stole the message in the last election. Hopefully, my party will wake up to that fact and not let it happen again. Hopefully, protecting the middle class, ensuring integrity in the markets and advocating a true ownership society will be a bigger part of our message in the future. Thank you so much for listening to me. I appreciate your patience.

# # #

Editor's note: I made minor punctuation and grammatical corrections, (as befits a former proofreader) especially since this was a speech and I'm sure Attorney General Sptizer would have corrected the written copy as he spoke. I apologize for any typographical errors I didn't catch.